iPhone®
For Seniors

FOR

DUMMIES®

A Wiley Brand

3rd Edition

iPhone® For Seniors

FOR

DUMMIES®

A Wiley Brand

3rd Edition

by Nancy C. Muir

iPhone® For Seniors For Dummies, 3rd Edition

Published by: John Wiley & Sons, Inc., 111 River Street, Hoboken, NJ 07030-5774, www.wiley.com

Contents at a Glance

Table of Contents

*I*f you bought this book (or are even thinking about buying it), you've probably already made the decision to buy an iPhone. The iPhone is designed to be easy to use, but still you can spend hours exploring the preinstalled apps, finding out how to change settings, and syncing the device to your computer or through iCloud. I've invested those hours so that you don't have to — and I've added advice and tips for getting the most out of your iPhone.

This book helps you get going with the iPhone quickly and painlessly so that you can move directly to the fun part.

About This Book

This book is specifically written for mature people like you, folks who may be relatively new to using a smartphone and want to discover the basics of buying an iPhone 5S or 5C, working with its preinstalled apps, and getting on the Internet. In writing this book, I've tried to consider the types of activities that might interest someone who is 50 years old or older and picking up an iPhone for the first time.

➤ Introduction

Conventions used in this book

This book uses certain conventions to help you find your way around, including

➡ Text you type in a text box is shown in **bold**. Figure references, such as "see **Figure 1-1**," are also in bold, to help you find them.

➡ Whenever I mention a website address, or *URL*, I put it in a different font, `like this`.

➡ Figure callouts draw your attention to actions you need to perform. In some cases, points of interest in a figure may be indicated. The text tells you what to look for; the callout line makes it easy to find.

 Tip icons point out insights or helpful suggestions related to tasks in the step lists.

 New icons highlight features of iPhone 5S, iPhone 5C, or iOS 7 that are new and exciting, in case you're moving up from earlier versions.

Foolish Assumptions

This book is organized by sets of tasks. These tasks start from the beginning, assuming that you've never laid your hands on an iPhone, and guide you through basic steps provided in nontechnical language.

This book covers going online using either a Wi-Fi or 3G/4G connection. I'm also assuming that you'll want to download and use the iBooks e-reader app, so I tell you how to download it in Chapter 13 and cover its features in Chapter 14.

Why You Need This Book

The iPhone 5S and 5C are cool and perfect for many seniors because they provide a simple, intuitive interface for making and receiving calls, and also for activities such as checking e-mail and playing music. The less expensive 5C could be a good option for you if you don't need quite as many bells and whistles in the camera or the Touch ID fingerprint sensor, pretty much the only difference in features offered on the 5S. But why should you stumble around, trying to figure out their features? Following the simple, step-by-step approach used in this book, you can get up to speed with the iPhone right away and overcome any technophobia you might have.

How This Book Is Organized

This book is conveniently divided into several handy parts to help you find what you need:

➟ **Part I: Making the iPhone Work for You:** If you're about to buy your iPhone or are ready to get started with the basics of using it, this part is for you. These chapters highlight the newest features in iPhone 5S, iPhone 5C, and iOS 7 (the phones' latest operating system) and help you explore the different specifications, styles, and price ranges for all iPhone models.

You find out how to set up your iPhone 5S or 5C out of the box, including

- Opening an iCloud account to register and push content to all your Apple devices automatically.

- Opening an iTunes account to buy entertainment content and additional apps.

- These chapters also provide information for exploring the iPhone Home screen when you first turn the phone on, for using the new Control Center feature, and for working with useful accessibility features to help out if you have hearing or vision challenges.

➡ **Part II: Start Using Your iPhone:** In this part, you discover the basics of making and receiving calls — this is a phone, after all! You find out how to set up and manage your contacts, how to get the most out of some useful utility apps, and how to take advantage of iPhone's accessibility features for those who have vision, hearing, or motor skill challenges.

In this part, you're also introduced to Siri, the iPhone's useful feature that allows you to talk to your phone and have it respond by providing information and performing tasks for you. You also explore the exciting FaceTime feature, used for making video calls to other people.

FaceTime works with people who use the iPhone 4, 4S, 5, 5S, or 5C; iPad 2 or third or later generation iPad; an iPad mini; an iPod touch (fourth generation or later); or a Mac running OS X, 10.6.6 or later.

You get acquainted with AirDrop, a new feature compatible with iPhone 5 or later for sharing content with somebody nearby, and new multitasking features.

Finally, you discover how integrated features for using Twitter, Facebook, and iMessage (the latter is accessed via the Messages instant-messaging app) help you to connect with others.

➡ **Part III: Taking the Leap Online:** Here, you find out how to connect to the Internet and use the built-in Safari browser and the stylish new Tab view. You putter with the preinstalled Mail app and set up your iPhone to access e-mail from your existing e-mail accounts. In this part, you also get to shop online at the iTunes Store for multimedia content, such as movies and music, and shop the App Store for additional iPhone apps.

➡ **Part IV: Having Fun and Consuming Media:** The iPhone has been touted by some as a great device for consuming media such as music (including the all new iTunes Radio), podcasts, and movies. Included with every iPhone are a Music app for playing music and the Videos app for watching video content. In addition, in this part, I explain how to use iBooks, the free e-reader app from Apple. You also explore playing games on your iPhone, which — trust me — is a lot of fun, and I help you experiment with the Maps app to find your favorite restaurant or bookstore with ease. You also discover the wonderful possibilities for using still and video cameras on iPhone, including sharing via photo streams and using new filters for taking photos. The latest Photos app provides new collections for viewing your images by year or location where they were taken, while the improved camera features on iPhone 5 offer slow motion for video and burst mode for capturing as much as 20 photos per second.

In this part, you also explore the Newsstand app for subscribing to and reading magazines.

➠ **Part V: Managing Your Life and Your iPhone:** For the organizational part of your brain, the iPhone makes available Calendar, Notification Center, Reminders, and Notes apps, all of which are covered in this part.

The Reminders app and Notification Center feature are also great for keeping you on schedule. Reminders is a great to-do list feature that allows you to enter tasks and details about them, and can also display tasks from your online calendars. Notification Center lists all your alerts and reminders in one place.

Finally, I offer advice in this part about keeping your iPhone safe and troubleshooting common problems that you might encounter, including using the Find My iPhone feature to deal with a lost or stolen iPhone and using the new Touch ID fingerprint sensor. You can also use the iCloud service to back up your content or restore your iPhone.

Where to Go from Here

You can work through this book from beginning to end or simply open a chapter to solve a problem or acquire a specific new skill whenever you need it. The steps in every task quickly get you to where you want to go, without a lot of technical explanation.

Note: At the time I wrote this book, all the information it contained was accurate for the iPhone 3GS, iPhone 4, and iPhone 4S, 5, 5S, and 5C, version 7 of the iOS (operating system) used by the iPhone, and version 11 of iTunes. Apple is likely to introduce new iPhone models and new versions of iOS and iTunes between book editions. If you've bought a new iPhone and its hardware, user interface, or the version of iTunes on your computer looks a little different, be sure to check out what Apple has to say at `www.apple.com/iphone`. You'll no doubt find updates on the company's latest releases. When a change is substantial, we may add an update or bonus information that you can download at this book's companion website, `www.dummies. com/extras/iphoneforseniors`.

Part I

Making the iPhone Work for You

Buying Your iPhone

Chapter 1

You've read about it. You've seen on the news the lines at Apple Stores on the day a new version of the iPhone is released. You're so intrigued that you've decided to get your own iPhone to have a smartphone that offers more than the ability to make and receive calls. iPhone also offers lots of fun apps; allows you to explore the online world; allows you to read e-books, magazines, and periodicals; allows you to organize your photos, and more.

Trust me: You've made a good decision, because the iPhone redefined the mobile phone experience in an exciting way. It's also an absolutely perfect fit for many seniors.

In this chapter, you learn about the advantages of iPhone, as well as where to buy this little gem and associated data plans from providers. After you have one in your hands, I help you explore what's in the box and get an overview of the little buttons and slots you'll encounter — luckily, the iPhone has very few of them.

Discover What's New in iPhone 5S, iPhone 5C, and iOS 7

Apple's iPhone gets its features from a combination of hardware and its software operating system (called iOS; the term is short for iPhone operating system, in case you need to know that to impress your friends). The most current operating system is iOS 7. It's helpful to understand which new features the iPhone 5S device and iOS 7 bring to the table (all of which are covered in more detail in this book). New features in iPhone 5S include

⟶ **Phone colors:** We were stuck with black and white iPhones for years, but now iPhone 5S comes in silver, gold, and a slightly darker gray called space gray. In addition, with the debut of iPhone 5C, a slightly less expensive version of iPhone lacking a few of iPhone 5S's features, you can choose from among five colors: green, white, blue, red, and yellow.

⟶ **Touch ID:** iPhone 5S comes with a fingerprint reader feature called Touch ID. Rather than enter a passcode again and again through the day to open your phone (keeping its contents safe), iPhone 5S can memorize your fingerprint, and a simple tap on the Home button gets you access to your iPhone and to iTunes.

⟶ **An A7 chip:** This chip gives you CPU and graphics performance that's up to twice as fast as the A6 chip in iPhone 5. The 64-bit chip is touted as being of desktop quality, though it may take some time for apps to truly take advantage of that.

⟶ **An M7 coprocessor:** This motion-sensing coprocessor makes it possible for your iPhone to detect monitor data that provides information about your motion. It's expected that this capability will enable lots of interesting new fitness apps.

➡ **New filtering features for camera:** The camera in iPhone 5S has a new sensor with a larger active area and a wider aperture. The improved auto functions include better white balance and autofocus. A flash feature and the ability to take photos using a slow motion feature make the camera experience better. Finally, Burst photo mode rounds out improvements. Burst allows you take up to 20 pictures in 2 seconds, and then the processor picks the best ones out of the bunch.

 Throughout this book, I highlight features that are relevant only in using the iPhone 5S and/or iPhone 5C, so you can use the majority of this book no matter which version of the iPhone you own as long as you have iOS 7 installed.

Any iPhone device more recent than the iPhone 3G can make use of most features of iOS 7 if you update the operating system (discussed in detail in Chapter 2); this book is based on version 7 of iOS. This update to the operating system adds many new features, including

➡ **A Whole New Look:** Apple has entirely redesigned the iPhone interface with iOS 7, providing flatter, more graphically bright buttons for your apps, and a simple clean look to areas such as the Lock screen and Settings. Love it or hate it, it's an overdue facelift for iPhone.

➡ **Control Center:** This handy group of buttons and sliders gives you access to the most commonly used settings such as volume, playback tools for music, on/off settings for AirDrop (see next item for more about this feature), Wi-Fi, Bluetooth, as well as buttons for a Flashlight, Clock, Calculator, and your Camera. Control Center appears when you flick up from the bottom of the iPhone screen.

⟶ **AirDrop:** Use this new feature to share pictures, videos, music, and more with somebody in your general vicinity who has an AirDrop-enabled device.

⟶ **Notification Center:** Swipe down on your iPhone screen and you reveal Notification Center. New Notification Center features in iOS 7 are the Today, All, and Missed views that help you see useful information such as events on your Calendar, Reminders, and stock values from three perspectives.

⟶ **Multitasking:** In iOS 7 Apple has made some changes to the way you work with more than one app at a time. You can press the Home button twice to get a view of all open apps to make it easier to switch among them. Also, your iPhone now pays attention to the time you typically use certain apps, such as a social app or stock tracker, and updates their content at that time to make the latest content available to you faster.

⟶ **Camera Improvements:** Now the Camera app makes various shooting formats (still, video, panorama, and the new square format) easily accessible. In addition, Apple has provided filters so you can add effects such as higher contrast or black and white to your photos.

⟶ **Photo Categories:** To help you organize your photos, iOS 7 has added Collections, Moments, and Years to group your images by the time and location where they were taken. In addition, you can now use iCloud to share photos with others, and photos or videos are streamed to everybody's devices. Others can also post items to your stream and even make comments.

➠ **A New Look for Safari:** Apple's browser, Safari, helps you get around the Internet. Now it also provides a unified search field so you can enter a website address or search term and Safari provides the best match for your entry. There's a new tab view that helps you move among open tabs more easily. The Shared Links feature lets you view information about your Twitter timeline, while Reading List helps you save and read articles to keep you informed. Finally, iCloud Keychain is a way to have iCloud store all your account names and passwords, as well as your credit card numbers safely. Keychain also helps out by entering information for you when you need it.

➠ **iTunes Radio:** iTunes Radio offers you streaming music from popular radio stations, but beyond that, it learns about you as you listen. This feature allows you to build new stations where you are in charge of how many familiar tunes are mixed in with new songs to help you expand your musical vocabulary. You can also view a History of what you've heard and build a musical Wish List.

➠ **Siri Grows Up:** Siri has jumped on the new look bandwagon with a simpler, cleaner look in iOS 7. You can choose between a male or female Siri voice, and enjoy the fact that Siri checks even more sources for its info, including Bing, Wikipedia, and even Twitter postings related to your verbal query.

➠ **App Store Apps Near Me:** In the App Store you'll find two new features. You can search for apps that are popular in your area, and browse the Kids category to find kid-friendly apps.

⟶ **Find My iPhone Security Features:** This app helps you locate a missing iPhone, and in iOS 7, new features help you display a message on the Lock screen that this is a lost phone and provide a phone number where someone can reach you; your phone cannot be used without your sign in information. If you get your iPhone back, you can easily deactivate the message and access your phone again.

⟶ **iOS in Your Car:** If you happen to have a car that's equipped with iOS in the Car, you can use your iPhone 5, 5C, or 5S to make calls and control a feature called Siri Eyes Free to access music and messages, and get directions.

⟶ **Important Free Apps:** Along with iPhone 5S and 5C, Apple announced that the iWork suite of productivity apps (word processing, spreadsheet, and presentation software), iMovie, and iPhoto would be free.

Choose the Right iPhone for You

iPhone 5, 5S, and 5C are bigger than previous iPhones with their four-inch screen (see **Figure 1-1**). You can get iPhone 5S in gold, silver, or space gray, or iPhone 5C in white, pink, yellow, blue, or green. Other differences between iPhone models come primarily from the current iOS, iOS 7.

iPhone 5S and 5C models have a few variations:

⟶ Color of the phone.

⟶ Amount of built-in memory ranging from 16GB to 64GB.

⟶ iPhone 5C models have a slightly slower processor (A6), do not have the Touch ID technology built into the Home button, and are missing a few camera features.

Figure 1-1

Read on as I explain these variations in more detail in the following sections.

Table 1-1 gives you a quick comparison of iPhone 3GS, 4, 4S, 5, 5S, and 5C. All costs are as of the time this book was written.

Table 1-1		iPhone Model Comparison			
Model	**Memory**	**Cost (with a Two-Year Contract)**	**Support for FaceTime**	**Siri**	**Carriers**
3GS	8GB	Free	No	No	AT&T
4	8GB	Free	Yes	No	AT&T, Verizon, Sprint
4S	16, 32, and 64GB	$99	Yes	Yes	AT&T, Verizon, Sprint
5	16, 32, and 64GB	$199–$399 with new service contract	Yes	Yes	AT&T, Verizon, Sprint
5S	16, 32, and 64GB	$199, $299, $399 with service plan; unlocked through T-Mobile $649, $749, $849	Yes	Yes	AT&T, Verizon, Sprint, T-Mobile
5C	16 and 32GB	$99 and $199 with service plan through AT&T, Verizon, Sprint; Unlocked through T-Mobile $549 and $649	Yes	Yes	AT&T, Verizon, Sprint, T-Mobile

Decide How Much Memory Is Enough

Memory is a measure of how much information — for example, movies, photos, and software applications (apps) — you can store on a computing device. Memory can also affect your iPhone's performance when handling tasks such as streaming favorite TV shows from the World Wide Web or downloading music.

Streaming refers to playing video or music content from the web (or from other devices) rather than playing a file stored on your computing device. You can enjoy a lot of material online without ever downloading its full content to your hard drive — and given that every iPhone model has a relatively small amount of memory, that's not a bad idea. See Chapters 15 and 17 for more about getting your music and movies online.

Your memory options with an iPhone 5S are 16, 32, or 64 gigabytes (GB) and with 5C either 32 or 64GB. You must choose the right amount of memory because you can't open the unit and add memory, as you usually can with a desktop computer. However, Apple has thoughtfully provided iCloud, a service you can use to back up content to the Internet (you can read more about that in Chapter 3).

So how much memory is enough for your iPhone? Here's a rule of thumb: If you like lots of media, such as movies or TV shows, you might need 64GB. For most people who manage a reasonable number of photos, download some music, and watch heavy-duty media such as movies online, 32GB is probably sufficient. If you simply want to check e-mail, browse the web, and write short notes to yourself, 16GB *might* be enough.

Do you have a clue how big a gigabyte (GB) is? Consider this: Just about any computer you buy today comes with a minimum of 250GB of storage. Computers have to tackle larger tasks than iPhones do, so that number makes sense. The iPhone, which uses a technology called *flash memory* for data storage, is meant (to a great extent) to help you experience online media and e-mail; it doesn't have to store much and in fact pulls lots of content from online. In the world of memory, 16GB for any kind of storage is puny if you keep lots of content and graphics on the device.

What's the price for larger memory? For the iPhone 5S, a 16GB unit costs $199 with a two-year contract; 32GB jumps the price to $299; and 64GB adds another $100, setting you back a pricey $399. iPhone 5C comes with 16GB under contract for $99 and with 32GB for $199

Understand What You Need to Use Your iPhone

Before you head off to buy your iPhone, you should know what other connections and accounts you'll need to work with it optimally.

At a bare minimum, to make standard cellular phone calls, you need to have a service plan with a cellular carrier such as AT&T, as well as a data plan that supports iPhone. The data plan allows you to exchange data over the Internet, such as e-mails.

You also need to be able to update the iPhone operating system and share media such as music among Apple devices. Though these things can be done without a phone carrier service plan, you have to plug your phone into your computer to update the iOS or update over a network using iCloud. You need to use a local Wi-Fi network to go online and make calls using an Internet service such as Skype. Given the cost and hi-tech nature of the iPhone, having to jury-rig these basic functions doesn't make much sense, so trust me, get an account and data plan.

You can open an iCloud account to store and share content online. You can also use a computer to download photos, music, or applications from non-Apple online sources such as stores or sharing sites like your local library and transfer them to your iPhone through a process called *syncing*. You can also use a computer or iCloud to register your iPhone the first time you start it, although you can have the folks at the Apple Store, AT&T, Sprint, or Verizon handle registration for you if you have one nearby.

Apple has set up its iTunes software and the iCloud service to give you two ways to manage content for your iPhone — including apps, music, or photos you've downloaded — and specify how to sync your calendar and contact information. Chapter 3 covers those settings in more detail.

Know Where to Buy Your iPhone

You can't buy iPhone from every major retail store. You can buy an iPhone at the Apple Store and from the mobile phone providers AT&T, Sprint, T-Mobile, and Verizon. You can also find an iPhone at major retailers such as Best Buy, Radio Shack, and Walmart, through whom you have to buy a two-year service contract for the phone carrier of your choice. You can also find iPhones at several online retailers such as Amazon.com and Newegg.com.

 Apple offers unlocked iPhones that can be used with any of the three iPhone cellular service providers, but though you save a lot on a service commitment, these phones without accompanying phone plans can be pretty pricey. T-Mobile is offering the iPhone 5C in an unlocked version with no service plan required.

Explore What's in the Box

When you fork over your hard-earned money for your iPhone, you'll be left holding one box about the size of a deck of tarot cards. Here's a rundown of what you'll find when you take off the shrink-wrap and open the box:

⟼ **iPhone:** Your iPhone is covered in a thick plastic sleeve-thingie that you can take off and toss (unless you think there's a chance you'll return it, in which case you might want to keep all packaging for 14 days — Apple's standard return period).

⟼ **Apple EarPods with Remote and Mic:** The EarPods are Apple's new breakthrough for earbud headphones. Plug these into your iPhone 5S for a free headset experience. If you buy an iPhone 4S or earlier, you get the Apple Earphones with Remote and Mic with your phone.

➠ **Documentation (and I use the term loosely):**
Notice, under the iPhone itself, a small, white enve-
~~lope about the size of a half-dozen index cards.~~
Open it and you'll find:

   - *A tiny pamphlet:* This pamphlet, named *Important
     Product Information Guide,* is essentially small print
     (that you mostly don't need to read) from folks
     like the FCC.

   - *A label sheet:* This sheet has two white Apple logos
     on it. (I'm not sure what they're for, but my hus-
     band and I use one sticker to differentiate my
     iPhone from his.)

   - *A small foldout card:* This card provides panels con-
     taining photos of the major features of iPhone 4S
     and information about where to find out more.
     (Prior to 4S, you got only a single card with a
     photo of the phone and callouts to major features;
     4S documentation expanded exponentially . . .
     which isn't saying much!).

➠ **Lightning to USB Cable:** Use this cable (see **Figure
1-2**) to connect the iPhone to your computer, or use
it with the last item in the box, the USB power
adapter. If you buy an iPhone 4S or earlier, you get
the Dock Connector to USB Cable, the larger, traditional 30-pin connector.

➠ **Apple USB power adapter:** The power adapter (refer
to **Figure 1-2**) attaches to the Lightning to USB
Cable so that you can plug it into the wall and
charge the battery.

➠ **SIM Eject Tool:** This tool, which you can use to eject
a SIM card from your phone if you have one (Sprint
doesn't use SIM cards), is provided with iPhone in
some areas.

Lightning to USB Cable   Apple USB power adapter

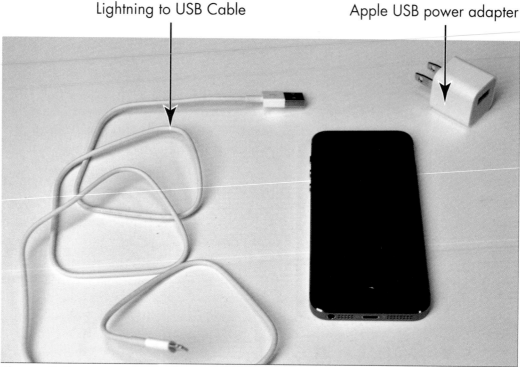

Figure 1-2

That's it. That's all there is in the box. It's kind of a study in Zen-like simplicity.

 Try searching for iPhone accessories online. You'll find iPhone cases ranging from leather to silicone; car chargers; and screen guards to protect your phone's screen.

Take a First Look at the Gadget

The little card contained in the documentation (see the preceding section) gives you a picture of the iPhone with callouts to the buttons you'll find on it. In this section, I give you a bit more information about those buttons and other physical features of the iPhone 5S and 5C. **Figure 1-3** shows you where each of these items is located.

Sleep/Wake button

FaceTime/iSight camera

Receiver

Status bar

Ring/Silent switch

iSight camera

Volume buttons

Rear microphone

SIM card tray

LED Flash

Multi-Touch display

Home button/ Fingerprint reader

Lightning Connector

Speaker

Bottom microphone

Headset jack

Figure 1-3

Here's the rundown on what the various hardware features are and what they do:

⟶ **(The all-important) Home button/Fingerprint reader:** On the iPhone, you can press this button to go back to the Home screen to find just about anything. The Home screen(s) displays all your installed and preinstalled apps and gives you access to your iPhone settings. No matter where you are or what you're doing, press the Home button and you're back at home base. You can also double-press the Home button to pull up a scrolling list of apps so you can quickly move from one to another. Finally, with iPhone 5S the Home button has been reengineered to contain a fingerprint reader used with the Touch ID feature.

⟶ **Sleep/Wake button:** You can use this button (whose functionality I cover in more detail in Chapter 2) to power up your iPhone, put it in Sleep mode, wake it up, or power it down.

⟶ **Lightning connector:** Plug in the Lightning connector to charge your battery or sync your iPhone with your computer (which you find out more about in Chapter 3).

⟶ **FaceTime/iSight cameras:** iPhone 4 and later models offer FaceTime (on the front of the phone) and iSight (on the back of the phone) cameras that you can use to make video calls and shoot photos or video. Make note of the location of the iSight camera on the back of the phone — you need to be careful not to put your thumb over it when taking shots (I have several very nice photos of my thumb already).

⟶ **Ring/Silent switch:** Slide this little switch to mute or unmute the sound on your iPhone.

➠ **(A tiny, mighty) Speaker:** One nice surprise when I first got my iPhone was hearing what a nice little

from this tiny speaker. The speaker is located on the bottom edge of the phone, below the Home button.

➠ **Volume buttons:** Tap the volume up button for more volume and the volume down button for less. You can use the volume up button as a camera shutter button when the camera is activated.

➠ **Headset jack and microphones:** If you want to listen to your music in private, you can plug in the EarPods (which gives you bidirectional sound) or 3.5mm minijack headphones. Three microphones (one on the front of the phone — this is also the Receiver — and one on the bottom of the phone, as well as one on the back of the phone) make it possible to speak into your iPhone. This feature allows you to do things such as make phone calls using the Internet, use video calling services like Skype, or work with other apps that accept audio input such as the Siri built-in assistant.

➠ **Receiver:** The mesh on the top front of the device that you hear through.

➠ **SIM card tray:** The little slot for placing your phone carrier's SIM card, which allows your phone to connect to the carrier and stores data such as contacts in memory. Note that iPhones have a smaller SIM card (called a nano-card) than other phones, and that Sprint doesn't use SIM cards at all.

➠ **LED flash:** The flash device for the built-in rear-facing camera.

Looking Over the Home Screen

I won't kid you: You have a slight learning curve ahead of you if you're coming from a more basic cell phone (although, if you own another smartphone, you've got a head start). For example, your previous phone might not have had a Multi-Touch screen and onscreen keyboard.

The good news is that getting anything done on the iPhone is simple, once you know the ropes. In fact, using your fingers instead of tiny plastic buttons to do things is a very intuitive way to communicate with your computing device, which is just what iPhone is.

In this chapter, you turn on your iPhone and register it and then take your first look at the Home screen. You also practice using the onscreen keyboard, see how to interact with the touchscreen in various ways, get pointers on working with cameras, and get an overview of built-in applications.

Get ready to . . .

Have a soft cloth handy, like the one you might use to clean your eyeglasses. Despite a screen that has

ton of fingerprints on your iPhone — one downside of a touchscreen device.

See What You Need to Use iPhone

You need to be able, at a minimum, to connect to the Internet to take advantage of most iPhone features, which you can do using a Wi-Fi network or a 3G/4G connection from your cellular provider. You might want to have a computer so that you can connect your iPhone to it to download photos, videos, music, or applications and transfer them to or from your iPhone through a process called *syncing* (see Chapter 3 for more about syncing). With iOS 5, a new Apple service called iCloud arrived that syncs content from all your Apple iOS devices, so anything you buy on your iPad that can be run on iPhone, for example, will automatically be pushed to your iPhone. In addition, you can sync without connecting a cable to a computer using a Wi-Fi connection to your computer (a wireless network you can set up in your home).

Your phone will probably arrive registered and activated, or if you buy it in a store, the person helping you can handle that procedure.

For an iPhone 5S and 5C, Apple's *iPhone User Guide* recommends that you have

⟶ A Mac or PC with a USB 2.0 port and one of these operating systems:

- Mac OS X Lion version 10.6.8 or later

- Windows 8, 7, Vista, or XP Home or Professional with Service Pack 3 or later

⟶ iTunes 11.1 or later, available at www.itunes.com/download

⟶ An Apple ID

⟶ Internet access

Apple has set up its iTunes software to help you manage content for your iPhone — which includes the movies, music, or photos you've downloaded — and specify from where to transfer your calendar and contact information. Chapter 3 covers these settings in more detail.

Turn On iPhone

1. The first time you turn on your iPhone, it will probably have been activated and registered by your phone carrier or Apple (if you buy it from Apple).

2. Press and hold the On/Off button on the top of your iPhone until the Apple logo appears. In another moment, a series of screens appears asking you to choose a language, country or region, and a Wi-Fi network to connect through.

3. Next you're asked if you'd like to set up the phone as a new iPhone or restore and back it up using iCloud or iTunes. If you choose iTunes follow Steps 4 and 5; if you're using iCloud skip to Step 6.

4. Plug the Lightning to USB Cable that comes with your device into your iPhone.

5. Plug the other end of the cable into a USB port on a computer. Both your computer and the iPhone think for a few moments while they exchange data.

6. Sign in with your Apple ID in the dialog that appears on your computer screen, and then accept Apple's terms and conditions. Follow the simple onscreen instructions in subsequent screens to register your iPhone and choose whether to use Apple's online storage service iCloud for backups, whether to use the voice controlled personal assistant Siri, and whether to automatically send diagnostic information to Apple. (You can change these settings later; these steps are covered in Chapter 3.) When you're done, your iPhone Home screen appears, and you're in business.

7. Unplug the Lightning to USB Cable.

 If you buy your iPhone at an Apple Store, an employee will register it for you, and you can skip this whole process.

 You can choose to have certain items transferred to your iPhone from your computer when you sync, including: music, videos, downloaded apps, contacts, audiobooks, calendars, e-books, podcasts, and browser bookmarks. You can also transfer to your computer any content you download directly to your iPhone using iTunes, the App Store, or non-Apple stores. See Chapters 12 and 13 for more about these features.

Register PC-Free Using iCloud

In Step 2 of the previous task, you can choose to register your device via iCloud. To use this PC-free process, you need to be within range of a Wi-Fi hotspot (your home Wi-Fi network or a public network at a location such as a café or hotel) or use your iPhone's 3G/4G connection — the connection over which it makes and receives calls — so you can connect directly to the Internet.

When you make this choice, rather than signing into iTunes, you enter your provider's ID. If you don't have an AT&T, Verizon, T-Mobile, or Sprint ID, you're offered the option of creating one right then and there. That ID is associated with your iCloud account, and you can use it for various iCloud-supported activities.

You'll also be asked to respond to various questions, such as your preferred language and country. When you finish answering these, your iPhone is registered without ever being plugged into a computer.

Meet the Multi-Touch Screen

When the iPhone Home screen appears (see **Figure 2-1**), you see a pretty background and two sets of icons. One set appears in the Dock, along the bottom of the screen. The *Dock* contains the Phone, Mail, Safari, and Music app icons by default, though you can swap out one app for another. The Dock appears on every Home screen. Other icons appear above the Dock and are closer to the top of the screen. (I cover all these icons in the "Take Inventory of Preinstalled Apps" task, later in this chapter.) Different icons appear in this area on each Home screen. You can add new apps to populate as many as 14 additional Home screens for a total of 15 Home screens.

App icons

The Dock

Figure 2-1

Treat the iPhone screen carefully. It's made of glass and will smudge when you touch it (and will break if you throw it at the wall).

The iPhone uses *touchscreen technology:* When you swipe your finger across the screen or tap it, you're providing input to the device just as you may have used a mouse or keyboard to provide input to a computer. You hear more about the touchscreen in the next task, but for now, go ahead and play with it for a few minutes — really, you can't hurt anything. Use the pads of your fingertips (not your fingernails) and follow these steps:

1. Tap the Settings icon. The various settings (which you read more about throughout this book) appear, as shown in **Figure 2-2**.

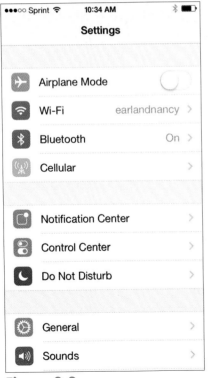

Figure 2-2

2. To return to the Home screen, press the Home button.

3. Swipe a finger or two from right to left on the Home screen. If downloaded apps occupy additional Home screens, then this action moves you to the next Home screen. Note that the little dots at the bottom of the screen, above the Dock icons, indicate which Home screen is displayed.

4. To experience the screen rotation feature, hold the iPhone firmly while turning it sideways. The screen flips to the horizontal orientation. To flip the screen back, just turn the device so it's oriented like a pad of paper again. (Note that some apps force iPhone to stay in one orientation or the other.)

5. Drag your finger down from the top of the screen to reveal the Notification Center (covered in Chapter 21); drag up from the bottom of the Home screen to display Control Central (discussed later in this chapter).

 You can customize the Home screen by changing its *wallpaper* (background picture) and brightness. You can read about making these changes in Chapter 7.

Say Goodbye to Endless Phone Menus, Say Hello to Tap and Swipe

You can use several methods for getting around and getting things done in iPhone using its Multi-Touch screen, including

➡ **Tap once.** To open an application on the Home screen, choose a field such as a search box, select an item in a list, select an arrow to move back or forward one screen, or follow an online link, and tap the item once with your finger.

➡ **Tap twice.** Use this method to enlarge or reduce the display of a web page (see Chapter 10 for more about using the *Safari* web browser) or to zoom in or out in the Maps app.

➡ **Pinch.** As an alternative to the tap-twice method, you can pinch your fingers together or move them apart on the screen (see **Figure 2-3**) when you're looking at photos, maps, web pages, or e-mail messages to quickly reduce or enlarge them, respectively.

You can use the three-finger tap to zoom your screen to be even larger or use multitasking gestures to swipe with four or five fingers. This method is handy if you have vision challenges. Go to Chapter 7 to discover how to turn on this feature using Accessibility settings.

➡ **Drag to scroll (known as *swiping*).** When you press your finger to the screen and drag to the right or left, the screen moves (see **Figure 2-4**). Swiping to the left on the Home screen, for example, moves you to the next Home screen. Swiping down while reading an online newspaper moves you down the page; swiping up moves you back up the page.

➡ **Flick.** To scroll more quickly on a page, quickly flick your finger on the screen in the direction you want to move.

➡ **Tap the Status bar.** To move quickly to the top of a list, web page, or e-mail message, tap the Status bar at the top of the iPhone screen.

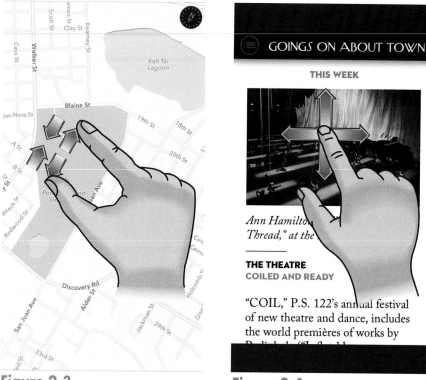

Figure 2-3

Figure 2-4

➡ **Press and hold.** If you're using Notes or Mail or any other application that lets you select text, or if you're on a web page, pressing and holding text selects a word and displays editing tools you can use to select, cut, or copy and paste the text.

Notice that when you rock your phone backward or forward the background moves as well. This parallax feature is new in iOS 7. You can disable this feature if it makes you seasick. Tap Settings⇨General⇨ Accessibility and then tap and turn off the Reduce Motion setting.

Try these methods now by following these steps:

1. Tap the Safari button in the Dock at the bottom of any iPhone Home screen to display the web browser. (You may be asked to enter your network password to access the network.)

2. Tap a link to move to another page.

3. Double-tap the page to enlarge it; then pinch your fingers together on the screen to reduce its size.

4. Drag one finger around the page to scroll.

5. Flick your finger quickly on the page to scroll more quickly.

6. Press and hold your finger on a word that isn't a link (links are usually blue and take you to another location on the web). The word is selected, and the Copy/Define tool is displayed, as shown in **Figure 2-5**. (You can use this tool to get a definition of a word or copy it.)

7. Press and hold your finger on a link or an image. A menu appears with commands you select to open the link or picture, open it in a new page, add it to your Reading List (see Chapter 10), or copy it. If you press and hold an image, the menu also offers the Save Image command. Tap Cancel to close the menu without making a selection.

8. Position your fingers slightly apart on the screen, and then pinch your fingers together to reduce the page; then, with your fingers already pinched together, place them on the screen, and then move them apart to enlarge the page.

9. Press the Home button to go back to the Home screen.

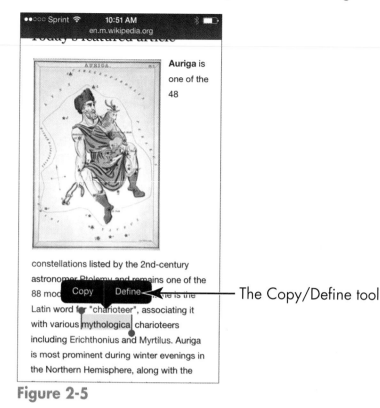

The Copy/Define tool

Figure 2-5

Display and Use the Onscreen Keyboard

1. The built-in iPhone keyboard appears whenever you're in a text-entry location, such as a search field or writing an e-mail message. Tap the Notes icon on the Home screen to open this easy-to-use notepad and try out the keyboard.

2. Tap the note page, or if you've already entered notes, tap one to display the page and tap anywhere on the note; the onscreen keyboard appears.

3. Type a few words using the keyboard, as shown in **Figure 2-6**. To make the keyboard display as wide as possible, rotate your iPhone to landscape (horizontal) orientation (note that if you've locked the screen orientation in Control Center you have to unlock it to do this).

4. If you make a mistake while using the keyboard — and you will, when you first use it — tap the Delete key (it's

to the left of the insertion point.

5. To create a new paragraph, tap the Return button, just as you would do on a regular computer keyboard.

6. To type numbers and symbols, tap the number key (labeled 123) on the left side of the spacebar (refer to **Figure 2-6**). The characters on the keyboard change (see **Figure 2-7**). If you type a number and then tap the spacebar, the keyboard returns to the letter keyboard automatically. To return to the letter keyboard at any time, simply tap the keys labeled ABC on the left side of the spacebar.

Figure 2-6

Figure 2-7

7. Use the Shift button (It's a thick, upward-facing arrow in the lower-left corner of the keyboard) just as you would on a regular keyboard to type uppercase letters or alternate characters. Tapping one of these buttons once causes just the next letter you type to be capitalized.

8. Double-tap the Shift key to turn on the Caps Lock feature so that all letters you type are capitalized until you turn the feature off. Tap the Shift key once to turn off Caps Lock. (You can control whether this feature is available in iPhone General Settings under Keyboard.)

9. To type a variation on a symbol or letter (for example, to see alternate presentations for the letter "A" when you press the "A" button on the keyboard), hold down the key; a set of alternate letters/symbols appears (see **Figure 2-8**). Note that this trick works with only certain letters and symbols.

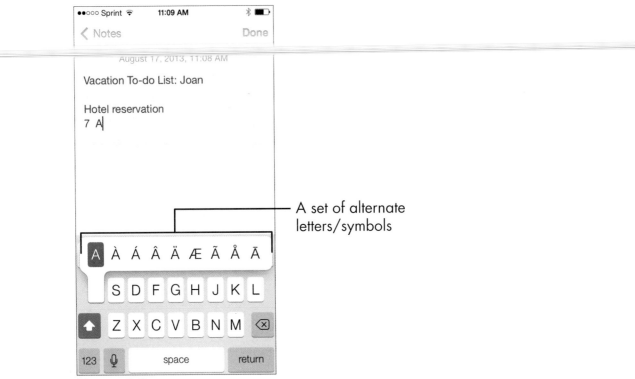

A set of alternate
letters/symbols

Figure 2-8

10. Press the Home button to return to the Home screen.

 To type a period and space, just double-tap the spacebar.

 Note that a small globe symbol will appear on the keyboard if you've enabled multi-language functionality in iPhone settings.

 If you want to add punctuation, such as a comma, and then return immediately to the letter keyboard, simply tap the 1, 2, 3 key and then drag up to the punctuation you want to use.

Flick to Search

1. The Spotlight Search feature in iPhone helps you find photos, music, e-mails, contacts, movies, and more. Swipe down from any Home screen (but not from the top or bottom of the screen) to reveal the Search feature.

2. Tap in the Search iPhone field (see **Figure** 2-9); the keyboard appears.

3. Begin entering a search term. In the example in **Figure 2-10,** after I typed the letters *No,* the search results displayed some contacts, the Notes app, and some music I had downloaded. As you continue to type a search term, the results narrow to match it.

Search iPhone field

Figure 2-9

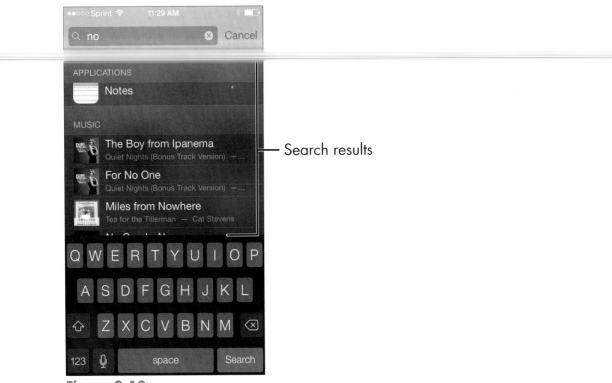

Search results

Figure 2-10

4. Tap an item in the search results to open it in its appropriate app or player.

Update the Operating System to iOS 7

1. This book is based on the latest version of the iPhone operating system at the time: iOS 7. To be sure you have the latest and greatest features, update your iPhone to the latest iOS now (and periodically to receive minor upgrades to iOS 7). If you have set up an iCloud account on your iPhone, updates will happen automatically, or you can update manually by tapping Settings, General, and then Software Update.

2. To update your iPhone using a physical connection, plug the Lightning end (the smaller end) of the Lightning to USB Cable into your iPhone and plug the USB end into your computer; or if you've set up wireless syncing, be within range of a Wi-Fi network.

3. When iTunes opens, click your iPhone (near the upper-right corner of the iTunes window or in the Sidebar along the left, if it's displayed) and then click the Summary tab if it isn't already displayed (see **Figure 2-11**).

4. Read the note next to the Check for Update button to see whether your iOS is up to date. If it isn't, click the Check for Update button. iTunes checks to find the latest iOS version and walks you through the updating procedure.

Click on the Summary tab

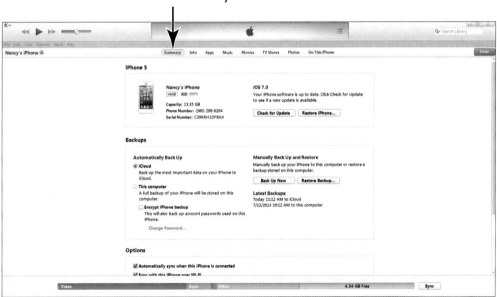

Figure 2-11

Learn Multitasking Basics

1. Multitasking lets you easily switch from one app to another without closing the first one and returning to the Home screen. With iOS 7, this is now accomplished by previewing all open apps and jumping from one to another; you quit an app by simply swiping upward. First, open an app.

2. Double-press the Home button.

3. On the app preview that appears (see **Figure 2-12**), flick to scroll to the left or right to locate another app you want to display.

4. Tap an app to open it.

App preview

The multitasking bar

Figure 2-12

Tap the Home button to remove the multitasking bar from the Home screen and return to the app you were working in.

Examine the iPhone Cameras

iPhone 5S and 5C have front- and back-facing cameras. You can use the cameras to take still photos (covered in more detail in Chapter 16) or shoot videos (covered in Chapter 17).

For now, take a quick look at your camera by tapping the Camera app icon on the Home screen. The app opens, as shown in **Figure 2-13.**

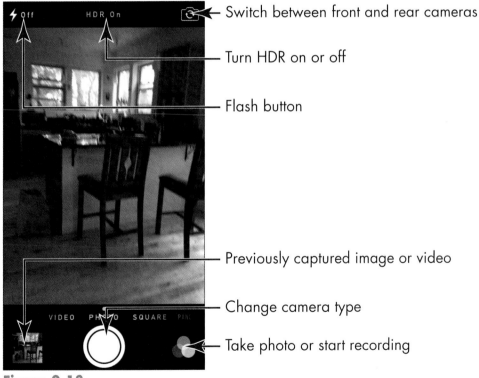

Switch between front and rear cameras

Turn HDR on or off

Flash button

Previously captured image or video

Change camera type

Take photo or start recording

Figure 2-13

You can use the controls on the screen to

➠ Switch between the front and rear cameras.

➠ Change from still-camera to video-camera operation by using the slider at the bottom of the screen.

➠ Take a picture or start recording a video.

➠ Turn HDR (high dynamic range for better contrast) on or off.

➠ Tap the Flash button to set flash to On, Off, or Auto.

➠ Open previously captured images or videos.

When you view a photo or video, you can use an iPhone sharing feature to send the image via AirDrop (fifth-generation iPhones only), in a tweet, post it to Facebook, or send as an e-mail attachment. You can also print images, use a still photo as wallpaper (your Home or lock screen background image) or assign it to represent a contact, run a slideshow, or edit a video. See Chapters 16 and 17 for more detail about using the iPhone cameras.

Lock Screen Rotation

Sometimes you don't want your screen orientation to flip around when you move your phone around. Use these steps to lock the iPhone into portrait orientation:

1. Swipe up from the bottom of any screen to open Control Center.

2. Tap the Lock Screen button; it's the button in the top-right corner of Control Center.

3. Swipe down on the screen to close Control Center.

Explore the Status Bar

Across the top of the iPhone screen is the *Status bar* (see **Figure** 2-14). Tiny icons in this area can provide useful information, such as the time, battery level, and wireless-connection status. **Table 2-1** lists some of the most common items you find on the Status bar.

●●●○○ Sprint 📶   12:36 PM   ✳ 🔋

Figure 2-14

Table 2-1	**Common Status Bar Icons**	
Icon	**Name**	**What It Indicates**
 📶	Wi-Fi	You're connected to a Wi-Fi network.
❋	Activity	A task is in progress — a web page is loading, for example.
 12:36 PM	Time	You guessed it: You see the time.
 🔒	Screen Rotation Lock	The screen is locked in portrait orientation and doesn't rotate when you turn the iPhone.
 ▶	Play	A media element (such as a song or video) is playing.
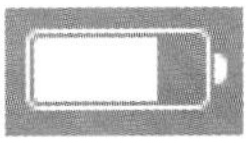 🔋	Battery Life	The charge percentage remaining in the battery. The indicator changes to a lightning bolt when the battery is charging.

 If you have GPS, 3G, 4G, cellular, or Bluetooth service or a connection to a virtual private network (VPN), a corresponding symbol appears on the Status bar whenever one of these features is active. (If you can't even conceive of what a virtual private network is, my advice is not to worry about it.)

Take Inventory of Preinstalled Apps

The iPhone comes with certain functionality and applications — or *apps*, for short — built in. When you look at the Home screen, you see icons for each app. This task gives you an overview of what each app does. (You can find out more about every one of them as you read different chapters in this book.) Here are the icons in the Dock (these are shown at the bottom of every Home screen; refer to **Figure 2-1**), from left to right:

➡ **Phone:** Use this app to make and receive phone calls, view recent calls, create a list of favorite contacts, access your voice mail, and view Contacts.

➡ **Mail:** You use this application to access e-mail accounts that you have set up in iPhone. Your e-mail is then displayed without you having to browse to the site or sign in. Then you can use tools to move among a few preset mail folders, read and reply to e-mail, and download attached photos to your iPhone. Read more about e-mail accounts in Chapter 11.

➡ **Safari:** You use the Safari web browser (see **Figure 2-15**) to navigate on the Internet, create and save bookmarks of favorite sites, and add web clips to your Home screen so that you can quickly visit favorite sites from there. You may have used this web browser (or another, such as Internet Explorer) on your desktop computer.

➡ **Music:** *Music* is the name of your media player. Though its main function is to play music, you can use it to play audio podcasts and audiobooks as well.

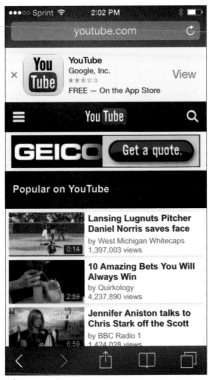

Figure 2-15

Apps with icons above the Dock on the Home screen include

➡ **Messages:** For those who love to instant message, the Messages app comes to the rescue. iMessage since iOS 5 brought more features to the Messages app than have been in iPhone for quite some time. Now you can engage in live text- and image-based conversations with others via their phones or other devices that use e-mail.

➡ **Calendar:** Use this handy onscreen daybook to set up appointments and send alerts to remind you about them.

➡ **Photos:** The Photos app in iPhone (see **Figure 2-16**) helps you organize pictures in folders, e-mail photos to others, use a photo as your iPhone wallpaper, and assign pictures to contact records. You can also run slideshows of your photos, open albums, pinch or unpinch to shrink or expand photos, and scroll photos with a simple swipe. Your iPhone has the capability to use the Shared Photo Streams feature to share photos among your friends. In iOS 7, Photos displays images by collections including Years and Moments.

➡ **Camera:** As you may have read earlier in this chapter, the Camera app is control central for the still and video cameras built into the iPhone.

➡ **Videos:** This media player is similar to Music but specializes in playing videos and offers a few features specific to this type of media, such as chapter breakdowns and information about a movie's plot and cast.

➡ **Maps:** In this iPhone mapping app you can view classic maps or aerial views of addresses, and find directions from one place to another by car, foot, or public transportation (though this last requires a third-party app be installed). You can even get your directions read out loud via a spoken narration feature.

➡ **Weather:** Get the latest weather for your location and others instantly with this handy app. You can easily add other locations to check for weather where you're going or where you've been (see **Figure 2-17**).

➡ **Passbook:** This feature lets you store a virtual wallet of plane or concert tickets, coupons, and more and use them with a swipe of your iPhone across a point of transaction device.

Wrapped up in the Utilities folder are some other handy tools: Contacts, Calculator, Compass, and Voice Memo apps. The Utilities folder is on the second Home screen by default.

⮕ **Notes:** Enter text or cut and paste text from a website into this simple notepad app. You can't do much except save notes or e-mail them — the app has no features for formatting text or inserting objects. You'll find Notes handy, though, for simple notes on the fly.

⮕ **Reminders:** This is a useful app that centralizes all your calendar entries and alerts to keep you on schedule, as well as allowing you to create to-do lists.

Figure 2-16

Figure 2-17

➠ **Clock:** This app, which appeared with iOS 6, allows you to display clocks from around the world, set

➠ **Stocks:** See the latest information about stock exchanges and individual stocks as well as trending information in one place anytime you like.

➠ **Newsstand:** Similar to an e-reader for books, Newsstand is a handy place to gather your subscriptions to magazines, newspapers, and other periodicals.

➠ **iTunes Store:** Tapping this icon takes you to the iTunes Store, where you can shop 'til you drop (or until your iPhone battery runs out of juice) for music, movies, TV shows, and audiobooks and then download them directly to your iPhone. (See Chapter 12 for more about how iTunes works.)

➠ **App Store:** Here you can buy and download applications that do everything from enabling you to play games to building business presentations. You can also subscribe to periodicals for use with the Newsstand app. Some of these are even free!

➠ **Game Center:** This app helps you browse games in the App Store and play them with other people online. You can add friends and track your scores. See Chapter 18 for more about Game Center.

➠ **Settings:** This isn't exactly an app, but it's an icon you should know about, anyway. It's the central location on the iPhone where you can specify settings for various functions and do administrative tasks such as set up e-mail accounts or create a password.

⟹ **FaceTime:** Use FaceTime to place phone calls using video of sender and receiver to have a more personal conversation.

The iBooks app isn't bundled with the iPhone out of the box. Though iBooks is free, you have to download it from the App Store. Because the iPhone has been touted as being a good small screen *e-reader* — a device that enables you to read books on an electronic device, similar to the Amazon Kindle Fire HD — you should definitely consider downloading the app as soon as possible. (For more about downloading applications for your iPhone, see Chapter 13. To work with the iBooks e-reader application itself, go to Chapter 14.)

With the coming of iPhone 5S/5C, Apple has made free several apps that used to cost you. These include iMovie, iPhoto, and the Pages, Keynote, and Numbers apps of the iWork suite.

Discover Control Center

1. With iOS 7 comes Control Center, a one-stop screen for common features and settings such as connecting to a network, increasing screen brightness or volume, and using the Calculator or Camera. To display Control Center, swipe up from the bottom of the screen.

2. In the screen that appears, tap on a button or slider to access or adjust a setting (see **Figure 2-18**).

3. Swipe the top of Control Center down to hide it.

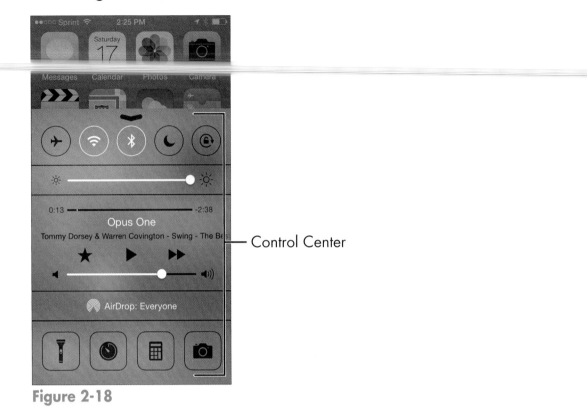

Control Center

Figure 2-18

Lock iPhone, Turn It Off, or Unlock It

Earlier in this chapter, I mention how simple it is to turn on the power to your iPhone. Now it's time to put it to *sleep* (a state in which the screen goes black, though you can quickly wake up the iPhone) or turn off the power to give your new toy a rest. Here are the procedures you use to put the phone to sleep or turn it off:

➔ **Press the Sleep/Wake button on the top of the phone.** The iPhone goes to sleep. The screen goes black and is locked.

➔ **From any app or Home screen press and hold the Sleep/Wake button until the Slide to Power Off bar appears at the top of the screen, and then swipe the bar.** You've just turned off your iPhone.

To wake the phone back up, do the following:

➡ **Press the Home button and swipe the onscreen arrow on the Slide to Unlock bar (see Figure 2-19).** The iPhone unlocks.

 The iPhone automatically enters sleep mode after a few minutes of inactivity. You can change the time interval at which it sleeps by adjusting the Auto-Lock feature in Settings. See this book's companion Cheat Sheet at www.dummies.com/cheatsheet/iphoneforseniors to review tables of various settings.

Figure 2-19

Getting Going

Chapter 3

*Y*our first step in getting to work with the iPhone is to make sure that its battery is charged. Next, if you want to find free or paid content for your iPhone from Apple, from movies to music to e-books to audiobooks, you'll need to open an iTunes account.

After you have an iTunes account and the latest iTunes software on your computer, you can connect your iPhone to your computer and sync them to exchange content between them (for example, to transfer your saved photos or music to the iPhone). You can also use the wireless sync feature to exchange content over a wireless network.

If you prefer, you can take advantage of the iCloud service from Apple to store and push all kinds of content and data to all your Apple devices — wirelessly.

This chapter also introduces you to the *iPhone User Guide*, which you access using the Safari browser on your iPhone. The guide essentially serves as your iPhone Help system, to provide advice and information about your magical new device.

Get ready to . . .

Charge the Battery

1. ~~~~~~ hope yours did, too. Because all batteries run down eventually, one of your first priorities is to know how to recharge your iPhone battery. Gather your iPhone and its Lightning to USB Cable (iPhone 5 and later; if you have an earlier model you have the older style cable) and the Apple USB power adapter.

2. Gently plug the Lightning connector end (the smaller of the two connectors) of the Lightning to USB Cable into the iPhone.

    Note that if you have a hard case for your iPhone, you should remove the phone from it while charging as these cases retain heat, which is bad for the phone and case.

3. Plug the USB end of the Lightning to USB Cable into the Apple USB power adapter (see **Figure 3-1**).

4. Plug the adapter into an electric outlet.

    Connector cables from earlier versions of iPhone or other Apple devices such as iPad or iPod will no longer work with your iPhone 5 or later. There are adapters available, however, from Apple.

Attach this end...   to the power adapter.

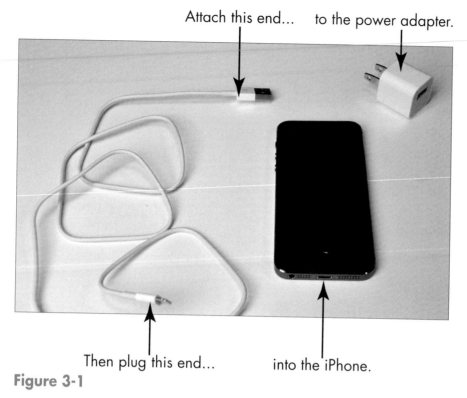

Then plug this end...   into the iPhone.

Figure 3-1

Download iTunes to Your Computer

1. If you're using a Mac, you already have iTunes installed, but to be sure you have the latest version (at the time of this writing it's version 11), open iTunes and choose Check for Updates. For Windows users, you should download the iTunes application to your computer so that you have the option of using it to *sync* (transfer) downloaded content to your iPhone. Go to www.apple.com/itunes using your computer's browser (in these steps I use Internet Explorer as an example).

2. Click the Download iTunes 11 link on the iTunes home page (see **Figure 3-2**). On the screen that opens, click the Download Now button.

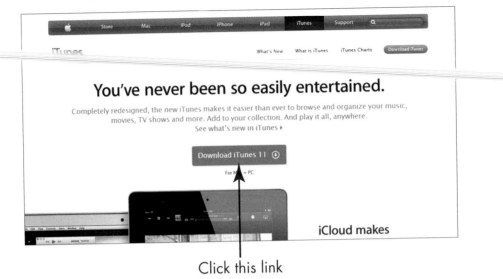

Click this link

Figure 3-2

3. In the dialog that appears, or using the Internet Explorer 10 download bar if you use that version (see **Figure** 3-3), click Run. The iTunes application downloads.

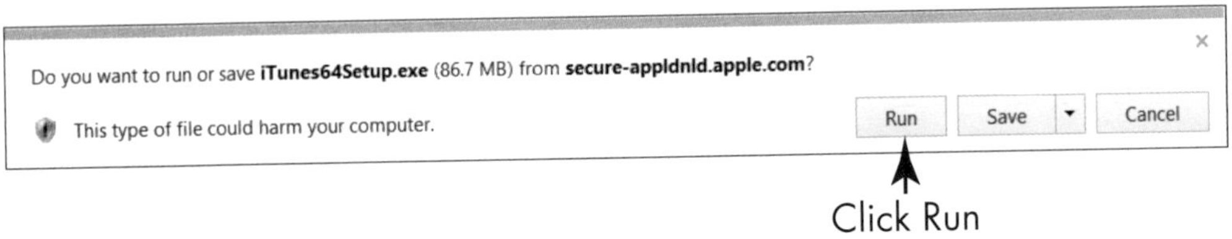

Do you want to run or save **iTunes64Setup.exe** (86.7 MB) from **secure-appldnld.apple.com**?

This type of file could harm your computer.   Run   Save ▾   Cancel

Click Run

Figure 3-3

4. When the download is complete, another dialog appears, asking whether you want to run the software. Click Run, and the iTunes Installer appears (see **Figure** 3-4).

5. Click Next.

6. Click the I Accept the Terms of the License Agreement check box in the following dialog and click Next.

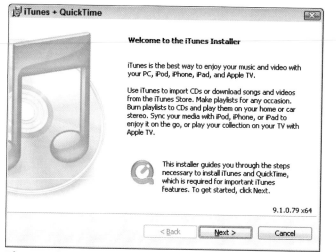

Figure 3-4

7. Review the installation options, click to deselect the ones you don't want to use, and then click the Install button, as shown in **Figure 3-5.** A dialog appears, showing the installation progress.

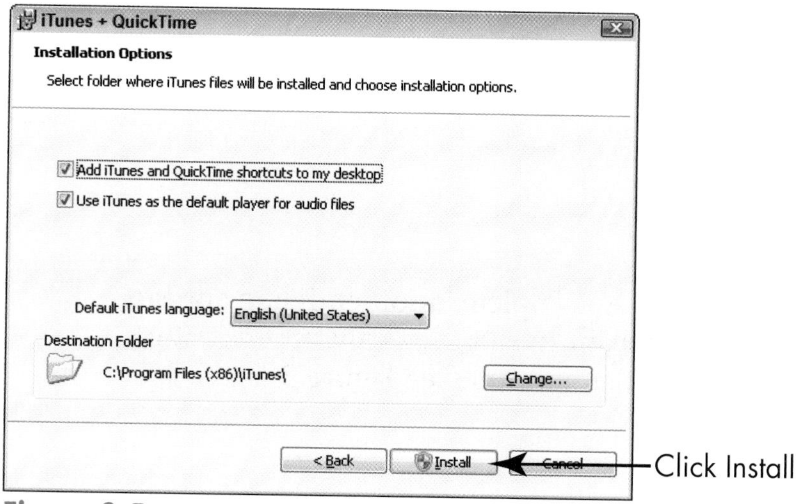

Click Install

Figure 3-5

8. When a dialog appears and tells you that the installation is complete, click Finish. You have to restart your computer for the configuration settings that were made during the installation to take effect.

As of this writing, iTunes 11 is the latest version and includes a paid feature called iTunes Match that allows you to store all your music, ~~~~~ you've copied from CDs, in the cloud and push it to all your Apple devices using iCloud. See Chapter 15 for more about music and iPhone.

Open an iTunes Account for Music, Movies, and More

1. To be able to buy or download free items from iTunes or the App Store on your computer or iPhone, you must open an iTunes account. First, open the iTunes app (you download it to your computer in the preceding task if you're running Windows). You can open iTunes by typing "iTunes" on your computer's Start screen in Windows or on a Mac by clicking the iTunes item in the Mac Dock or Launchpad.

2. Click the iTunes iStore button to open the Store and click the Sign In button on the screen that appears (see **Figure** 3-6).

Click this button

Figure 3-6

3. In the dialog that appears, click the Create Apple ID button and in the next screen that appears click Continue.

4. On the following screen click to select the I Have Read and Agree to the These Terms and Conditions check box (see **Figure 3-7**), and then click the Agree button.

5. In the Provide Apple ID Details screen that follows (see **Figure 3-8**), fill in the information fields, click the last two check boxes to deselect them if you don't want to receive e-mail from Apple, and then click the Continue button.

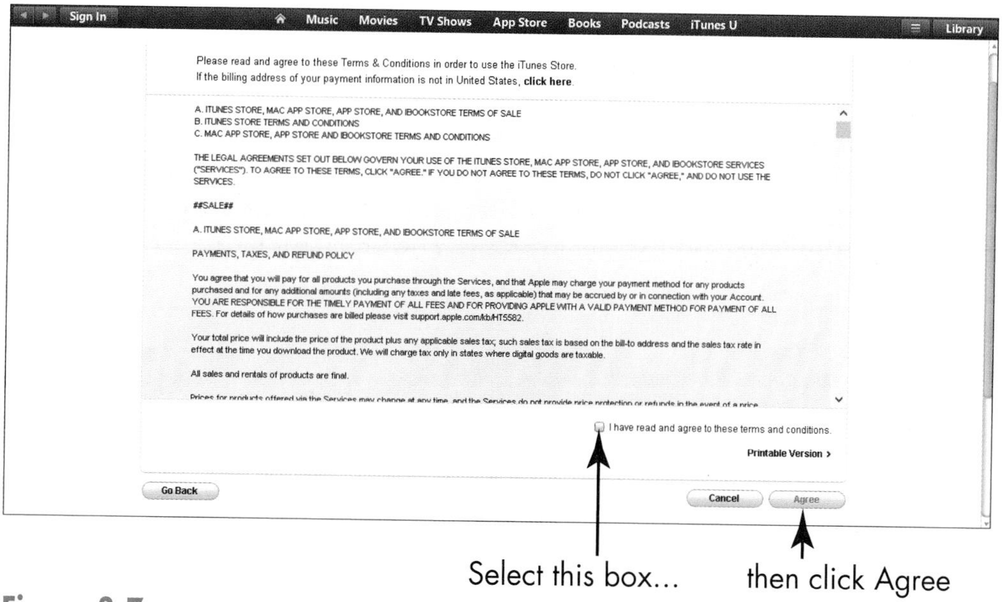

Select this box...   then click Agree

Figure 3-7

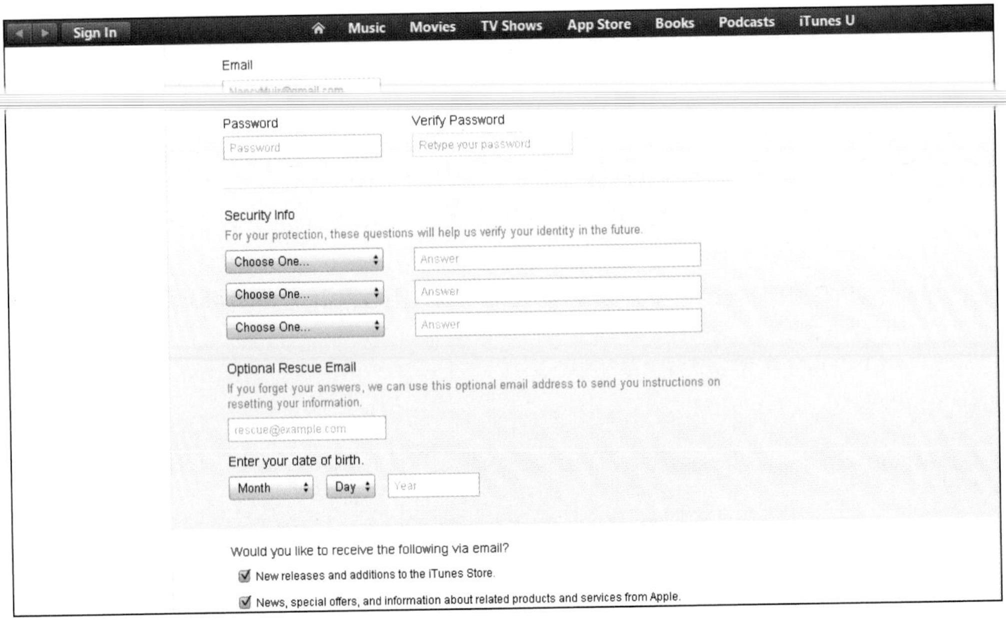

Figure 3-8

6. On the Provide a Payment Method screen that appears (see **Figure 3-9**), enter your payment information and click the Create Apple ID button.

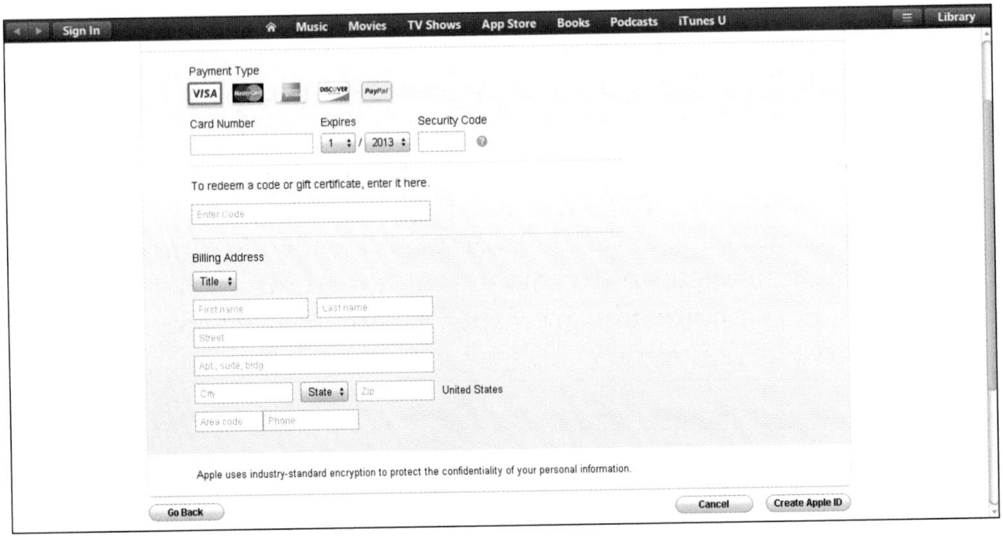

Figure 3-9

7. A screen appears, confirming that your account has been opened. Click the Done button to return to the iTunes Store.

 If you prefer not to leave your credit card info with Apple, one option is to buy an iTunes gift card and provide that as your payment information. You can replenish the card periodically through the Apple Store.

Make iPhone Settings Using iTunes

1. Open your iTunes software. (On a Windows 8 computer, begin to type iTunes on the Start screen and then click iTunes in the search results; on a Mac, click the iTunes icon in the Dock or Launchpad; if you still have iTunes open in the iTunes Store from the previous task, just click the Library button.)

2. iTunes opens, and if you've connected it to your computer using the Lightning to USB Cable, your iPhone is listed near the upper right corner, as shown in **Figure 3-10** (if you display the Sidebar you'll find your iPhone listed there, instead). Click your iPhone, and a series of tabs displays. The tabs offer information about your iPhone and settings to determine how to download music, movies, or podcasts, for example. (You can see the choices on the Summary tab in **Figure 3-11**.) The settings relate to the kind of content you want to download and whether you want to download it automatically (when you sync) or manually. See **Table 3-1** for an overview of the settings that are available on each tab.

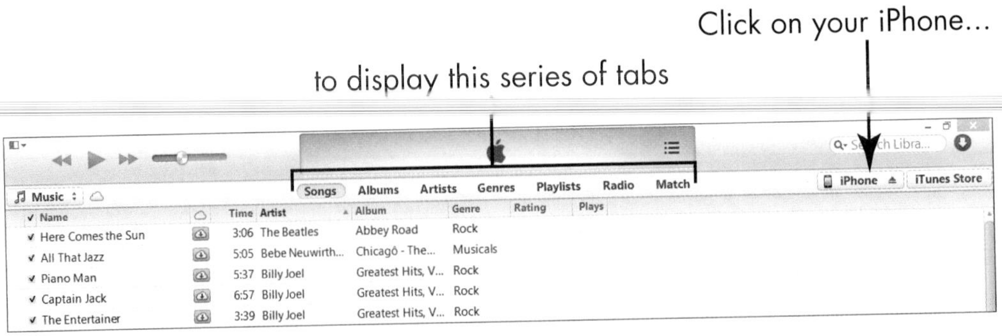

Click on your iPhone...

to display this series of tabs

Figure 3-10

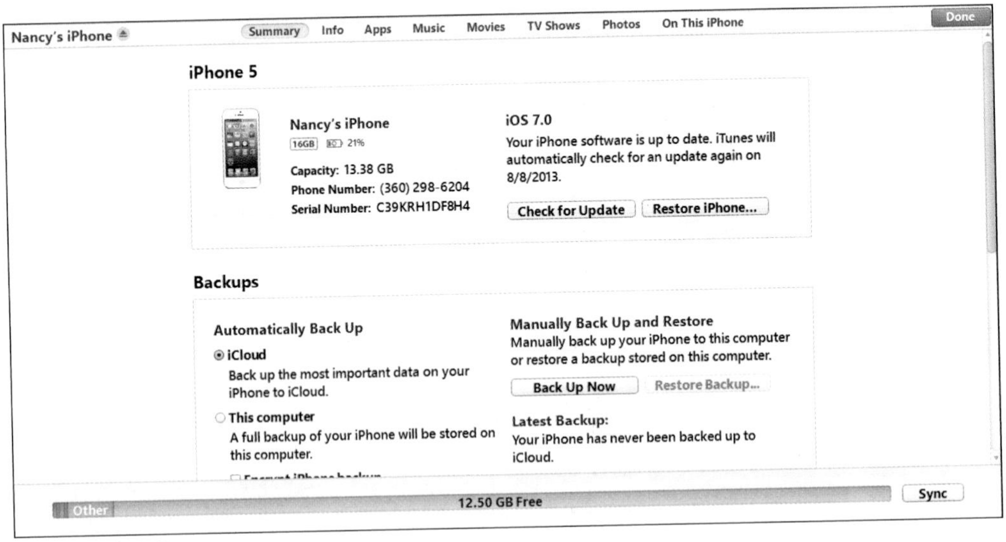

Figure 3-11

3. Make all settings for the types of content you plan to obtain on your computer. **Table 3-1** provides information about settings on the different tabs. Note that if you've downloaded content through apps like iTunes and Podcast, you may see additional tabs.

Table 3-1	iPhone Settings in iTunes
Tab Name	**What You Can Do with the Settings on the Tab**
Summary	Perform updates to the iPhone software and set general backup and syncing options.
Info	Specify which information to sync: Contacts, Calendars, E-mail accounts, Bookmarks, and/or Notes. Perform an advanced replacement of info on the phone with info from the computer.
Apps	Sync with iPhone the apps you've downloaded to your computer and manage the location of those apps and folders, as well as associating data files with your various apps. Choose whether to automatically install new apps.
Music	Choose which music to download to your iPhone when you sync.
Movies	Specify whether to automatically download movies and which movies to sync.
TV Shows	Choose shows and episodes to sync automatically.
Photos	Choose the applications or folders from which you want to download photos or albums.
On This iPhone	Select music on the iPhone to copy to iTunes.

Sync the iPhone to Your Computer Using iTunes

1. After you specify which content to download in iTunes (see the preceding task), you can use the Lightning to USB Cable to connect your iPhone and computer at any time and sync files, contacts, calendar settings, and more. After iTunes is downloaded to your computer and your iTunes account is set up, plug the data connection cord into your iPhone (using the smaller connector).

2. Plug the other end of the cord into a USB port on your computer.

3. iTunes opens and shows an item for your iPhone near upper right corner (refer to **Figure 3-10**). Click the Sync button in the lower-right corner and your iPhone screen shows the phrase *Syncing [Your Phone's Name] iPhone.*

4. When the syncing is complete, the Lock screen returns on the iPhone. Disconnect the cable. Any media you chose to transfer in your iTunes settings and any new photos in albums or folders on your computer you've specified for syncing to iPhone have been transferred to your iPhone.

Sync Wirelessly

You can also use the iTunes Wi-Fi Sync setting to allow cordless syncing if you're within range of a Wi-Fi network that has a computer connected to it with iTunes installed. There are a few steps you have to take with your iPhone connected to your computer before you can perform a wireless sync with iTunes:

1. Open iTunes and connect your iPhone to your computer using the Lightning to USB Cable.

2. Click on your phone (refer to **Figure 3-10**), click the Summary tab, and then scroll down and click the check box labeled Sync with this iPhone over Wi-Fi.

3. Disconnect your iPhone from your computer.

After you complete the above steps you'll be able to wirelessly sync your iPhone with your computer. To do so, follow these steps:

1. To initiate a wireless sync, tap Settings⇨General⇨iTunes Wi-Fi Sync.

2. In the dialog that appears, tap Sync Now to sync with a computer connected to the same Wi-Fi network (choose Settings⇨Wi-Fi and tap on a network to join a network from your iPhone).

If you have your iPhone set up to sync wirelessly to your Mac or PC and both are within range of the same Wi-Fi network, iPhone will appear in your iTunes Source list. This allows you to sync and manage syncing from within iTunes.

Understand iCloud

There's an alternative to syncing content by using iTunes. Concurrent with the launch of iOS 5, iCloud became available. iCloud is a service offered by Apple that allows you to back up most of your content to online storage (however, some content, such as videos, aren't backed up, so consider an occasional backup of content to your computer, as well). That content is then pushed automatically to all your Apple devices through a wireless connection. All you need to do is get an iCloud account, which is free, and make settings on your devices and in iTunes for which types of content you want pushed to each device. After you've done that, content you create or purchase on one device — such as music, apps, and TV shows, as well as documents created in Apple's iWork apps, photos, and so on — is synced among your devices automatically.

When you get an iCloud account, you get 5GB of free storage. Content you purchase (such as apps, books, music, iTunes Match content, Photo Stream contents, and TV shows) won't be counted against your storage. If you want additional storage, you can buy an upgrade from one of your devices. 10GB costs $20 per year; 20GB is $40 per year; and 50GB is $100 per year. Most people will do just fine with the free 5GB of storage.

To upgrade your storage, go to iCloud in Settings, tap Storage & Backup, and then tap Buy More Storage. Tap the amount you need and then tap Buy.

 You can make settings for backing up your content to iCloud in the iCloud section of General Settings. Here you can choose to have content backed up automatically or to back up content manually. See Chapter 24 for more about this topic.

If you pay $24.99 a year for the iTunes Match service, you can sync up to 25,000 songs in your iTunes ~~library to your devices, which may be a less expensive~~ way to go than paying for added iCloud storage. Tap Match in iTunes or visit `www.apple.com/itunes/` `itunes-match` for more information.

Get an iCloud Account

Before you can use iCloud, you need an iCloud account, which is tied to the Apple ID you probably already have. You can turn on iCloud when first setting up your iPhone or use Settings to sign up using your Apple ID.

1. When first setting up your phone after upgrading to iOS 7, in the sequence of screens that appear, you'll see the one in **Figure 3-12**. Tap Use iCloud.

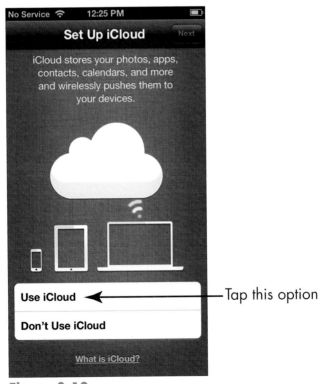

Figure 3-12

2. In the next dialog, tap Backup to iCloud. Your account is now set up based on the Apple ID you entered earlier in the setup sequence.

Here are the steps to set up iCloud on your iPhone if you didn't do so when first setting up iPhone:

1. Tap Settings, then tap Mail, Contacts, Calendars, and then under Accounts tap iCloud.

2. Scroll to the bottom of the next screen and tap Storage and Backup and then tap the On/Off button to turn on iCloud Backup (see **Figure 3-13**).

3. A message appears letting you know that your iPhone will no longer backup to your computer when you sync with a cable; tap OK.

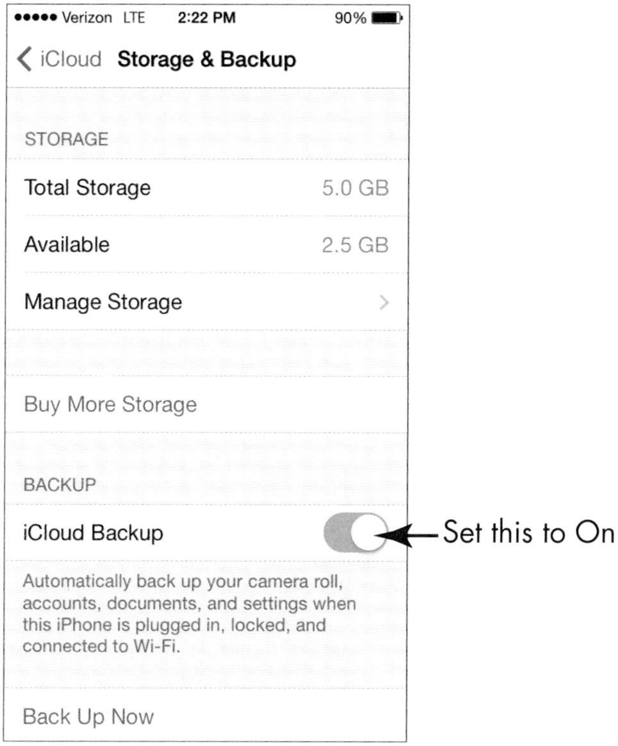

Figure 3-13

4. A dialog may appear asking if you want to allow iCloud
to use the location of your iPhone. Tap OK to use iCloud
~~and features such as Find My iPhone.~~ Your account is
now set up.

Make iCloud Sync Settings

1. When you have an iCloud account up and running (see
the previous task), you have to specify which type of content should be synced with your iPhone via iCloud. To
do so, tap Settings and then tap iCloud.

2. In the iCloud settings shown in **Figure 3-14,** tap the On/
Off button for any item that's turned off that you want to
turn on (or vice versa). You can sync Mail, Contacts,
Calendars, Reminders, Safari, Notes, Passbook, Keychain
(an app that stores all your passwords across all Apple
devices), Photos, and Documents & Data.

 If you want to allow iCloud to provide a service for
locating a lost or stolen iPhone, tap the On/Off button in the Find My iPhone field to activate it. This
service helps you locate, send a message to, or delete
content from your iPhone if it falls into other hands.

3. To enable automatic downloads of music, apps, and
books, return to the main Settings screen by tapping the
Settings button in the top-left corner of the screen (refer
to **Figure** 3-14), and then tap iTunes & App Stores.

4. Scroll down and tap the On/Off button for Music, Apps,
or Books to set up automatic downloads of any of this
content to your iPhone via iCloud.

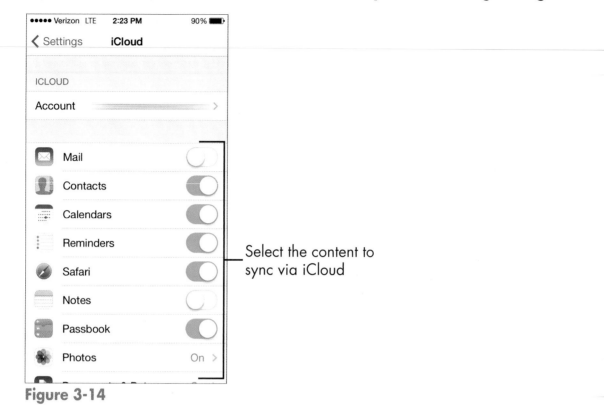

Figure 3-14

View the iPhone User Guide Online

1. The *iPhone User Guide* is equivalent to the Help system you may have used on a Windows or Mac computer. You access the guide online using the Safari browser. From the iPhone Home screen, tap the Safari icon.

2. Go to http://support.apple.com/manuals/ #iphone and on the screen that appears (see **Figure 3-15**), tap iPhone User Guide (For iOS 7 Software). The User Guide downloads and opens.

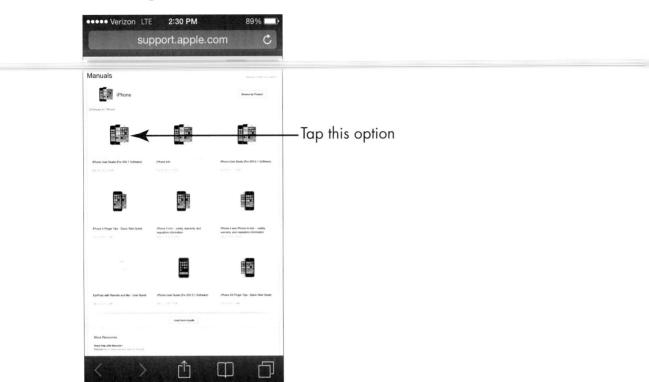

Tap this option

Figure 3-15

3. Scroll down to Contents (see **Figure 3-16**).

4. Tap a subtopic to display information about it, as shown in **Figure 3-17**.

5. Tap any link in the subtopic information to access additional topics.

6. Press the Home button to close the browser.

 To save the User Guide to your iPhone so you can use it when you don't have an Internet connection, with the User Guide open tap in the middle of the screen and then tap the Open in "iBooks" link in the top-right corner. The User Guide is now saved in iBooks.

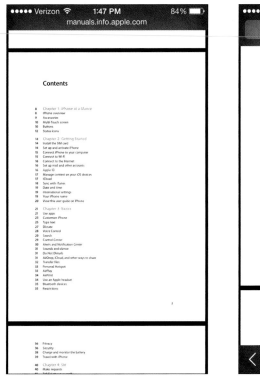

Figure 3-16

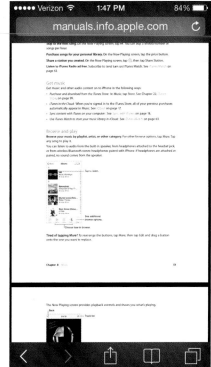

Figure 3-17

Part II

Start Using Your iPhone

Visit www.dummies.com/extras/iphoneforseniors for ideas about the many ways to use Siri with sample commands for interacting with various apps.

Making and Receiving Calls

*I*f you're the type who wants a cell phone only to make and receive calls, you probably didn't buy an iPhone. Still, making and receiving calls is one of the primary functions of any phone, smart or not.

In this chapter, you discover all the basics of placing calls, receiving calls, and using available tools during a call to mute sound, turn on speakerphone, and more. You also explore new features that help you manage how you respond to a call you can't take at the moment.

Use the Keypad to Place a Call

1. Dialing a call with a keypad is an obvious first skill for you to acquire, and it's dead simple. On any Home screen, tap Phone in the Dock, and the app opens; tap the keypad button at the bottom of the screen and the keypad appears (see **Figure** 4-1). (Note that if anything other than the keypad appears, you can just tap the Keypad button at the bottom of the screen to display the keypad.)

2. Enter the number you want to call by tapping the number buttons; as you do, the number appears above the keypad.

3. If you enter a number incorrectly, use the Delete button that appears on the keypad once you've begun to enter a number (a backward-pointing arrow with an X in it) to clear numbers one at a time.

4. Tap Call. The call is placed, and tools appear as shown in **Figure** 4-2.

Figure **4-1**

Figure **4-2**

When you enter a phone number, before you place the call, you can tap Add to Contacts under the phone number to add the person to your Contacts app. You can create a new contact or add the phone number to an existing contact using this feature.

 If you're on a call that requires that you punch in numbers or symbols such as a pound sign, tap the Keypad button on the tools that appear during a call to display the keypad. See more about using calling tools in the "Use Tools During a Call" task later in this chapter.

End a Call

In the following tasks, I tell you several other ways to place calls; however, I don't want to leave you on your first call without a way out. When you're on a phone call, the Call button changes to a red End button (see **Figure 4-3**). Tap End, and the call is disconnected.

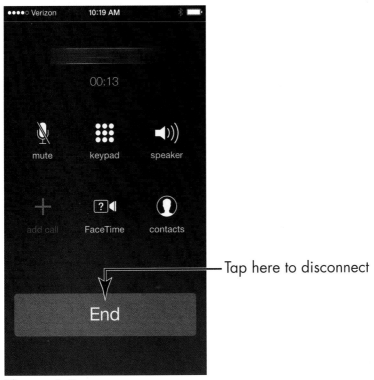

Figure 4-3

Place a Call Using Contacts

1. If you've created a contact and included a phone number in that contact record, you can use the Contacts app to place a call. Tap the Phone icon in any Home screen Dock.

2. Tap the Contacts button at the bottom of the screen.

3. In the Contacts list that appears (see **Figure** 4-4), scroll up or down to locate the contact you need or tap a letter along the right side to jump to that section of the list.

4. Tap the contact to display his or her record. In the record that appears (see **Figure** 4-5), tap the phone number field. The call is placed.

Contacts button   Tap the phone number

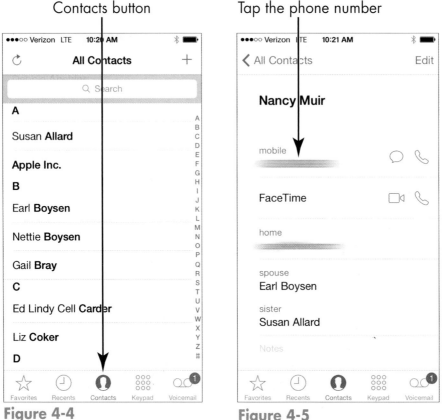

Figure 4-4   **Figure 4-5**

If you locate a contact and the record doesn't include a phone number, you can add it at this point by tapping the Edit button, entering the number, and then tapping Done. Place your call following Step 4 in the preceding steps.

Return a Recent Call

1. If you want to dial a number from a call you've recently made or received, you can use Recents. Tap Phone in the Dock on any Home screen.

2. Tap the Recents button at the bottom of the screen. A list of recent calls that you've both made and received appears (see **Figure** 4-6). Missed calls appear in red.

3. If you want to view only the calls you've missed, tap the Missed tab at the top of the screen.

4. Tap the "i" button to the right of any item to view information about calls to or from this person (see **Figure** 4-7).

5. Tap the Recents button to return to the Recents list, and then tap any call record to place a call to that number.

 To delete calls from your Recents list, with the list displayed, swipe across the contact name in the list, to the left or right, and a Delete button appears. Tap the button and the item is deleted.

Recents button

Figure 4-6

Figure 4-7

Use Favorites

1. You can save up to 50 contacts to Favorites in the Phone app so you can quickly make calls to your A-list folks or businesses. Tap Phone on any Home screen.

2. Tap the Favorites button at the bottom of the screen.

3. In the Favorites screen that displays (see **Figure** 4-8), tap the Add button.

4. Your Contacts list appears. Locate a contact you want to make a Favorite and tap it. In the contact record, tap Voice Call or FaceTime depending on which type of call you prefer to make to this person most of the time. (see **Figure** 4-9). The Favorites list reappears with your new favorite contact on it.

5. To place a call to a Favorite, display the Phone app, tap Favorites, and then tap a person on the list to place a call.

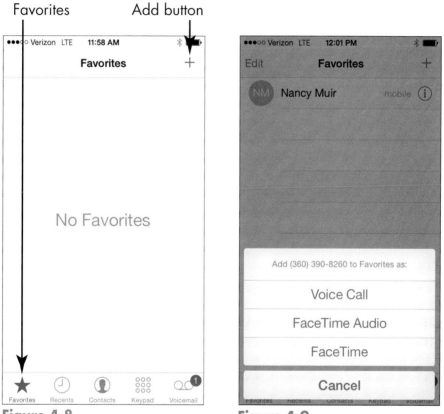

Favorites   Add button

Figure 4-8   Figure 4-9

If you decide to place a FaceTime call to a Favorite you've created using the Voice Call setting, just tap ~~the Information icon that appears to the right of the~~ favorite's listing and tap the FaceTime call button in the contact record that appears. You can also create two contacts for the same person, one with a cell phone and one with a land phone, for instance, and place one or both in Favorites. See Chapter 9 for more about making FaceTime calls.

Receive a Call

There's one step to receiving a call. When a call comes in to you, the screen shown in **Figure 4-10** appears. Tap Answer to pick up the call, or Decline to end the call without picking up, which sends the caller to your voice mail. If you don't tap either button, the call goes to your voice mail after a few rings.

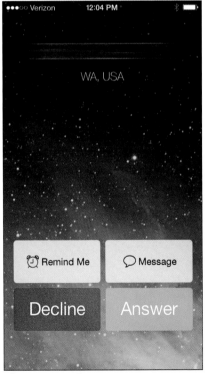

Figure 4-10

There's another quick way to send a call to voice mail or decline it; single-click the Sleep/Wake button on the top of your phone to send a call to voice mail or double-click the same button to decline the call.

Use Tools During a Call

When you're on a call, whether you initiated it or received it, a set of tools, shown in **Figure 4-11**, is displayed.

Here's what these six buttons allow you to do, starting with the top-left corner:

➡ **Mute:** Silences the phone call so the caller can't hear you, though you can hear the caller. The Mute button background turns white, as shown in **Figure 4-12,** when a call is muted. Tap again to unmute the call.

➡ **Keypad:** Displays the numeric keypad.

➡ **Speaker:** Turns the speakerphone feature on and off. If you are near a Bluetooth device and have Bluetooth turned on in your iPhone Settings, you will see a list of sources (such as a car Bluetooth connection for hands-free calls) and you can choose the one you want to use.

➡ **Add Call:** Displays Contacts so you can add a caller to a conference call.

➡ **FaceTime:** Begins a video call with somebody who has an iPhone 4, 4S, or 5, iPod touch (4th generation or later), iPad 2 or third-generation or later, an iPad mini, or a Mac running OS X 10.7 or later.

➡ **Contacts:** Displays a list of contacts.

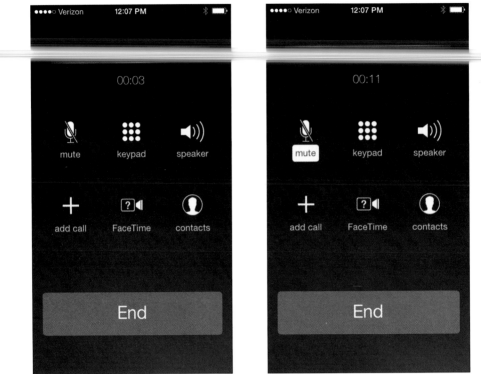

Figure 4-11   Figure 4-12

Turn On Do Not Disturb

1. Do Not Disturb is a feature that arrived with iOS 6 that has iPhone silence incoming calls when iPhone is locked, only displaying a moon-shaped icon to let you know a call is coming in. To turn the feature on, tap Settings.

2. Tap Do Not Disturb and then tap the On/Off button labeled Manual to turn the feature on.

 When you turn on the Do Not Disturb feature, be aware that calls from Favorites are automatically allowed through by default, though you can change that in Settings.

Set Up Exceptions for Do Not Disturb

1. If there are people whose calls you want to receive even when the Do Not Disturb feature is turned on, you can set that up. You can also set up a feature that allows a second call from the same number made within three minutes of the first to ring through. The theory with this feature is that two calls within a few minutes of each other might suggest an emergency situation you'll want to respond to. With the Do Not Disturb feature turned on (see the previous task), tap Settings.

2. Tap Do Not Disturb, and on the Do Not Disturb screen, tap the Repeated Calls On/Off button (see **Figure** 4-13).

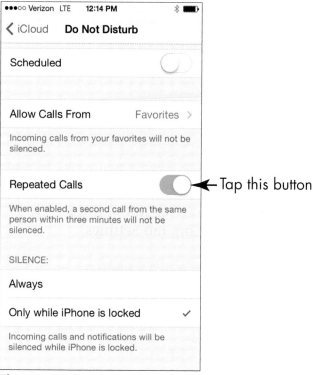

Figure 4-13

If you want to schedule Do Not Disturb to be active only during a certain time period, such as your lunch hour, tap the Scheduled feature shown in **Figure 4-13** and then set a from and to time.

Reply to a Call via Text or Set a Reminder to Callback

1. With iOS 6 came the ability to reply with a text message to callers whose calls you can't answer. You can also set up a reminder to call the person back later. When a call comes in that you want to deal with in one or both of these ways, swipe up on the screen.

2. Tap Message.

3. Tap on a preset reply, or tap Custom and then enter your own message.

4. To set up a reminder, tap Remind Me Later and then tap In One Hour, When I Get to Work, or When I Leave to be reminded when you leave your current location.

Managing Contacts

Chapter 5

*C*ontacts is the iPhone equivalent of the dog-eared address book that sits by your phone. The Contacts app is simple to set up and use, and it has some powerful features beyond simply storing names, addresses, and phone numbers.

For example, you can pinpoint a contact's address in iPhone's Maps app. You can use your contacts to address e-mail and Facebook messages and Twitter tweets quickly. If you store a contact record that includes a website, you can use a link in Contacts to view that website instantly. And, of course, you can easily search for a contact by a variety of criteria, including how people are related to you, such as family or mutual friends.

In this chapter, you discover the various features of Contacts, including how to save yourself time spent entering contact information by syncing a contacts list from services such as Google, Facebook, or Yahoo! to your iPhone.

Add a Contact

Contacts icon. An alphabetical list of contacts appears, like the one shown in **Figure 5-1**.

2. Tap the Add button, the button with the small plus sign (+) on it. A blank Info page opens (see **Figure 5-2**). Tap in any field, and the onscreen keyboard displays.

3. Enter any contact information you want. (Only one of the First, Last, or Company fields is required.)

4. To scroll down the contact page and see more fields, flick up on the page with your finger.

Add button

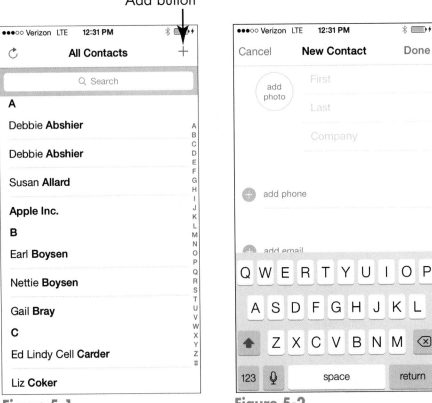

Figure 5-1

Figure 5-2

5. If you want to add information such as a mailing or street address, you can tap the relevant Add field, which opens additional entry fields.

6. To add an information field such as Nickname or Job Title, tap Add Field towards the bottom of the page. In the Add Field dialog that appears (see **Figure 5-3**), choose a field to add. (You may have to flick the page up with your finger to view all the fields.)

7. Tap the Done button when you finish making entries. The new contact appears in your address book. Tap it to see details (see **Figure 5-4**).

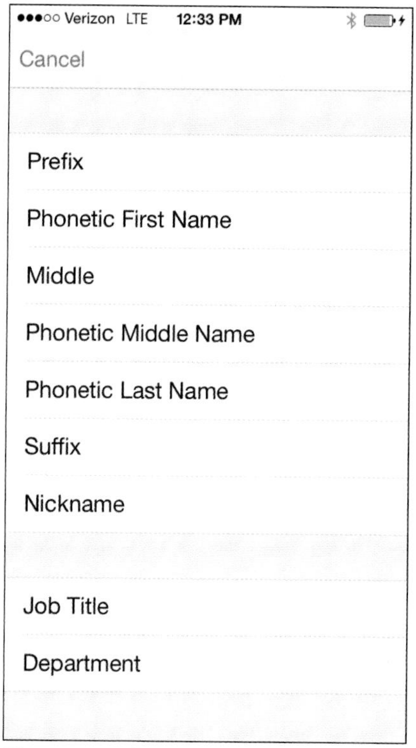

Figure 5-3

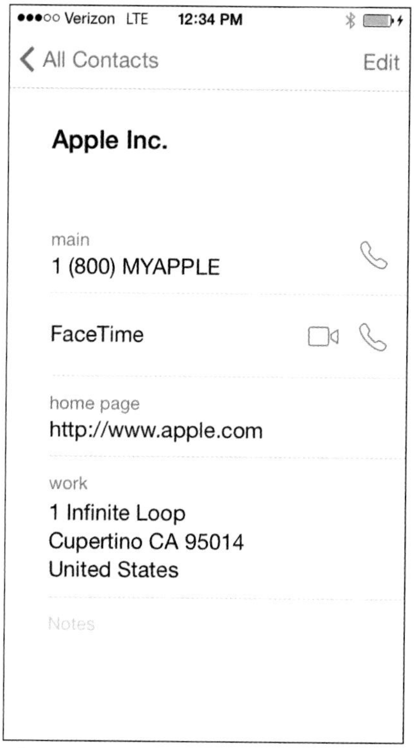

Figure 5-4

If your contact has a name that's difficult for you to pronounce, consider adding the Phonetic First Name or Phonetic Last Name field, or both, to that person's record (refer to Step 6).

You can choose a distinct ringtone or text tone for a new contact. Just tap the Ringtone or Text Tone field in the New Contact form to see a list of options. When that person calls either on the phone or via FaceTime, or texts you via SMS, MMS, or iMessage, you will recognize him or her from the tone that plays.

Sync Contacts with iCloud

1. You can use your iCloud account to sync contacts from your iPad to iCloud to back them up. These also become available to your iCloud e-mail account, if you set one up. Tap Settings and then tap iCloud.

2. In the iCloud settings shown in **Figure 5-5,** make sure the On/Off button for Contacts is set to On in order to sync contacts.

3. Tap the Back button in the top-left corner of the screen to return to Settings.

4. To choose which e-mail account to sync with, tap Mail, Contacts, Calendars, and tap iCloud.

5. In the following screen (see **Figure 5-6**), tap to turn Contacts on to merge contacts from that account via iCloud.

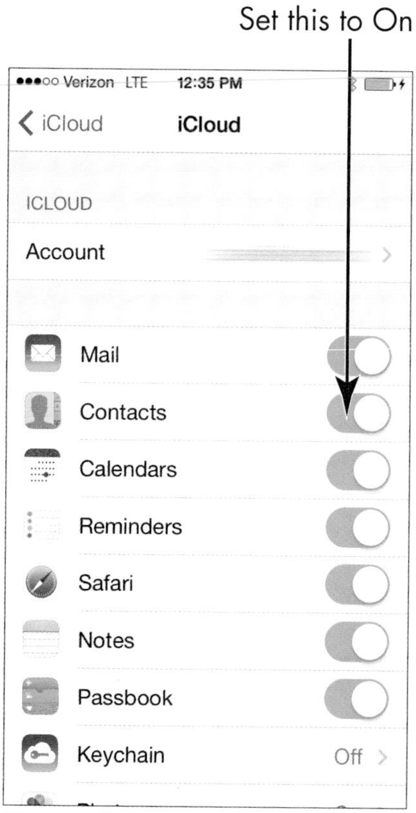

Set this to On   Set this to On

Figure 5-5

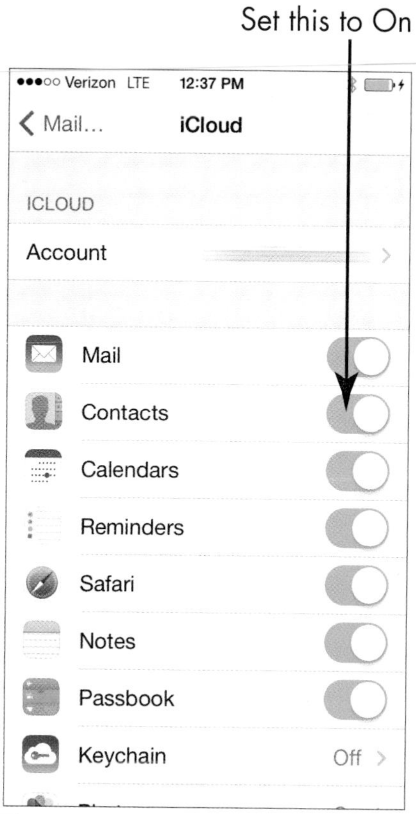

Figure 5-6

 You can also use iTunes to sync contacts among all your Apple devices and even a Windows PC. See Chapter 3 for more about making iTunes settings.

 You can also use the iTunes Wi-Fi sync feature in iPhone General Settings to sync with iTunes wirelessly from a computer connected to the same Wi-Fi network.

Assign a Photo to a Contact

1. With Contacts open, tap a contact to whose record you want to add a photo.

2. Tap the Edit button.

3. On the Info page that appears (see **Figure 5-7**), tap Add Photo.

4. In the dialog that appears, tap Choose Photo to choose an existing photo. You could also choose Take Photo to take that contact's photo on the spot.

5. In the Photos dialog that appears, choose a source for your photo (such as Camera Roll, Photo Stream, or other album).

6. In the photo album that appears, tap a photo to select it. The Move and Scale dialog, shown in **Figure 5-8**, appears.

Tap here to add a photo

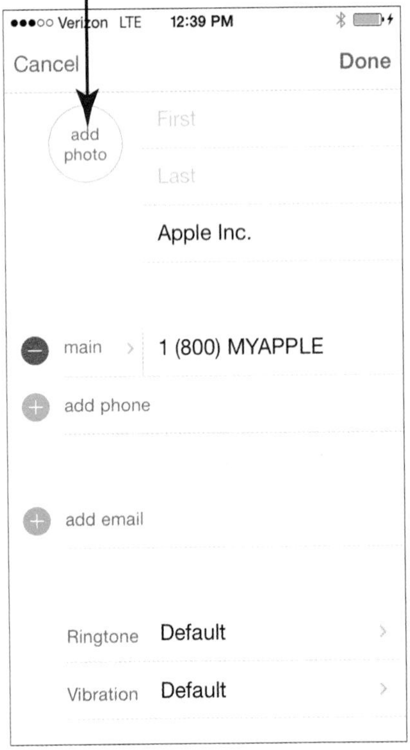

Figure 5-7

Figure 5-8

7. Tap the Choose button to use the photo for this contact.

8. Tap Done to save changes to the contact. The photo appears on the contact's Info page (see **Figure** 5-9).

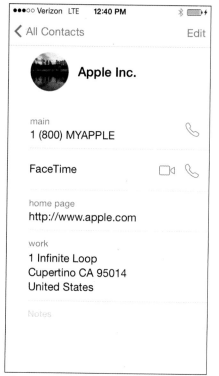

Figure 5-9

 While in the Photos dialog, in Step 6, you can modify the photo before saving it to the contact information. You can unpinch the iPhone screen to expand the photo and move it around the space to focus on a particular section and then tap the Choose button to use the modified version.

Add Twitter or Facebook Information

1. Since iOS 5, iPhone users have been able to add Twitter information to their Contacts so they can quickly tweet (send a short message to) others using Twitter. You can also add Facebook or LinkedIn information so you can post a message to your contact's Facebook or LinkedIn account. With Contacts open, tap a contact.

2. Tap the Edit button.

3. Scroll down and tap Add Field.

4. In the list that appears (see **Figure 5-10**), tap Add Social Profile.

5. Tap in the Twitter Social Profile field and enter the contact's username information for an account.

 If you prefer to add Facebook information instead of Twitter, tap Add Social Profile just under the Twitter field in Step 5 and enter the contact's Facebook information. (You can also tap the Add Social Profile link again and choose Flickr, LinkedIn, Myspace, or Add Custom Service in the fields that appear.)

6. Tap Done, and the information is saved. The account is now displayed when you select the contact, and you can send a tweet or Facebook message by simply tapping the username, then tapping the service you want to use to contact them, and then tapping the appropriate command (such as Facebook posting, as shown in **Figure 5-11**).

Tap this option

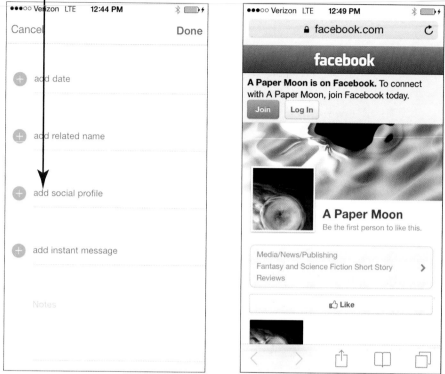

Figure 5-10   **Figure 5-11**

Designate Related People

1. You can quickly designate relationships in a contact record if those people are saved to Contacts. One great use for this is using Siri to simply say "Call Manager" to call someone who is designated in your contact information as your manager. Tap a contact and then tap Edit.

2. Scroll down the record and tap Add Related Name.

3. The field labeled Mother (see **Figure 5-12**) now appears.

4. Tap the Add Related Name and the Father field appears. Tap a field to change the label if you wish.

5. Tap the blue Information arrow in the field, and your
contact list appears. Tap the person's name, and it
appears in the field (see Figure 5-13)

Figure 5-12

Figure 5-13

After you add relations to a contact record, when you
select the person in the Contacts main screen, all the
related people for that contact are listed there.

Set Ringtones and Text Tones

1. If you want to hear a unique tone when you receive a
phone or FaceTime call from a particular contact, you can
set up this feature in Contacts. For example, if you want
to be sure you know instantly if your spouse, sick friend,
or boss is calling, set a unique tone for that person. Tap
to add a new contact or select a contact in the list of contacts and tap Edit.

2. Tap the Ringtone field in a new contact or tap Edit and then the Ringtone field in an existing contact, and a list of tones appears (see **Figure 5-14**).

3. Tap a tone, and it previews. When you hear one you like, tap Done.

 If you set a custom tone for someone, that tone will be used when they call or FaceTime you. You can also set a custom text tone to be used when they send you a text message — tap Text Tone instead of Ringtone in Step 2 in the preceding steps and follow the remaining steps.

 If your Apple devices are synced via iCloud, setting a unique ringtone for an iPhone contact will also set it for use with FaceTime and Messages on your iPad and Mac. See Chapter 3 for more about iCloud.

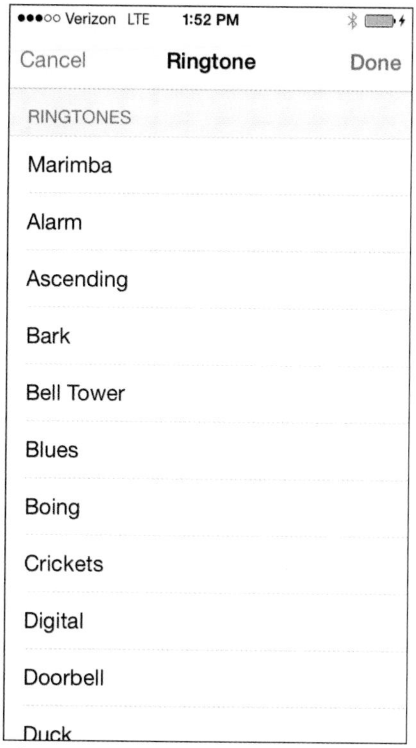

●●○○ Verizon LTE   1:52 PM   ⚮ ▭▸⚡

| Cancel | **Ringtone** | Done |

RINGTONES

Marimba

Alarm

Ascending

Bark

Bell Tower

Blues

Boing

Crickets

Digital

Doorbell

Duck

Figure 5-14

Search for a Contact

~~1. With Contacts open, tap in the Search field at the very~~ top of your contacts list (see **Figure 5-15**). The onscreen keyboard opens.

2. Type the first letter of either the first or last name or company. All matching results appear, as shown in **Figure 5-16**. For example, typing *Ea* might display *Earl* and email addresses including *@earthlink* in the results, all of which have *Ea* as the first two letters of the first or last part of the name or address.

Search field   Search results

Figure 5-15   Figure 5-16

3. Tap a contact in the results to display that person's Info page.

 You can search by phone number simply by entering the phone number in the search field until the list narrows to the person you're looking for. This might be a good way to search for all contacts in your town or company, for example.

 You can also use the alphabetical listing to locate a contact. Tap and drag to scroll down the list of contacts on the All Contacts page on the left. You can also tap on any tabbed letter along the left side of the page to scroll quickly to the entries starting with that letter.

Go to a Contact's Website

1. If you entered website information in the Home Page field, it automatically becomes a link in the contact's record. Tap the Contacts app icon in the Utilities folder to open Contacts.

2. Tap a contact's name to display the organization or person's contact information, locate the Home Page field, and then tap the link (see **Figure 5-17**).

3. The Safari browser opens with the web page displayed (see **Figure 5-18**).

Tap this link

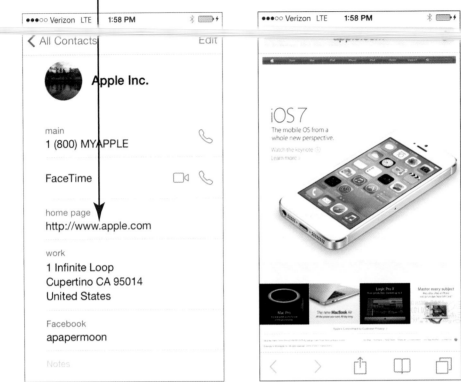

Figure 5-17

Figure 5-18

 You can't go directly back to Contacts after you follow a link to a website. You have to press the Home button and then tap the Contacts app again to reenter the application or use the multitasking feature by double-pressing the Home button and choosing Contacts from the icons that appear along the bottom of the screen.

Address E-mail Using Contacts

1. If you entered an e-mail address for a contact, the address automatically becomes a link in the contact's record. Tap the Contacts app icon on the Home screen to open Contacts.

2. Tap a contact's name to display the person's contact information, and then tap the e-mail address link in the field labeled Home (see **Figure 5-19**).

3. The New Message dialog appears, as shown in **Figure 5-20**. Initially, the title bar of this dialog reads *New Message,* but as you type a subject, *New Message* changes to the specific title.

4. Use the onscreen keyboard to enter a subject and message.

5. Tap the Send button. The message goes on its way!

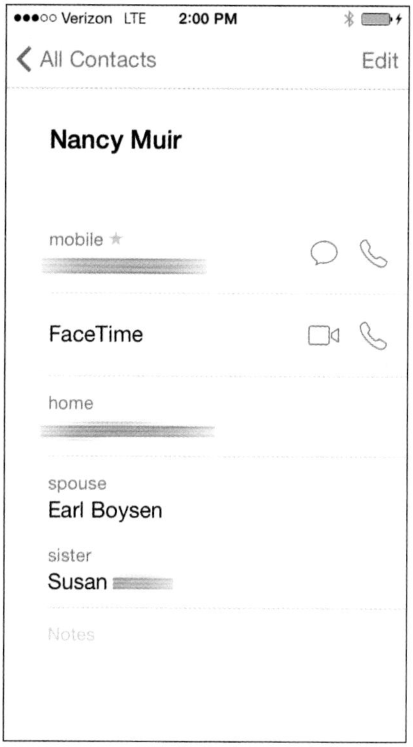

Figure 5-19

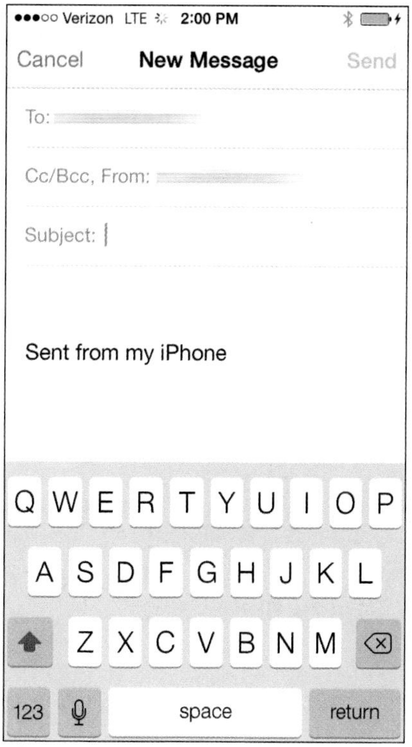

Figure 5-20

Share a Contact

~~1. After you've entered contact information, you can share it~~
with others via an e-mail message, text message, or tweet.
With Contacts open, tap a contact name to display its
information.

2. On the information page, scroll down and tap the Share
Contact button. In the dialog that appears shown in
Figure 5-21, tap Mail (at this point you could also tap
Message or Twitter). A New Message form appears.

 To share with an AirDrop-enabled device that is
nearby, use the AirDrop button in the screen shown
in **Figure 5-21**. Just select a nearby device and your
contact is transmitted to that person's device (such as
smartphone or tablet).

Figure 5-21

3. In the New Message form use the onscreen keyboard to enter the recipient's e-mail address. Note that if the person is saved in Contacts, you can just type his or her name here.

4. Enter information in the Subject field.

5. If you like, enter a message and then tap the Send button. The message goes to your recipient with the contact information attached as a .vcf file. (This *vCard* format is commonly used to transmit contact information.)

 When somebody receives a vCard containing contact information, he or she needs only to click the attached file to open it. At this point, depending on the e-mail or contact management program, the recipient can perform various actions to save the content. Other iPhone, iPod touch, iPad, or iPhone users can easily import .vcf records as new contacts in their own Contacts apps.

View a Contact's Location in Maps

1. If you've entered a person's address in Contacts, you have a shortcut for viewing that person's location in the Maps application. Tap the Phone app on the Home screen and then tap Contacts.

2. Tap the contact you want to view to display his information.

3. Tap Add Address and enter the address information. Tap Done and then tap the Address field. Maps opens and displays a map of the address (see **Figure 5-22**).

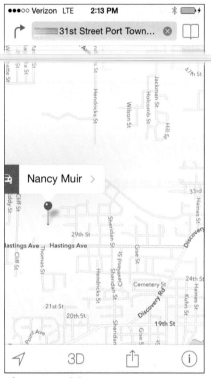

Figure 5-22

 This task works with more than your friends' addresses. You can save information for your favorite restaurant or movie theater or any other location and use Contacts to jump to the associated website in the Safari browser or to the address in Maps. For more about using Safari, see Chapter 10. For more about the Maps application, see Chapter 19.

Delete a Contact

1. When it's time to remove a name or two from your Contacts, it's easy to do. With Contacts open, tap the contact you want to delete.

2. On the information page (refer to **Figure** 5-4), tap the Edit button.

3. On the Info page that displays, drag your finger upward to scroll down and then tap the Delete Contact button at the bottom (see **Figure 5-23**).

4. The confirming dialog shown in **Figure 5-24** appears; tap the Delete Contact button to confirm the deletion.

 During this process, if you change your mind before you tap Delete, tap the Cancel button in Step 4. But be careful: After you tap Delete, there's no going back!

Tap this button   Tap this button

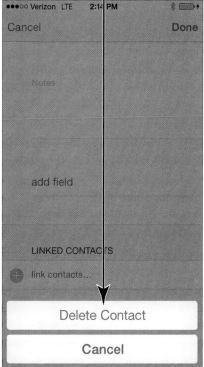

Figure 5-23   **Figure 5-24**

Using Handy Utilities

*U*tilities are simple apps that can be very useful indeed to help with common tasks such as calculating your meal tip or finding your way on a hike in the woods.

In this chapter, I help you explore two apps from the Utilities folder, Calculator to keep your numbers in line and Compass to help you find your way, as well as the Voice Memos app on the Home screen so you can record your best ideas for posterity. (Note that the third app in the Utilities folder, Contacts, is covered in Chapter 5).

Use the Calculator

1. This one won't be rocket science. The Calculator app works just about like every calculator app you've ever used. Go to the second Home screen and locate the Utilities folder.

2. Tap the Utilities folder to display the contents shown in **Figure 6-1**.

3. Tap the Calculator icon. The Calculator app appears.

4. Tap a few numbers (see **Figure** 6-2) and then use any of these functions and additional numbers to perform calculations:

- **+, −, x, and ÷:** These familiar buttons add, subtract, multiply, and divide the number you've entered.

- **+/−:** If the calculator is displaying a negative result, tap this to change it to a positive result, and vice versa.

- **AC/C:** This is the clear button; its name will change depending on whether you've entered one item or several (AC clears all; C clears just the last entry).

- **=:** This button produces the result of whatever calculation you've entered.

Figure 6-1

Figure 6-2

If you have a scientific nature, you'll be delighted to see that if you turn your phone to a landscape orientation, you get additional features that turn the basic calculator into a scientific calculator so you can play with calculations involving such functions as cosines and tangents. You can also use memory functions to work with stored calculations.

Find Your Way with Compass

1. Compass is a handy tool for finding your way, assuming that you get 3G or 4G reception wherever you are. Tap the Utilities folder and then tap the Compass app. The first time you do this, a message appears, asking if iPhone can use your current location to provide information. Tap OK.

2. If you're using Compass for the first time, you'll be asked to tilt the screen to roll a little red ball around a circle; this helps iPhone to calibrate the Compass app. When you've completed this exercise, the Compass app appears (see **Figure 6-3**). Move around with your iPhone, and the compass indicates your current orientation in the world.

3. Tap the bold white line indicating your current location as shown in **Figure 6-4,** and the display changes to True North; tap it again to display Magnetic North.

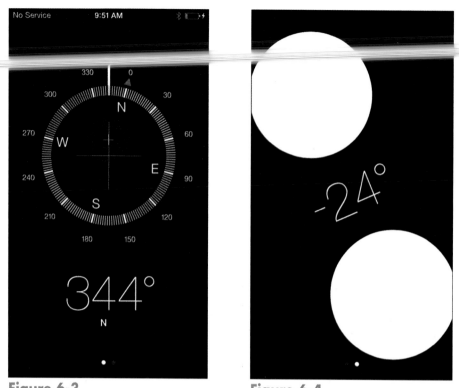

Figure 6-3

Figure 6-4

4. Swipe to the left to view a compass view with information about how many degrees off of zero a surface is (see **Figure 6-5**). If a surface beneath your phone is flat, the screen turns green. Use this to check to see if a surface is level.

 True North refers to the direction you follow from where you are to get to the North Pole; Magnetic North is correlated relative to the Earth's magnetic field. True North is the more accurate measurement because of the tilt of the Earth.

 You will know that you have a 4G connection if you see LTE in the Status bar. Not every location has this capability yet, so this is a good way to check if you're connected.

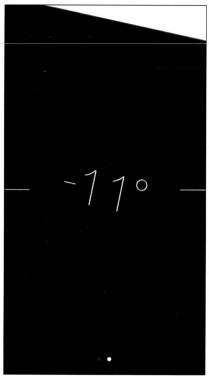

Figure 6-5

Record Voice Memos

1. Voice Memos is perhaps the most robust of the three apps covered in this chapter. The app allows you to record memos, edit memos by trimming them down, share them via e-mail or instant message with Messages, and label recordings so you find them again. On the Home screen, tap the Voice Memos icon.

2. In the Voice Memos app (see **Figure 6-6**), tap the red Record button to record a memo. (This button changes to a red Pause button when you're recording.)

3. A blue line moving from left to right shows that you're in recording mode (see **Figure 6-7**). While recording, you can tap the red Pause button to pause the recording or tap Done to stop recording.

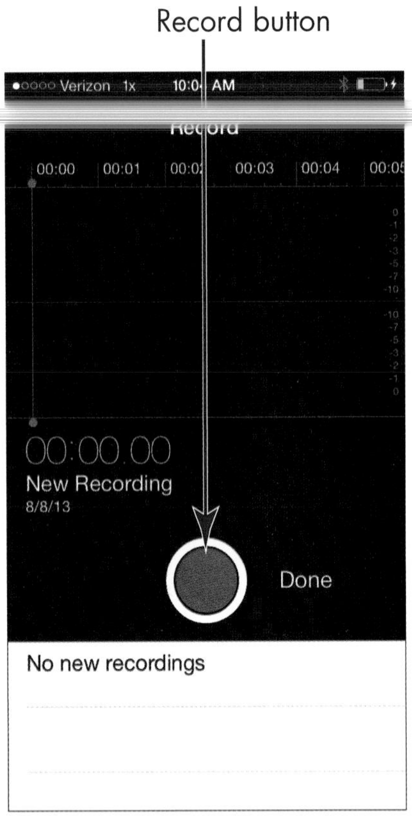

Record button   Pause button

●○○○○ Verizon 1x 10:0 AM   ●●○○○ Verizon 1x 10:0 AM

Record   Record

00:00 00:01 00:0 00:03 00:04 00:0   0:00 00:01 00:02 0 :03 00:04 00:05 0

00:00.00   00:03.25

New Recording   New Recording 2
8/8/13   8/8/13

Done   Done

No new recordings   New Recording 2
                           8/8/13   0:00:03

                           New Recording
                           8/8/13   0:00:05

Figure 6-6 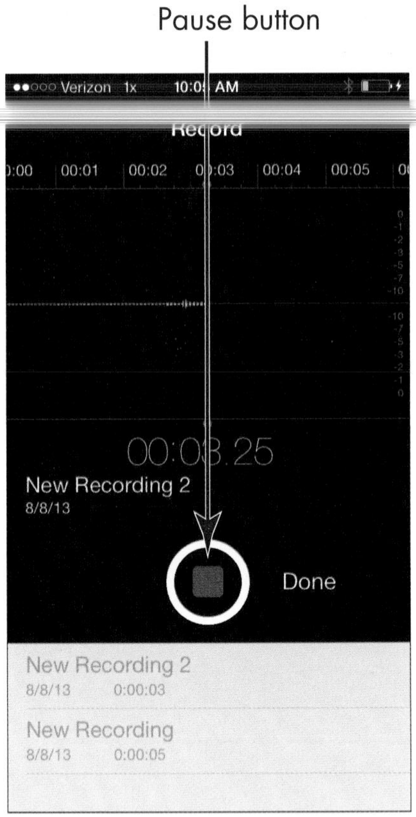   **Figure 6-7**

4. When you're done recording, a New Voice Memos dialog appears where you can enter a name for the recording and tap OK. A list of recorded memos appears (see **Figure 6-8**). Tap one to play it back, share it via AirDrop, iMessage, or Mail; edit it, or delete it.

 AirDrop is a feature new with iOS 7 that, with a fifth-generation iPhone, allows you to share items such as photos, voice memos, music, and more with another person who has an AirDrop-enabled device and is nearby. Learn more about AirDrop in Chapter 9.

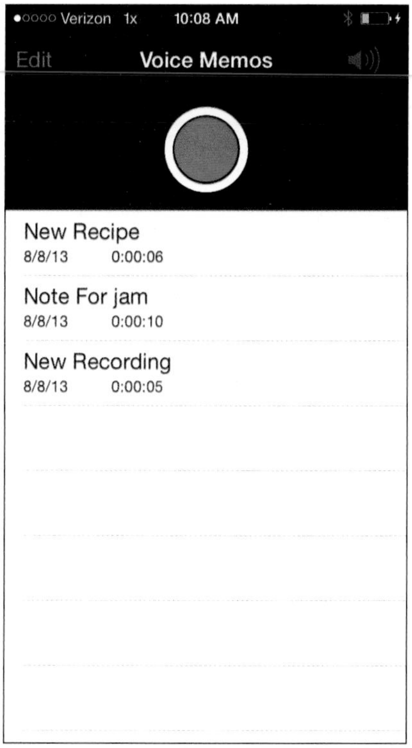

Figure 6-8

Trim a Voice Memo

1. Perhaps you repeated yourself at the beginning of your memo. If you want to cut part of a recorded memo out, you can trim it. With the list of recordings displayed (refer to **Figure 6-8**), tap any recording. The recording details display as shown in **Figure 6-9**.

2. Tap Edit.

3. In the Edit screen shown in **Figure 6-10**, tap the Trim button (it's a little square with dots coming off of the left and right side) and then drag the lines on the right or left of the memo bar and drag inward to trim a portion of the recording.

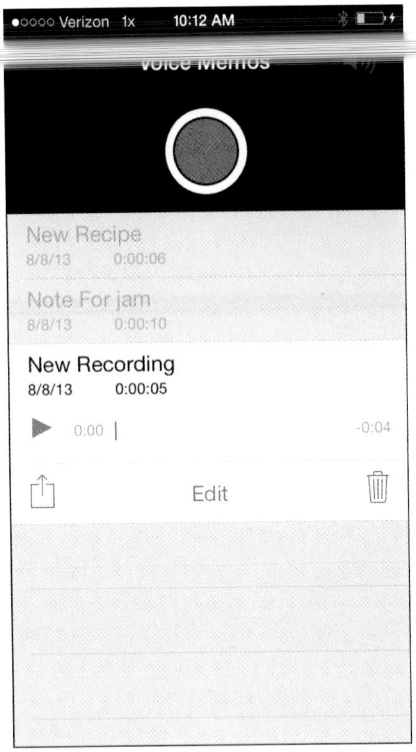

Trim button

New Recipe
8/8/13   0:00:06

Note For jam
8/8/13   0:00:10

New Recording
8/8/13   0:00:05

▶   0:00 | -0:04

Edit

Figure 6-9

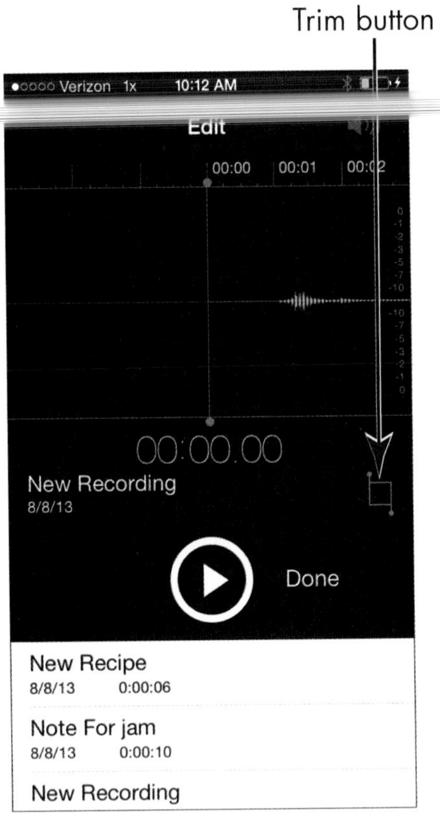

Edit

00:00   00:01   00:02

00:00.00

New Recording
8/8/13

▶   Done

New Recipe
8/8/13   0:00:06

Note For jam
8/8/13   0:00:10

New Recording

Figure 6-10

4. Tap Trim and a dialog appears. Tap Trim Original to apply the trim and save the recording, or Save As New Recording to apply the trim and save it as a new version of the recording.

 If you begin to trim a memo and change your mind, tap the Cancel button in the dialog mentioned in Step 4.

Rename a Voice Memo

1. You may occasionally have to rename a voice memo. With the list of memos displayed (refer to **Figure 6-8**), tap a memo to display its details.

2. Tap the name of the recording to display the New Voice Memo settings shown in **Figure 6-11**.

3. Tap Backspace on your iPhone keyboard to delete the current name; enter a new name and then tap Done to return to the list of memos where you see the memo now named with the label you just gave it (see **Figure 6-12**).

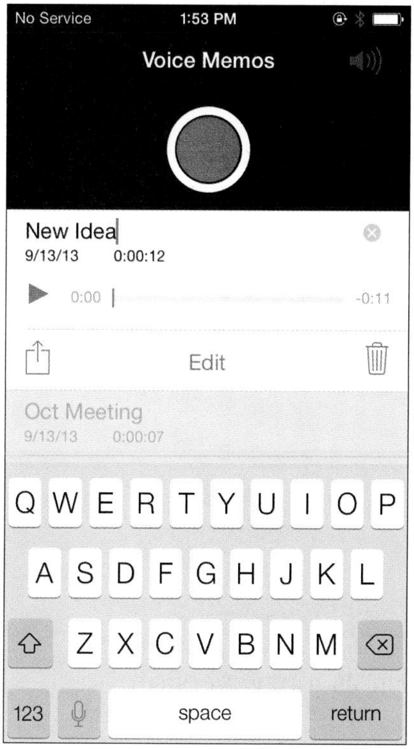

Figure 6-11 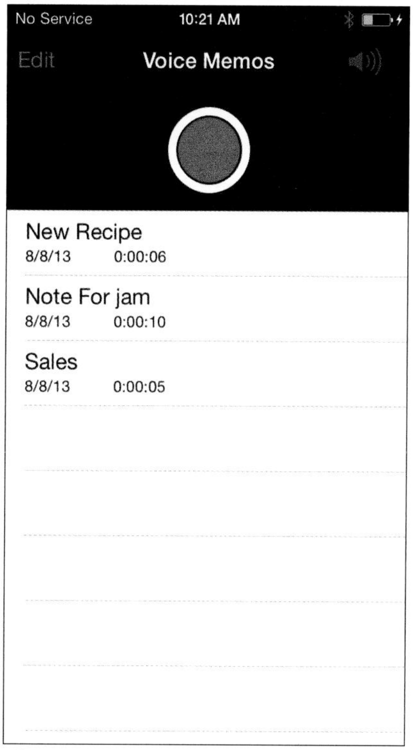   Figure 6-12

Share a Voice Memo

1. Tap a memo in the list of memos (refer to **Figure 6-8**) to select it.

2. Tap the Share button (the box with an arrow pointing out of the top) shown in **Figure 6-13**.

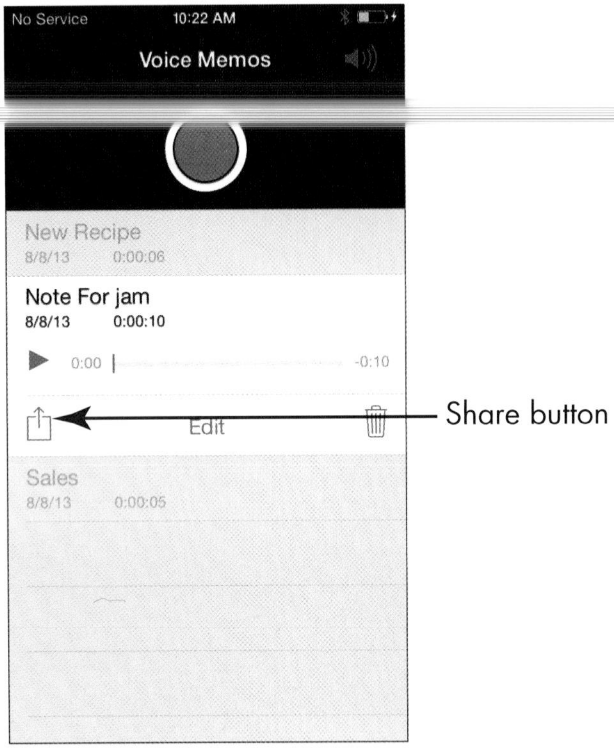

No Service   10:22 AM

Voice Memos

New Recipe
8/8/13   0:00:06

Note For jam
8/8/13   0:00:10

▶   0:00 | -0:10

                Edit   Share button

Sales
8/8/13   0:00:05

Figure 6-13

3. In the menu shown in **Figure 6-14,** tap Mail to display
an e-mail form or Message to display an iMessages form
to send an instant message with the voice memo attached
(see **Figure 6-15**).

4. Fill in the recipient's information, a subject if you're
sending an e-mail, and a message, and tap Send. The
voice memo and your message go on their way.

Tap this option

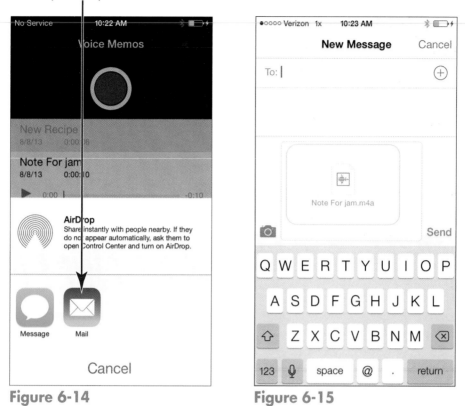

Figure 6-14

Figure 6-15

Making Your iPhone More Accessible

*i*Phone users are all different; some face visual, motor, or hearing challenges. If you're one of these folks, you'll be glad to hear that iPhone offers some handy accessibility features, with iOS 7 adding a handful more.

To make your screen easier to read, you can adjust the brightness or change wallpaper. You can also set up the VoiceOver feature to read onscreen elements out loud. Then there are a slew of features you can turn on or off including Zoom, Invert Colors, Speak Selection, Large Type, and more.

If hearing is your challenge, you can do the obvious and adjust the system volume. If you wear hearing aids you can choose the correct settings for using Bluetooth or another hearing aid mode. The iPhone also has settings for mono audio (useful when you're wearing headphones), Speak Auto-Text, using an LED Flash when an alert sounds, and a Phone Noise Cancellation feature. Features that help you deal with physical and motor challenges include an AssistiveTouch feature for those who have difficulty using the iPhone touch-screen, Switch Control for working with

Get ready to . . .

adaptive accessories, and the new Home Click Speed and Incoming Calls settings that allow you to adjust how quickly you have to tap the iPhone screen to work with features and whether you can use a head set or speaker to answer calls.

Finally, the Guided Access feature introduced with iOS 6 provides help for those who have difficulty focusing on one task and also provides a handy mode for showing presentations of content in settings where you don't want users to flit off to other apps, as in school or a public kiosk.

Set Brightness

1. Especially when using iPhone as an e-reader, you may find that a slightly less-bright screen reduces strain on your eyes. To adjust screen brightness, tap the Settings icon on the Home screen.

2. In the Settings dialog, tap Wallpapers & Brightness.

3. To control brightness manually, tap the Auto-Brightness On/Off button (see **Figure 7-1**) to turn off this feature.

4. Tap and drag the Brightness slider (refer to **Figure 7-1**) to the right to make the screen brighter, or to the left to make it dimmer.

5. Press the Home button to close the Settings dialog.

 If glare from the screen is a problem for you, consider getting a *screen protector*. This thin film not only protects your screen from damage but can also reduce glare.

 In the iBooks e-reader app, you can set a sepia tone for the page, which might be easier on your eyes. See Chapter 14 for more about using iBooks.

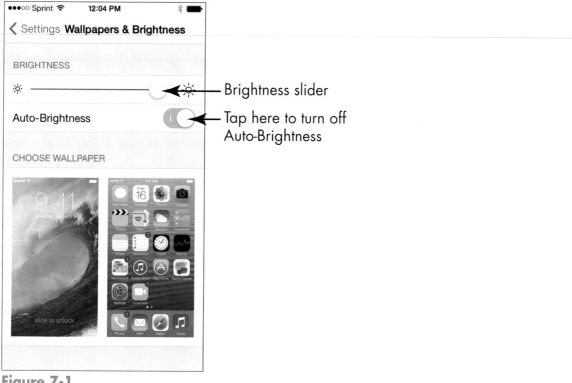

Brightness slider

Tap here to turn off
Auto-Brightness

Figure 7-1

Change the Wallpaper

1. The picture of rippling water — the default iPhone background image — may be pretty, but it may not be the one that works best for you. Choosing different wallpaper may help you to see all the icons on your Home screen. Start by tapping the Settings icon on the Home screen.

2. In the Settings dialog, tap Wallpapers & Brightness.

3. In the Wallpaper settings that appear, tap a wallpaper category such as Dynamic to view choices as shown in **Figure 7-2**. Tap on a sample to select it, or tap on an album in Photos to locate a picture to use as your wallpaper and tap on it.

4. In the preview that appears, tap Set.

5. In the menu on the following screen (see Figure 7-3) use your fingers to move and shrink or expand the image to manage exactly what portion of the image will be used and then tap Set.

6. In the following menu, tap either Set Lock Screen (the screen that appears when you lock the iPhone by tapping the power button), Set Home Screen, or Set Both.

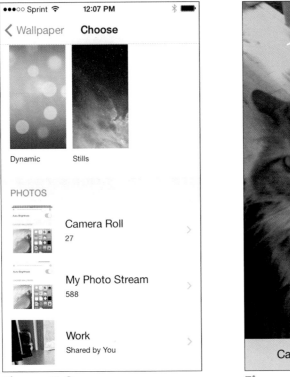

Figure 7-2

Figure 7-3

7. Press the Home button to return to your Home screen with the new wallpaper set as the background.

Set Up VoiceOver

1. VoiceOver reads the names of screen elements and settings to you, but it also changes the way you provide input to the iPhone. In Notes, for example, you can have VoiceOver read the name of the Notes buttons to you, and when you enter notes, it will read words or characters you've entered. It can also tell you whether features such as Auto-Correction are on. To turn on this feature, tap the Settings icon on the Home screen. Tap General and then scroll down and tap Accessibility.

2. In the Accessibility pane shown in **Figure 7-4**, tap the VoiceOver button.

3. In the VoiceOver pane shown in **Figure 7-5**, tap the VoiceOver On/Off button to turn on this feature. With VoiceOver on, you must first single-tap to select an item such as a button, which causes VoiceOver to read the name of the button to you. Then you double-tap the button to activate its function. (VoiceOver reminds you about this if you turn on Speak Hints, which is helpful when you first use VoiceOver, but it soon becomes annoying.)

4. Tap the VoiceOver Practice button to select it, and then double-tap the button to open VoiceOver Practice. (This is the new method of tapping that VoiceOver activates.) Practice using gestures such as pinching or flicking left, and VoiceOver tells you what action each gesture initiates.

5. Tap the Done button and then double-tap it to return to the VoiceOver dialog. Tap the Speak Hints field, and VoiceOver speaks the name of each tapped item. Double-tap the slider to turn off Speak Hints.

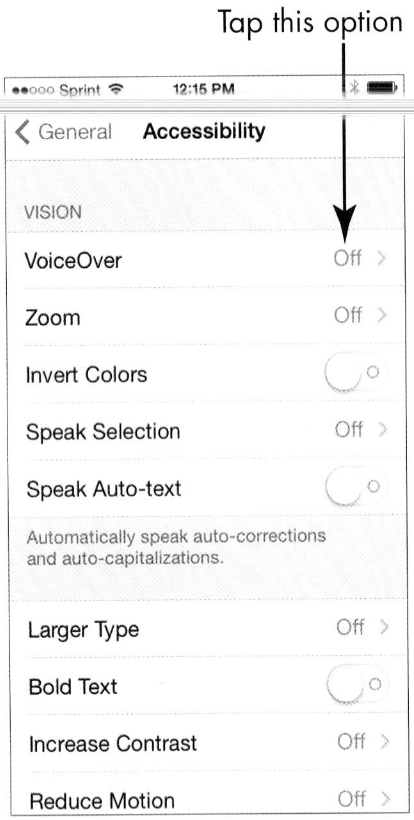

Tap this option   Tap to turn on VoiceOver

●●○○○ Sprint 📶   12:15 PM   ❋ ▬▬▮   ●●○○○ Sprint 📶   12:15 PM   ❋ ▬▬▮

‹ General **Accessibility**   ‹ Accessibility **VoiceOver**

VISION

VoiceOver   Off ›   VoiceOver   ○

Zoom   Off ›   VoiceOver speaks items on the
                                  screen:
Invert Colors   ○   • Tap once to select an item
                                  • Double-Tap to activate the selected
Speak Selection   Off ›   item
                                  • Swipe three fingers to scroll
Speak Auto-text   ○
                                  SPEAKING RATE
Automatically speak auto-corrections
and auto-capitalizations.
                                  🐢 ———————————————— 🐇
Larger Type   Off ›

Bold Text   ○   Speak Hints   ⬤

Increase Contrast   Off ›   Use Pitch Change   ⬤

Reduce Motion   Off ›   Use Sound Effects   ⬤

                                  Use Compact Voice   ○

Figure 7-4 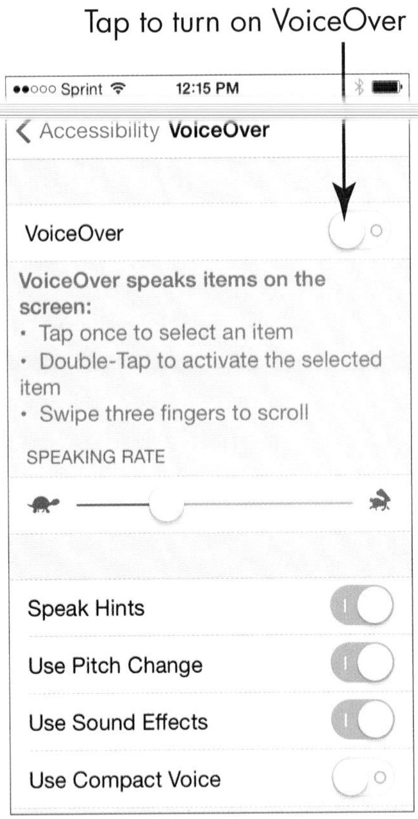   **Figure 7-5**

6. If you want VoiceOver to read words or characters to you
(for example, in the Notes app), tap and then double-tap
Typing Feedback.

7. In the Typing Feedback dialog, tap and then double-tap
to select the option you prefer. The Words option causes
VoiceOver to read words to you, but not characters, such
as the "dollar sign" ($). The Characters and Words
option causes VoiceOver to read both, and so on.

8. Press the Home button to return to the Home screen.
Read the next task to find out how to navigate your
iPhone after you've turned on VoiceOver.

You can change the language that VoiceOver speaks. In General settings, choose International and then Language and select another language. This action, however, also changes the language used for labels on Home icons and various settings and fields in iPhone.

 You can use the Accessibility Shortcut setting to help you more quickly turn the VoiceOver, Zoom, Switch Control, AssistiveTouch, or Invert Colors features on and off. In the Accessibility dialog, tap Accessibility Shortcut. In the dialog that appears, choose what you want a triple-click of the Home button to activate. Now a triple-click with a single finger on the Home button provides you with the option you selected wherever you go in iPhone.

Use VoiceOver

After VoiceOver is turned on, you need to figure out how to use it. I won't kid you — using it is awkward at first, but you'll get the hang of it! Here are the main onscreen gestures you should know how to use:

➡ **Tap an item to select it.** VoiceOver then speaks its name.

➡ **Double-tap the selected item.** This action activates the item.

➡ **Flick three fingers.** It takes three fingers to scroll around a page with VoiceOver turned on.

Table 7-1 provides additional gestures to help you use VoiceOver. I suggest that if you want to use this feature often, you read the VoiceOver section of the iPhone online *User Guide*, which goes into a great deal of detail about the ins and outs of using VoiceOver. You'll find the *User Guide* in the Bookmarks section of the Safari browser.

Table 7-1	VoiceOver Gestures
Gesture	**Effect**
Flick right or left.	Select the next or preceding item.
Tap with two fingers.	Stop speaking the current item.
Flick two fingers up.	Read everything from the top of the screen.
Flick two fingers down.	Read everything from the current position.
Flick three fingers up or down.	Scroll one page at a time.
Flick three fingers right or left.	Go to the next or preceding page.
Tap three fingers.	Speak the scroll status (for example, line 20 of 100).
Flick four fingers up or down.	Go to the first or last element on a page.
Flick four fingers right or left.	Go to the next or preceding section (as on a web page).

 If tapping with two or three fingers seems difficult for you, try tapping with one finger from one hand and one or two from the other. When double- or triple-tapping, you have to perform these gestures as quickly as you can for them to work.

 Check out some of the settings for VoiceOver, including a choice for Braille, Language Rotor for making language choices, the ability to navigate images, and a setting to have iPhone speak notifications.

Make Additional Vision Settings

Several Vision features are simple on/off settings, so rather than give you the steps to get to those settings repeatedly, I provide this useful bullet list of additional features you can turn on or off after you tap Settings⇨General⇨Accessibility:

➠ **Zoom:** The Zoom feature enlarges the contents displayed on the iPhone screen when you double-tap the screen with three fingers. The Zoom feature works almost everywhere in iPhone: in Photos, on web pages, on your Home screens, in your Mail, in Music, and in Videos — give it a try!

➠ **Invert Screen Colors**: The Invert Screen Colors setting reverses colors on your screen so that white backgrounds are black and black text is white.

The Invert Colors feature works well in some places and not so well in others. For example, in the Photos application, pictures appear almost as photo negatives. Your Home screen image will likewise look a bit strange. And don't even think of playing a video with this feature turned on! However, if you need help reading text, White on Black can be useful in several apps.

➠ **Turn On Large Text:** If having larger text in apps such as Contacts, Mail, and Notes would be helpful to you, you can turn on the Large Text feature and choose the text size that works best for you.

➠ **Bold Text:** Turning on this setting will first restart your iPhone (after asking you for permission to do so) and then cause text in various apps and in Settings to be bold. This is a handy setting as text in the iOS 7 redesign was simplified, meaning thinner!

➠ **Increase Contrast:** Use this setting to set up backgrounds in some areas of iPhone and apps with greater contrast which should improve visibility.

➠ **Reduce Motion:** Tap this accessibility feature and then tap the On/Off setting to turn off the parallax ~~effect new with iOS 7, which causes the background~~ of your Home screens to appear to float as you move the phone around.

➠ **On/Off Labels:** If you have trouble making out colors, and so have trouble telling when an On/Off setting is On (and green) and Off (White), use this setting to add a circle to the right of a setting when it's off and a white vertical line to a setting when it's on (see **Figure 7-6**).

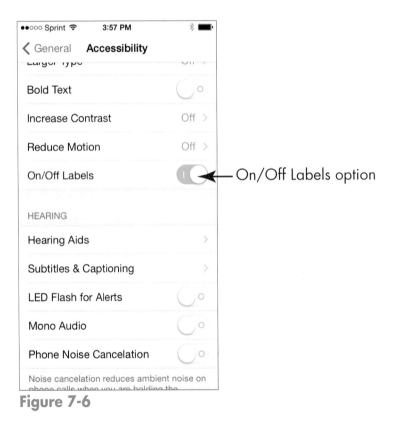

Figure 7-6

Use iPhone with Hearing Aids

1. If you have Bluetooth enabled or another style of hearing aid, your iPhone may be able to detect it and work with its settings to improve sound on your phone calls. Tap Settings and then tap General.

2. Tap Accessibility and then tap Hearing Aids.

3. On the following screen shown in **Figure 7-7**, your iPhone will search for hearing aid devices; when yours appears, tap on it.

4. Tap Hearing Aid Mode to turn on a feature that could improve audio quality using your hearing aid.

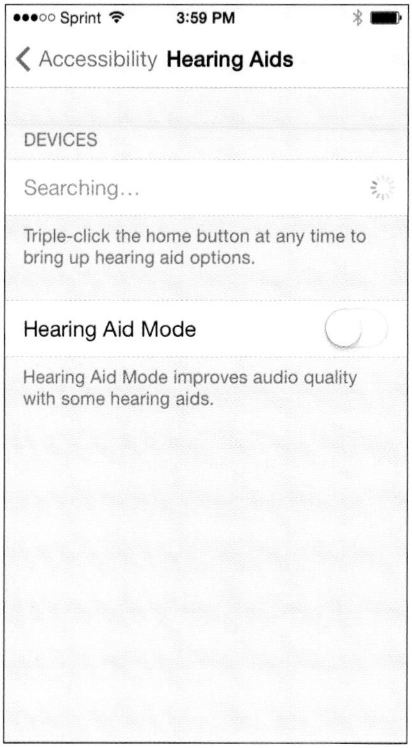

Figure 7-7

Adjust the Volume

1. ~~Though individual apps such as Music and Video have~~ their own volume settings, you can set your iPhone system volume for your ringer and alerts as well to help you better hear what's going on.

2. Tap Sounds.

3. In the Sounds pane that appears (see **Figure 7-8**), tap and drag the Ringer and Alerts slider to the right to increase the volume of these audible attention grabbers, or to the left to lower it.

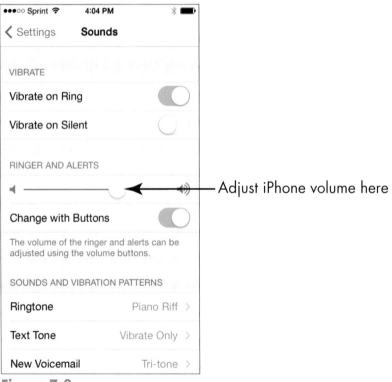

Adjust iPhone volume here

Figure 7-8

4. Press the Home button to close Settings.

 In the Sounds pane, you can turn on or off the sounds that iPhone makes when certain events occur (such as receiving new mail or Calendar alerts). These sounds are turned on by default.

 Even those of us with perfect hearing sometimes have trouble hearing a phone ring, especially in busy public places. Consider using the Vibrate settings in the Sounds pane to have your phone vibrate when a call is coming in.

Set Up Subtitles and Captioning

1. Closed captioning and subtitles help folks with hearing challenges enjoy entertainment and educational content. From the Accessibility Settings screen tap Subtitles and Captioning.

2. On the following screen shown in **Figure 7-9**, tap the On/Off button to turn on Closed Captions and SDH (Subtitles for the Deaf and Hard of Hearing).

3. Tap the Home button to return to the Home screen.

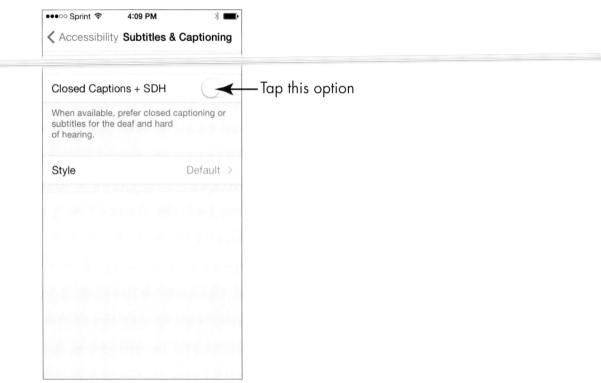

Figure 7-9

Manage Other Hearing Settings

Several hearing accessibility settings, including several new with iOS 7, are simple on/off settings, including:

➡ **Use Mono Audio:** Using the stereo effect in head-phones or a headset breaks up sounds so that you hear a portion in one ear and a portion in the other ear, to simulate the way your ears process sounds unless there is only one channel of sound in which case that sound is sent to both ears. However, if you're hard of hearing or deaf in one ear, you're hearing only a portion of the sound in your hearing ear, which can be frustrating. If you have such hearing challenges and want to use iPhone with a headset connected, you should turn on Mono Audio. When it's turned on, all sound is combined and distributed to both ears.

➡ **Have iPhone Speak Auto-text:** The Speak Auto-text feature speaks autocorrections and autocapitaliza- tions (you can turn on both these features using Keyboard settings). When you enter text in an app such as Notes or Mail, the app then makes either type of change, while Speak Auto-text lets you know what change was made.

Why would you want iPhone to tell you whenever an autocorrection has been made? If you have vision challenges and you know that you typed *ain't* when writing dialogue for a character in your novel, but iPhone corrected it to *isn't*, you would want to know. Similarly, if you type the poet's name *e.e. Cummings* and autocapitalization corrects it (incorrectly), you need to know immediately so that you can change it back again!

➡ **LED Flash:** If you need a visual clue when an alert is spoken, turn this setting on.

➡ **Phone Noise Cancellation:** If you're annoyed at ambient noise when you make a call in public (or noisy private) settings, turn on the Phone Noise Cancellation feature. When you hold the phone to your ear during a call, this feature reduces back- ground noise to some extent.

Turn On and Work with AssistiveTouch

1. The AssistiveTouch Control panel helps those who have challenges working with buttons to provide input to iPhone using the touchscreen. To turn on AssistiveTouch, tap Settings on the Home screen, and then tap General and Accessibility.

2. In the Accessibility pane, scroll down and tap AssistiveTouch. In the pane that appears, tap the On/Off button for AssistiveTouch to turn it on (see Figure 7-10). A gray square (called the AssistiveTouch Control panel) then appears on the top left of the pane. This square now appears in the same location in whatever apps you display on your iPhone.

3. Tap the AssistiveTouch Control panel to display options, as shown in **Figure 7-11**.

Tap to turn on AssistiveTouch

Figure 7-10   **Figure 7-11**

4. You can tap Favorites or Device on the panel to see additional choices, tap Siri to activate the personal assistant feature, or tap Home to go directly to the Home screen. Once you've chosen an option, tapping the Back arrow takes you back to the main panel.

Table 7-2 shows the major options available in the AssistiveTouch Control panel and their purpose.

Table 7-2	AssistiveTouch Controls
Control	**Purpose**
Siri	Activates the Siri feature, which allows you to speak questions and make requests of your iPhone.
Favorites	Displays a set of gestures with only the Pinch gesture preset; you can tap any of the other blank squares to add your own favorite gestures.
Device	You can rotate the screen, lock the screen, turn volume up or down, mute or unmute sound, or shake iPhone to undo an action using the presets in this option.
Home	Sends you to the Home screen.

 In addition to using Siri, don't forget about using the Dictation key on the keyboard (iPhone 4S and later) to speak text entries and basic keyboard commands.

Turn On Additional Physical and Motor Settings

Use these On/Off settings to help you deal with how fast you tap and how you answer phone calls:

➡ **Home Click Speed**: Sometimes if you have dexterity challenges it's hard to double-tap or triple-tap the Home button fast enough to make an effect. Choose the Slow or Slowest setting when you tap this setting to allow you a bit more time to make that second or third tap.

⟹ **Incoming Calls:** If you prefer to use your speaker phone to receive incoming calls, or you typically use a headset with your phone that allows you to tap a button to receive a call, choose Headset or Speaker when you tap this setting. Speakers and headsets can both provide a better hearing experience for many.

 If you have certain adaptive accessories that allow you to control devices with head gestures, you can use them to control your iPhone, highlighting features in sequence and then selecting one. Use the Switch Control feature in the Accessibility settings to turn this mode on and make settings.

Focus Learning with Guided Access

1. Guided Access is a feature that arrived with iOS 6. You can use it to limit a user's access to iPhone to a single app, and even limit access in that app to certain features. This is considered useful in several settings, ranging from a classroom, for use by someone with attention deficit disorder, and even to a public setting such as a kiosk where you don't want users to be able to open other apps. Tap Settings and then tap General.

2. Tap Accessibility and then tap Guided Access and on the screen that follows (see **Figure 7-12**), tap Guided Access to turn the feature on.

3. Tap Set Passcode to activate a passcode so those using an app cannot return to the Home screen to access other apps. In the Set Passcode dialog that appears (see **Figure 7-13**), enter a passcode using the numeric pad. Enter the number again when prompted.

4. Press the Home button and tap an app to open it.

Tap to turn on Guided Access

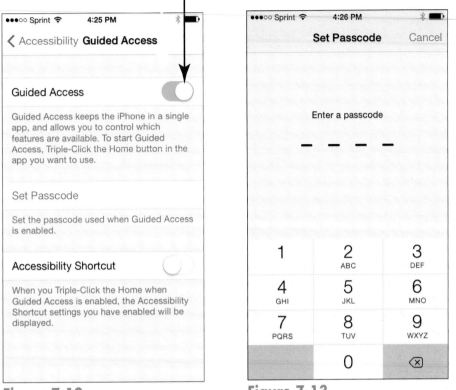

Figure 7-12   **Figure 7-13**

5. Triple-click the Home button. You are presented with an Option button along the bottom of the screen; tap the button to display three options:

- **Sleep/Wake Button:** You can put your iPhone to sleep or wake it up with a triple-tap of the Home button.

- **Volume Buttons:** You can tap to turn this Always On or Always Off. If you don't want users to be able to adjust volume using the volume toggle on the side of the iPhone, for example, use this setting.

- **Touch:** If you don't want users to be able to use the touchscreen, turn this off.

- **Motion:** Turn this setting off if you don't want users to move the iPhone around — for example, to play a race car driving game.

6. At this point, you can also use your finger to circle areas of the screen you want to disable, such as a Store button in the Music app.

7. Triple-click the Home button and then enter your passcode, if you set one, to return to the Home screen.

Talking to Your iPhone with Siri

*O*ne of the hottest features on iPhone 4S, 5, and 5S/5C is Siri, a personal assistant feature that responds to the commands you speak to your phone. With Siri, you can ask for nearby restaurants, and a list appears. You can dictate your e-mail messages rather than typing them. You can open apps with a voice command. Calling your mother is as simple as saying, "Call Mom." Want to know the capital of Rhode Island? Just ask. Siri checks several online sources to answer questions ranging from the result of a mathematical calculation to the next scheduled flight to Dubai. You can also have Siri perform tasks such as returning calls and controlling iTunes Radio.

If you have an iPhone 4 or 3GS, you don't have Siri but you do have a Voice Control feature you can explore by holding down the Home button for about two seconds until you hear a beep. This feature is more limited, and you have to state commands in a very specific way such as "Call Joe" or "Play Music." Note that, with an iPhone 4S, iPhone 5, and iPhone 5S, when you activate Siri, you override Voice Control, which is just as well, because Siri leaves Voice Control in the dust.

If you don't have an iPhone 4S, 5, or 5S, you can skip this chapter and dream of the day when you can upgrade (or jailbreak your iPhone 4 and port Siri to it). But if you have your iPhone 4S, 5, or 5S/5C in hand, you're about to discover an absolutely awesome feature.

Activate Siri

When you first go through the process of registering your phone, making settings for your location, using iCloud, and so on, at one point you will see the screen in **Figure 8-1**. To activate Siri at this point, just tap Use Siri. As you begin to use your phone, iPhone reminds you about using Siri by displaying a message.

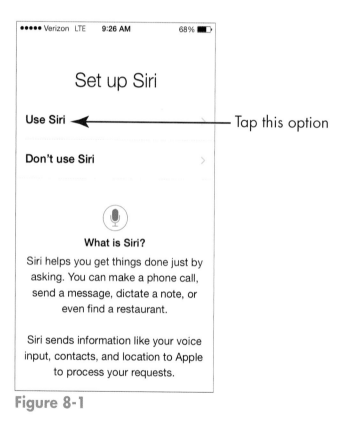

Figure 8-1

If you didn't activate Siri during the registration process, you can use Settings to turn Siri on by following these steps:

1. Tap the Settings icon on the Home screen.

2. Tap General, and then tap Siri (see **Figure 8-2**).

3. In the dialog in **Figure 8-3**, tap the On/Off button to turn Siri on.

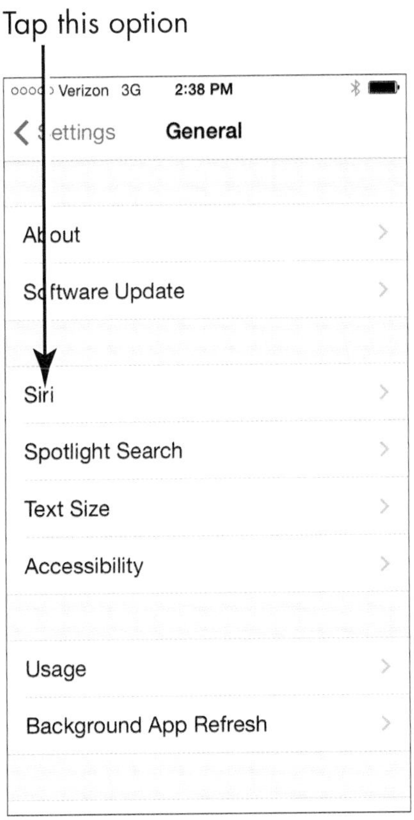

Tap this option

Tap to turn Siri on

Figure 8-2

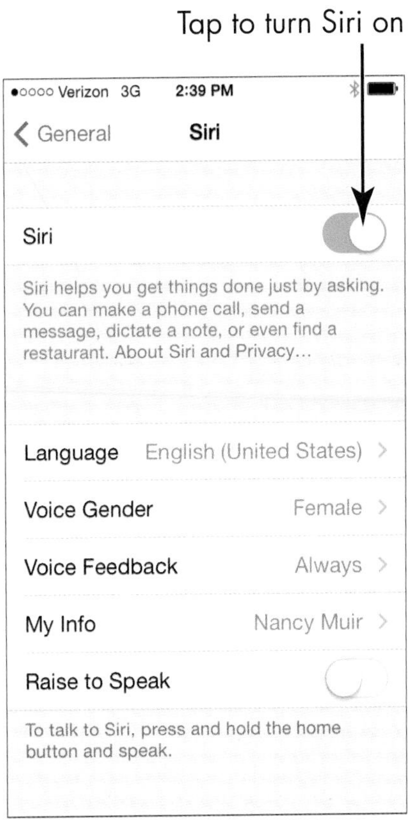

Figure 8-3

4. If you wish to change the language Siri uses, tap Language and choose a different language in the list that appears.

5. To change the gender of Siri's voice from female to male, tap Voice Gender and then tap Male.

 If you only want Siri to verbally respond to your requests when the handset isn't in your hands, tap Voice Feedback and choose Handsfree Only. Here's how this setting works and why you might want to use it: In general, if you're holding your iPhone, you can read responses on the screen so you might choose not to have your phone talk to you out loud. In addition, if you are, say, puttering with an electronics project and want to speak requests for mathematical calculations and hear the answers rather than have to read them, Handsfree is a useful setting.

 Siri is only available on iPhone 4S, 5, or 5S/5C with Internet access, and cellular data charges could apply when Siri checks online sources. In addition, Apple warns that available features may vary by area.

Understand All That Siri Can Do

Siri allows you to interact by voice with many apps on your iPhone. You can pose questions or ask to do something like make a call or add an appointment to your calendar, for example. Siri can also search the Internet or use an informational service called Wolfram|Alpha to provide information on just about any topic.

 With the arrival of iOS 7, Siri also checks with Wikipedia, Bing, and Twitter to get you the information you ask for. In addition, you can now use Siri to tell iPhone to return a call, play your voice mail, or control iTunes Radio playback.

Siri knows what app you're using, though you don't have to have that app open to make a request involving it. However, if you are in the Messages app, you can make a statement like "Tell Susan I'll be late.", and Siri knows you want to send a message.

Siri requires no preset structure for your questions; you can phrase things in several ways. For example, you might say, "Where am I?" to see a map of your current location, or you could say, "What is my current location?" or "What address is this?" and get the same results.

Siri responds to you both verbally and with text information (see **Figure** 8-4), in a form as with e-mail, or in a graphic display for some items such as maps. When a result appears, you can tap it to make a choice or open a related app.

Siri works with Phone, Music, Messages, Reminders, Calendar, Maps, Mail, Weather, Stocks, Clock, Contacts, Notes, social media apps such as Twitter, Safari, and iTunes Radio (see **Figure** 8-5). In the following tasks, I provide a quick guide to some of the most useful ways you can use Siri.

 If you want to dictate text in an app like Notes, use the Dictation key on the onscreen keyboard in iPhone 4S and later to do so. See the task "Use Dictation" later in this chapter for more about this feature.

Note that no matter what kind of action you wish to perform, first press and hold the Home button until Siri opens. Remember this only works with iPhone 4S and later models; for iPhone 4, this action activates Voice Control. The rest of this chapter assumes you're working with a 4S, 5, 5S, or 5C model.

Siri's reply   Related info

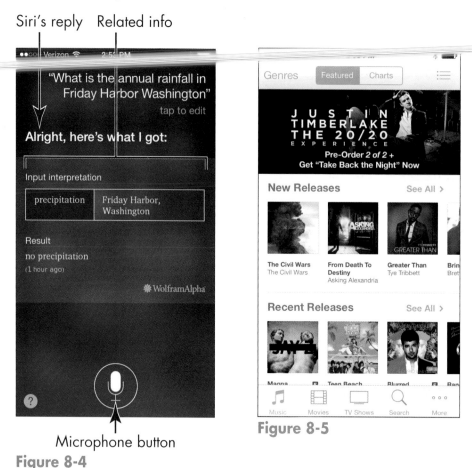

"What is the annual rainfall in
Friday Harbor Washington"

tap to edit

Alright, here's what I got:

Input interpretation

precipitation	Friday Harbor, Washington

Result

no precipitation
(1 hour ago)

✴ WolframAlpha

Microphone button

Figure 8-4

Genres   Featured   Charts

JUSTIN
TIMBERLAKE
THE 20/20
E X P E R I E N C E
Pre-Order 2 of 2 +
Get "Take Back the Night" Now

New Releases   See All >

The Civil Wars   From Death To   Greater Than   Brin
The Civil Wars   Destiny   Tye Tribbett   Bret
                  Asking Alexandria

Recent Releases   See All >

Magna   Teen Beach   Blurred   Ran
Music   Movies   TV Shows   Search   More

Figure 8-5

Call Contacts

First, make sure the person you want to call is entered in your
Contacts app and include that person's phone number in his record. If
you want to call somebody by stating your relationship to her, such as
"Call sister", be sure to enter that relationship in the related field in
her contact record and make sure that the settings for Siri (refer to
Figure 8-3) include your contact name in the My Info field. (See
Chapter 5 for more about creating contact records.)

1. Press and hold the Home button until Siri appears.

2. Speak a command such as "Call Harold Smith." "Return Joe's call" or "Call Mom." If you want to make a FaceTime call, you can say "FaceTime Mom."

3. If there are two contacts who might match a spoken name, Siri responds with a list of possible matches (see **Figure 8-6**). Tap one in the list or state the correct contact's name to proceed.

Figure 8-6

4. The call is placed. To end it before it completes, you can press the Home button and then tap End.

To cancel any spoken request, you have three options: You can say, "Cancel", tap the Microphone Button on the Siri screen, or press the Home button. If you're using a headset or Bluetooth device, you can tap the end button on the device.

 You can now access your voice mail using Siri. Just press and hold the Home button until Siri activates, then say something like "Check Voicemail." Siri responds by telling you if you have a new voice mail and displays a list of any new messages. Tap on one and you can then tap the Play button to play it back. If you want to get rid of it, tap Delete. It's that simple.

Create Reminders and Alerts

1. You can also use Siri with the Reminders app. To create a reminder or alert, press and hold the Home button and then speak a command, such as "Remind me to call Dad on Thursday at 10 a.m." or "Wake me up tomorrow at 7 a.m."

2. A preview of the reminder or alert is displayed (see **Figure** 8-7), and Siri asks you if it should create the reminder. Tap or say Confirm to create it or Cancel.

3. If you want a reminder ahead of the event you created, activate Siri and speak a command, such as "Remind me tonight about the play on Thursday at 8 p.m." A second reminder is created, which you can confirm or cancel.

Figure 8-7

Add Tasks to Your Calendar

1. You can also set up events on your Calendar using Siri. Press and hold the Home button and then speak a phrase, such as "Set up meeting at 10 a.m. on October 12th."

2. A sample calendar entry appears, and Siri asks if you want to confirm it.

3. If there's a conflict with the appointment, Siri tells you that there's already an appointment at that time (see **Figure 8-8**) and asks if you still want to set up the new appointment. You can say Yes or Cancel at that point or tap the Yes or Cancel button.

Figure 8-8

Play Music

1. You can use Siri to play music from the Music app and iTunes Radio. Press and hold the Home button until Siri appears.

2. To play music, speak a command, such as "Play music" or "Play Jazz radio station." to play a specific song, album, or radio station.

3. When music is playing, use commands, such as "Pause music.", "Next track.", or "Stop music." to control playback.

One of the beauties of Siri is that you don't have to follow a specific command format as you do with Voice Control. You could say "Play the next track" or "Next track" or "Jump to the next track on this album" and Siri will get your meaning. If you're stuck with Voice Control, check the *iPhone User Guide* for the correct syntax for all commands.

Get Directions

You can use the Maps app and Siri to find your current location, find nearby businesses such as restaurants or a bank, or get a map of another location. Be sure to turn on Location Services to allow Siri to know your current location (go to Settings and tap Privacy⇨Location Services and make sure Location Services are on and that Siri is turned on further down in that dialog).

Here are some of the commands you can try to get directions or a list of nearby businesses:

➡ **"Where am I?"**

   Displays a map of your current location.

➡ **"Where is Apache Junction, Arizona?"**

   Displays a map of that city.

➡ **"Find restaurants."**

   Displays a list of restaurants near your current location; tap one to display a map of its location.

➡ **"Find Bank of America."**

Displays a map with the location of the indicated business (or in some cases, several nearby locations, such as a bank branch and all ATMs), as shown in Figure 8-9.

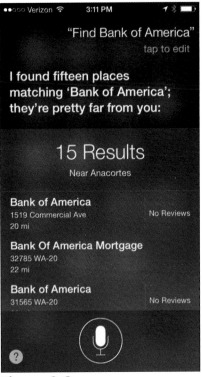

Figure 8-9

 Once a location is displayed in a map, tap the information button on the location's label to view its address, phone number, and website address, if available.

Ask for Facts

Wolfram|Alpha is a self-professed online computational knowledge engine. That means it's more than a search engine because it provides specific information about a search term rather than multiple search results. If you want facts without having to spend time browsing websites to find those facts, Wolfram|Alpha is a very good resource.

Siri uses Wolfram|Alpha and sources such as Wikipedia and Bing to look up facts in response to questions, such as "What is the capital of Kansas?" "What is the square root of 2003?" or "How large is Mars?" Just press and hold the Home button and ask your question; Siri consults its resources and returns a set of relevant facts.

You can also get information about the weather, stocks, or the time. Just say a phrase like one of these to get what you need:

➡ **"What is the weather?"**

This shows the weather report for your current location. If you want weather in another location, just specify the location in your question.

➡ **"What is the price of Apple stock?"**

Siri tells you the current price of the stock or the price of the stock when the stock market last closed.

➡ **"What time is it?"**

Siri tells you the time and displays a clock for your location (see **Figure 8-10**).

Figure 8-10

 Note that with the arrival of iOS 6, Siri could understand more languages than before, and continuing with iOS 7 therefore works in more countries. If you love to travel, Siri could help make your next trip much easier.

Search the Web

While Siri can use its resources to respond to specific requests such as "Who is the Queen of England?" more general requests for information will cause Siri to search further on the web. Siri can also search Twitter for comments related to your search.

For example, if you speak a phrase, such as "Find a website about birds" or "Find information about the World Series.", Siri can respond in a couple of ways. The app can simply display a list of search results using the default search engine specified in your settings for Safari or suggesting, "If you like, I can search the web for such-and-such." In the first instance, just tap a result to go to that website. In the second instance, you can confirm that you want to search the web or cancel.

Send E-mail, Messages, or Tweets

You can create an e-mail or an instant message using Siri. For example, if you say, "E-mail Jack Wilkes.", a form opens already addressed to that contact. Siri asks you what to say; speak your message and then say, "Send." to speed your message on its way.

Siri also works with messaging apps such as the iMessage feature of Messages. If you have the Messages app open and you say, "Tell Sarah I'll call soon.", Siri creates a message for you to approve and send.

 Siri can also tweet and post to Facebook. Go to Settings and turn on Twitter or Facebook support and provide your account information. Now you can say things to Siri such as "Post Tweet" or "Post to Facebook" and Siri asks what you want to say, lets you review it, and posts it.

Use Dictation

1. Text entry isn't Siri's strong point. Instead, you can use a microphone key that appears on the onscreen keyboard (see **Figure 8-11**) to speak text rather than type it. This feature is called Dictation. Go to any app where you enter text, such as Notes or Mail, and tap in the document or form. The onscreen keyboard appears.

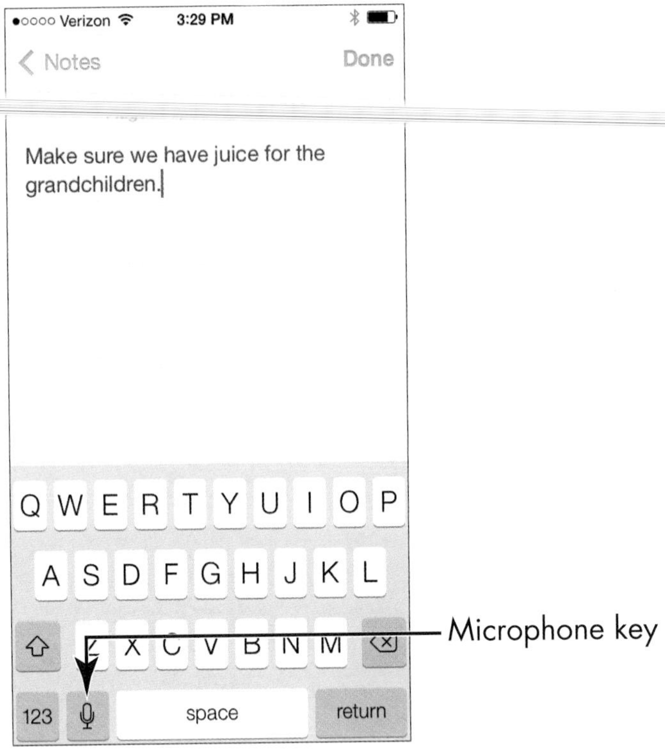
●○○○○ Verizon
3:29 PM
Notes
Done
Make sure we have juice for the grandchildren.
Q W E R T Y U I O P
A S D F G H J K L
Z X C V B N M
123
space
return
Microphone key

Figure 8-11

2. Tap the microphone key on the keyboard and speak your text.

3. To end the dictation, tap Done.

When you finish speaking text, you can use the keyboard to make edits to the text Siri entered, although as voice recognition programs go, Siri is pretty darn accurate. If a word sports a blue underline, which means there may be an error, you can tap to select it and make edits to it.

Get Helpful Tips

I know you're going to have a wonderful time learning the ins and outs of Siri, but before I close this chapter, here are some tips to get you going:

➡ **Activating Raise to Speak:** Go to Settings, General, and under the Siri setting, use the Raise to Speak setting to activate Siri when you put your phone to your ear rather than pressing and holding the Home button.

➡ **If Siri doesn't understand you:** When you speak a command and Siri displays what it thought you said, if it misses the mark, you have a few options. To correct a request you've made, you can tap Tap to Edit under the command Siri heard and edit the question by typing or tapping the microphone key on the onscreen keyboard and dictating the correct information. If a word is underlined in blue, it's a possible error. Tap the word and then tap an alternative that Siri suggests. You can also simply speak to Siri and say something like, "I meant Sri Lanka." or "No, send it to Sally." If even corrections aren't working, you may need to restart your phone to reset the Siri software.

➡ **Headsets and earphones:** If you're using iPhone earphones or a Bluetooth headset to activate Siri, instead of pressing the Home button, press and hold the center button (the little button on the headset that starts and stops a call).

➡ **Using Find My Friends:** There is a free app you can download from the App Store called Find My Friends that allows you to ask Siri to locate your friends geographically.

➡ **Getting help:** To get help with Siri features, just press and hold the Home button and ask Siri, "What can you do?"

 If you're becoming a Siri aficionado, you might want to purchase *Siri For Dummies* by Marc Saltzman.

Getting Social with FaceTime, Twitter, and iMessage

*F*aceTime is an excellent video-calling app that's been available since the release of iPhone 4 in mid-2010. With the arrival of iOS 7, FaceTime gets its own slot on the iPhone Home page. The app lets you call people who have FaceTime on their devices using either a phone number or an e-mail address. You and your friend, colleague, or family member can see each other as you talk, which makes for a much more personal calling experience.

Twitter is a social networking service referred to as a *microblog,* because it involves only short posted messages. Twitter has been incorporated into iOS 7 in a way that allows you to tweet people from within Safari, Photos, Camera, Maps, and many other apps. You can also set up Twitter credentials in iPhone Settings and use it to post tweets whenever you like.

Finally, iMessage is a feature available through the preinstalled Messages app for instant messaging (IM). IM involves sending a text ~~message to somebody's iPhone (using their phone number), iPod~~ touch, Mac running OS X 10.8 or later, or iPad (using their e-mail address) to carry on an instant conversation.

In this chapter, I introduce you to FaceTime, Twitter, and iMessage and review their simple controls. In no time, you'll be socializing with all and sundry.

Understand Who Can Use FaceTime

Here's a quick rundown of what device and what information you need for using FaceTime's various features:

⟹ You can use FaceTime to call people who have an iPhone 4 or later, an iPad 2 or a third-generation iPad or later, a fourth-generation iPod touch or later, or a Mac (running Mac OS X 10.6.6 or later).

⟹ You can use a phone number to connect with iPhone 4 or later.

⟹ You can connect using an e-mail address with a Mac, an iPod touch, an iPad 2, or a third-generation iPad or later.

Get an Overview of FaceTime

FaceTime works with the Camera app and iPhone's built-in cameras so you can call other folks who have a device that supports FaceTime. You can use FaceTime to chat while sharing video images with another person. This preinstalled app is useful for seniors who want to keep up with distant family members and friends and see (as well as hear) the latest-and-greatest news.

You can make and receive calls with FaceTime using a phone number (on iPhone 4 or later) or an e-mail account (iPad 2 or later, iPod touch, or Mac) and show the person on the other end what's going on around you. Just remember that you can't adjust audio volume from within the app or record a video call. Nevertheless, on the positive side, even though its features are limited, this app is straightforward to use.

You can use your Apple ID and e-mail address to access FaceTime, so it works pretty much right away. See Chapter 3 for more about getting an Apple ID.

 If you're having trouble using FaceTime, make sure the FaceTime feature is turned on. That's quick to do: Tap Settings on the Home screen, tap FaceTime, and then tap the On/Off button to turn it on, if necessary. On this Settings page, you can also select the phone number that others can use to make phone calls to you.

Make a FaceTime Call with Wi-Fi or 3G/4G

1. If you know that the person you're calling has FaceTime on an iPhone 4 or later, an iPad 2 or later, an iPod touch, or a Mac, first be sure you've added that person to your iPhone Contacts (tap Phone in the Dock, tap Contacts, and then tap the plus sign Add button; see Chapter 5 for how to do this).

2. Tap the FaceTime icon on the Home page.

3. Scroll to locate a contact who has associated a device with FaceTime and tap the contact's name to display their information (see **Figure 9-1**).

4. Tap the FaceTime button. If the contact has both an e-mail address registered with FaceTime and phone num-

~~ber, a dialog displays them both. Tap on the one you~~

want to use. You've just placed a FaceTime call! (Note that if the contact has only a phone or e-mail recorded, when you tap the FaceTime button the call goes through immediately, assuming the recipient has FaceTime enabled on his or her device.)

 You have to use the appropriate method for placing a FaceTime call, depending on the kind of device the person you're calling has. If you're calling an iPhone 4, 4S, 5, 5S, or 5C user, you should use a phone number the first time you call, and thereafter you can use the phone number or a FaceTime registered e-mail address; if you're calling an iPad 2 or later, an iPod touch, or a FaceTime for a Mac user, you have to make the call using that person's e-mail address.

 When you call somebody using an e-mail address, the person must be signed in to his Apple ID account and have verified that the address can be used for FaceTime calls. iPhone 4 and later, iPad 2 and later, and iPod touch (fourth generation and later) users can make this setting by tapping Settings and then FaceTime⇨Use Your Apple ID for FaceTime; FaceTime for Mac users make this setting by selecting FaceTime⇨Preferences.

5. When the person accepts the call, you see a large screen that displays the recipient's image and a small screen referred to as a Picture in Picture (PiP) containing your image superimposed (see **Figure 9-2**).

Tap this button

Figure 9-1

Figure 9-2

 To view recent calls, tap the Phone app icon and then tap the Recents button. Tap a recent call, and iPhone displays that person's information. You can tap the contact to call the person back.

 You can also open the Messages app, choose a recipient, and then tap the Call button and tap FaceTime Audio to initiate a FaceTime call.

 If you have iOS 6 or 7, you can use FaceTime over both a Wi-Fi network and your iPhone 3G or 4G connection. However, remember that if you use FaceTime over a phone connection, you may incur costly data usage fees.

Accept and End a FaceTime Call

1. If ~~you're on the receiving end of a FaceTime call, accept~~ing the call is about as easy as it gets. When the call comes in, tap the Accept button to take the call or tap the Decline button to reject it (see **Figure 9-3**).

2. Chat away with your friend, swapping video images. To end the call, tap the End button (see **Figure 9-4**).

Switch Camera
End   Mute

Figure 9-3

Figure 9-4

To mute sound during a call, tap the Mute button, which looks like a microphone with a line through it (refer to **Figure** 9-4). Tap the button again to unmute your iPhone.

 If you'd rather not be available for calls, you can go to Settings and turn on the Do Not Disturb feature. This stops any incoming calls or notifications other than for the people you've designated as exceptions to Do Not Disturb. After you turn on Do Not Disturb, you can schedule when it's active, allow calls from certain people, or allow a second call from the same person in a three-minute interval to go through by using the Do Not Disturb settings under Notifications.

Switch Views

1. When you're on a FaceTime call, you might want to use iPhone's built-in rear-facing camera to show the person you're talking to what's going on around you. Tap the Switch Camera button (refer to **Figure** 9-4) to switch from the front-facing camera that's displaying your image to the back-facing camera that captures whatever you're looking at (see **Figure** 9-5).

2. Tap the Switch Camera button again to switch back to the front camera displaying your image.

Figure 9-5

Experience Twitter on iPhone

Twitter is a social networking service for *microblogging*, which involves posting very short messages (limited to 140 characters) online so your friends can see what you're up to. You can go to your iPhone Settings and install the app from the Twitter selection in Settings. After you have an account, you can post tweets for all to see, have people follow your tweets, and follow the tweets that other people post.

With iOS 5, the ability to tweet became integrated into several apps. You can post tweets using the Menu button within Safari, Photos, Camera, and Maps. First, sign up for an account. (See Chapter 13 for more about downloading apps.) Go to iPhone Settings and tap Twitter. Then tap Install, sign into the iTunes Store, and add your account information. iPhone installs the Twitter app automatically.

Now when you're using Safari, Photos, Camera, or Maps, you can choose Twitter in the screen that appears when you tap a Menu button (see **Figure 9-6**). You'll see a Tweet form. Just type your message in the form and then tap Send.

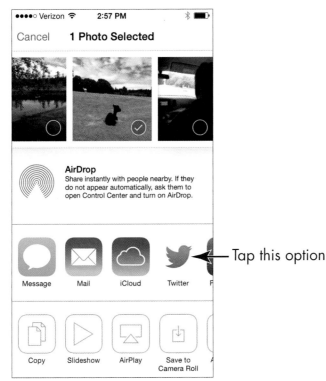

Tap this option

Figure 9-6

 See Chapters 10 and 16 for more about tweeting in the Safari and Photos apps.

Set Up an iMessage Account

1. iMessage is a feature available through the preinstalled Messages app that allows you to send and receive instant messages (IMs) to others using an Apple iOS device or suitably configured Macs. Instant messaging differs from e-mail or tweeting in an important way. Where you might e-mail somebody and wait days or weeks before that person responds, or you might post a tweet that could sit there awhile before anybody views it, with instant messaging, communication happens almost immediately. You send an IM, and it appears on somebody's Apple device right away — and assuming the person wants to participate in a live conversation, the chat begins immediately, allowing a back-and-forth dialogue in real time. To set up iMessage, tap Settings on the Home screen.

2. Tap Messages, and the settings shown in **Figure** 9-7 appear.

3. If iMessage isn't set to On (refer to **Figure** 9-7), tap the On/Off button to turn it on.

4. Check to be sure the phone number and/or e-mail account associated with your iPhone under the Send & Receive setting is correct. (This should be set up automatically based on your Apple ID.) If it's not, tap the Send & Receive field and then add an e-mail or phone and then tap Messages to return to the previous screen.

5. To allow a notice to be sent when you've read somebody's messages, tap the On/Off button for Send Read Receipts. You can also choose to show a subject field in your messages.

6. Press the Home button to leave the settings.

To change the e-mail account used by Messages, tap Send & Receive, tap the information icon to the right of an e-mail address, and then tap Remove This Email; then follow the preceding steps to add another account.

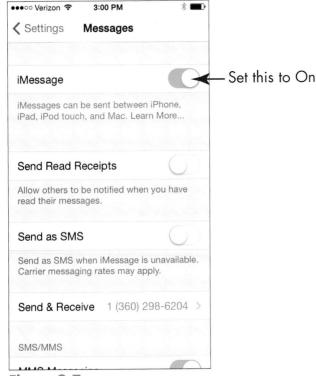

Figure 9-7

Use iMessage to Address, Create, and Send Messages

1. Now you're ready to use iMessage. From the Home screen, tap the Messages icon. Tap the New Message button in the top-right corner to begin a conversation.

2. In the form that appears (see **Figure 9-8**), you can address a message in a couple of ways:

- Begin to type an address in the To: field, and a list of matching contacts appears.

- Tap the Dictation key on the onscreen keyboard and speak the address.

- Tap the plus icon on the right side of the address field, and the All Contacts list is displayed.

3. Tap a contact on the list you chose from in Step 2. If the contact has both an e-mail address and a phone number stored, the Info dialog appears, allowing you to tap one or the other, which addresses the message.

4. To create a message, simply tap in the message field near the bottom of the screen (see **Figure** 9-9) and type your message.

5. To send the message, tap the Send button (refer to **Figure** 9-9). When your recipient(s) responds, you'll see the conversation displayed on the screen. Tap in the message field again to respond to the last comment.

 You can address a message to more than one person by simply choosing more recipients in Step 2 of the preceding list.

 If you want to include a photo or video with your message, tap the Camera icon to the left of the message field (refer to **Figure** 9-9). Tap Take Photo or Video or Choose Existing (depending on whether you want to create a new photo/video or send one you've already taken), and then tap Use to attach a photo or video. When you send your message, the photo or video will go along with your text.

Message field   Send button

Figure 9-8   **Figure 9-9**

Clear a Conversation

1. When you're done chatting, you might want to delete a conversation to remove the clutter before you start a new one. With Messages open and conversations displayed, tap the Edit button in the top-left corner.

2. Tap the Delete button next to the conversation you want to get rid of (see **Figure 9-10**).

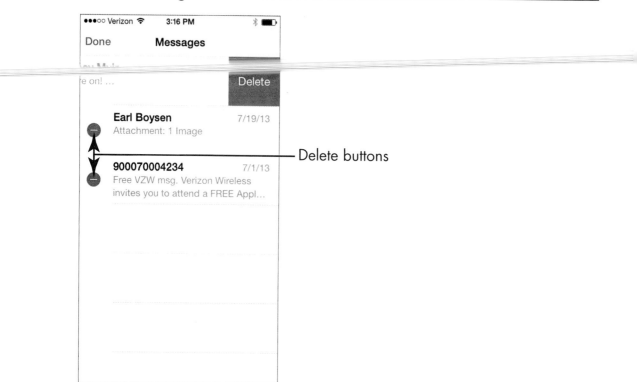

Figure 9-10

3. Tap Delete.

 You can tap the Contact button in the top right corner of a conversation screen and choose to place a call, FaceTime call, or get more information about a participant at any time.

Part III
Taking the Leap Online

Visit www.dummies.com/extras/iphoneforseniors for more ideas about apps you can buy in the App Store that you might find useful.

Browsing the Internet with Safari

etting on the Internet with your iPhone is easy, using its Wi-Fi or 3G/4G capabilities. After you're online, the built-in browser (software that helps you navigate the Internet's contents), *Safari,* is your ticket to a wide world of information, entertainment, education, and more. Safari will look familiar to you if you've used it on a PC or Mac device before, though the way you move around by using the iPhone touchscreen might be new to you. If you've never used Safari, this chapter takes you by the hand and shows you all the basics of using it.

In this chapter, you discover how to go online with your iPhone and navigate among web pages and use iCloud tabs to share your browsing experience among devices. Along the way, you see how to place a bookmark for a favorite site or place a web clip on your Home screen. You can also view your browsing history, save online images to your Photo Library, post photos to sites from within Safari, or e-mail or tweet a hotlink to a friend. Two new Safari features are Shared Links to see URLs posted to your Twitter timeline and iCloud Keychain used for storing passwords in one handy, safe place online. You also explore Safari's Reader

Get ready to . . .

and Reading List features and learn how to keep yourself safer while online using private browsing. Finally, you review the simple steps involved in printing what you find online.

Connect to the Internet

How you connect to the Internet depends on what connections are available:

➡ You can connect to the Internet via a Wi-Fi network. You can set up this type of network in your own home using your computer and some equipment from your Internet provider. You can also connect over public Wi-Fi networks, referred to as *hotspots*. You'll probably be surprised to discover how many hotspots your town or city has. Look for Internet cafés, coffee shops, hotels, libraries, and transportation centers such as airports or bus stations, for example. Many of these businesses display signs alerting you to their free Wi-Fi.

➡ You can also use the paid data network provided by AT&T, Sprint, or Verizon to connect using 3G or 4G from just about anywhere you can get cell phone coverage via a cellular network.

To enable 3G/4G data, tap Settings, then Cellular. Tap to turn on the Cellular Data setting. Do note that browsing the Internet using a 3G/4G connection can eat up your data plan allotment quickly if your plan doesn't include unlimited data access.

To connect to a Wi-Fi network, you have to complete a few steps.

1. Tap the Settings icon on the Home screen and then tap Wi-Fi. Be sure Wi-Fi is set to On and choose a network to connect to. Network names should appear automatically when you're in range of networks. When you're in range of a public hotspot, if access to several nearby networks is available, you may see a message asking you to tap a network name to select it. After you select one (or if only one network is available), you may see a message asking for your password. Ask the owner of the hotspot (for example a hotel desk clerk or business owner) for this password or enter your home network password.

2. If you're required to enter a network password, do so.

3. Tap the Join button, and you're connected.

 Free public Wi-Fi networks typically don't require passwords or the password is posted prominently for all to see. However, it's then possible for someone else to track your online activities over these *unsecured* networks. Avoid accessing financial accounts or sending e-mails with sensitive information in them when connected to a public hotspot.

Explore Safari

1. After you're connected to a network, tap the Safari icon on the Home screen. Safari opens, probably displaying the Apple iPhone home page the first time you go online (see **Figure 10-1**).

2. Put two fingers together on the screen and unpinch to enlarge the view. Double-tap the screen with a single finger to restore the default view size.

3. Put your finger on the screen and flick upward to scroll down on the page.

4. To return to the top of the web page, put your finger on the screen and drag downward or tap the Status bar at the top of the screen.

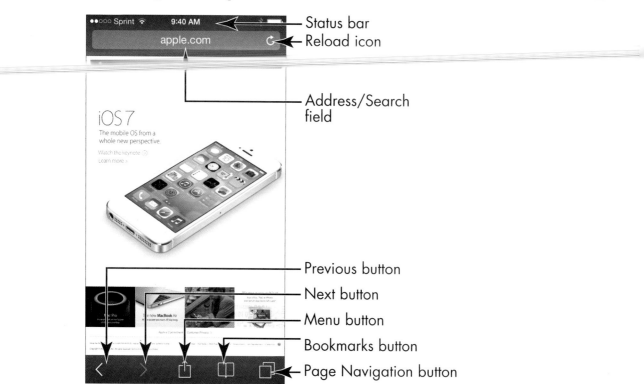

Figure 10-1

 Using the pinch method to enlarge or reduce the size of a web page on your screen allows you to view what's displayed at various sizes, giving you more flexibility than the double-tap method.

 When you enlarge the display, you gain more control using two fingers to drag from left to right or from top to bottom on the screen. On a reduced display, one finger works fine for making these gestures.

Navigate Among Web Pages

1. Tap in the Address field just under the Status bar. The onscreen keyboard appears (see **Figure 10-2**).

2. To clear the field, tap the Delete key on the keyboard. Enter a web address; for example, you can go to www. wiley.com.

3. Tap the Go key on the keyboard (see **Figure 10-2**). The website appears.

- If, for some reason, a page doesn't display, tap the Reload icon at the right end of the Address field.

- If Safari is loading a web page and you change your mind about viewing the page, you can tap Cancel, which appears at the right end of the Address field during this process, to stop loading the page.

4. Tap the Previous arrow to go backward to the last page you displayed.

5. Tap the Next arrow to go forward to the page you just backed up from.

6. To follow a link to another web page (links are typically indicated by colored text or graphics), tap the link with your finger. To view the destination web address of the link before you tap it, just touch and hold the link; a menu appears that displays the address at the top, as shown in **Figure 10-3**.

By default, AutoFill is turned on in iPhone, causing entries you make in fields such as the Address field to automatically display possible matching entries. You can turn off AutoFill by using iPhone Settings for Safari.

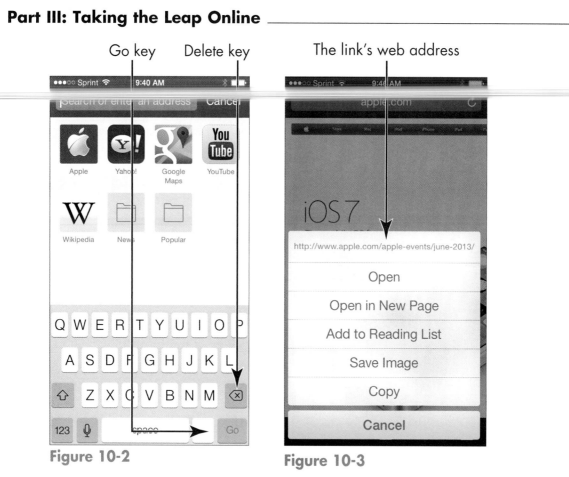

Go key   Delete key   The link's web address

Figure 10-2   Figure 10-3

Use Tabbed Browsing

1. *Tabbed browsing* is a feature that allows you to have several websites open at once so you can move easily among those sites. With Safari open and a web page already displayed, tap the Page Navigation button (refer to **Figure 10-1**). The new Tab view appears.

2. To add a new page (meaning you're opening a new website), tap the New Page button in the lower middle of the screen and tap the New Page button (see **Figure 10-4**). A page with some frequently used sites and an address bar appears. (Note you can get to the same new page by simply tapping in the address bar from any site).

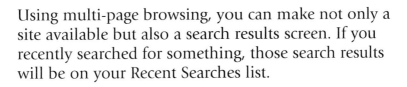
New Page button

Figure 10-4

3. Tap in the address field, use the onscreen keyboard to enter the web address for the website you want to open, and then tap the Go key. The website opens on the page.

 Repeat Steps 1–3 to open as many new web pages as you like.

4. You can now switch among open sites by tapping the Page Navigation button and scrolling among recent sites, finding the one you want, and tapping on it.

5. To delete a tab, tap the Page Navigation button, scroll to locate the tab, and then tap the Close button in the upper left corner of the tab.

 Using multi-page browsing, you can make not only a site available but also a search results screen. If you recently searched for something, those search results will be on your Recent Searches list.

View Browsing History

1. As you move around the web, your browser keeps a record of your browsing history. This record can be handy when you want to visit a site that you viewed previously but you've now forgotten its address. With Safari open, tap the Bookmarks button.

2. On the menu shown in **Figure 10-5**, tap the History item .

3. In the History list that appears (see **Figure 10-6**), tap a date if available, and then tap a site to navigate to it.

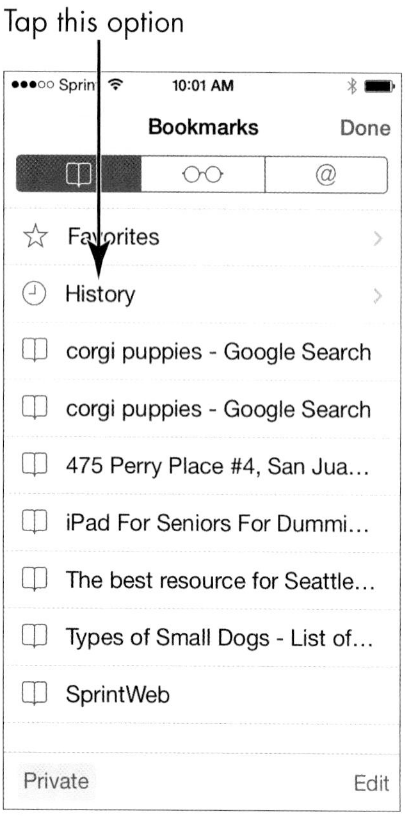

Tap this option

History list   Clear button

••••○ Sprint 📶 10:01 AM 💲 🔋	••○○○ Sprint 📶 10:10 AM 💲 🔋
Bookmarks Done	‹ Bookmarks **History** Done
📖 ◯◯ @	📖 ◯◯ @
☆ Favorites ›	**This Morning**
🕒 History ›	Nanotechnology
📖 corgi puppies - Google Search	understandingnano.com
📖 corgi puppies - Google Search	Kim Kardashian on Katie Couric s…
📖 475 Perry Place #4, San Jua…	t.entertainment.msn.co…ly-bashing-me?toc=celebs
📖 iPad For Seniors For Dummi…	Teen faces trial in killing of baby i…
📖 The best resource for Seattle…	news.msn.com/crime-ju…-killing-of-baby-in-stroller
📖 Types of Small Dogs - List of…	
📖 SprintWeb	
Private Edit	Private Clear

Figure 10-5 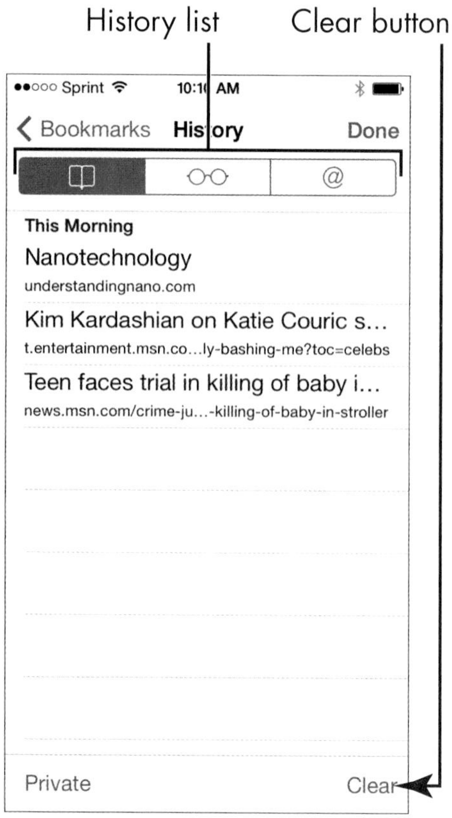   **Figure 10-6**

After you master using the Bookmarks button options, you might prefer a shortcut to view your History list. Tap and hold the Previous button on any screen and your browsing history for the current session appears. You can also tap and hold the Next button to look at sites you backtracked from.

 To clear the history, tap the Clear button (refer to **Figure 10-6**) and on the dialog that appears, tap Clear History. This button is useful when you don't want your spouse or grandchildren to see where you've been browsing for anniversary, birthday, or holiday presents!

Search the Web

1. If you don't know the address of the site you want to visit (or you want to research a topic or find other information online), get acquainted with Safari's Search feature on iPhone. By default, Safari uses the Google search engine. With Safari open, tap in the Search field (refer to **Figure 10-1**). The onscreen keyboard appears.

2. Enter a search term, which with the latest version of Safari can be a topic or a web address using the Unified smart search field. You can tap one of the suggested sites or complete your entry and tap the Go key (see **Figure 10-7**) on your keyboard.

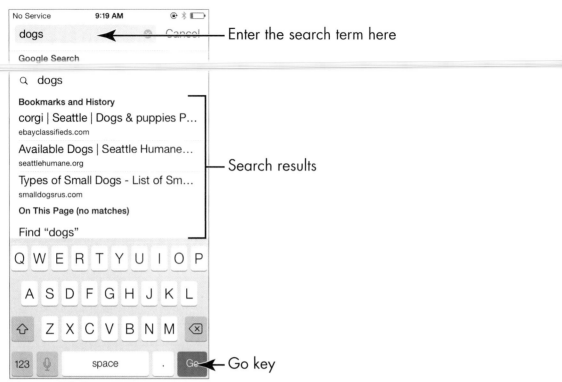

Enter the search term here

Search results

Go key

Figure 10-7

3. In the search results that are displayed, tap a link to visit that site.

 To change your default search engine from Google to Yahoo! or Bing, in iPhone Settings, tap Safari and then tap Search Engine. Tap Yahoo! or Bing, and your default search engine changes.

 You can browse for specific items such as images, videos, or news by tapping the corresponding link at the top of the Google results screen. Also, tap the More button in this list to see additional options to narrow your results, such as searching for books or shopping resources on the subject.

Add and Use Bookmarks

1. Bookmarks are a way to save favorite sites so you can easily visit them again. With a site you want to bookmark displayed, tap the Menu button.

2. On the menu that appears (see **Figure 10-8**), tap Bookmark.

3. In the Add Bookmark dialog, shown in **Figure 10-9**, edit the name of the bookmark if you want. To do so, tap the name of the site and use the onscreen keyboard to edit its name.

Tap this option

Edit the name here

Figure 10-8

Figure 10-9

4. Tap the Save button.

5. To go to the bookmark, tap the Bookmarks button.

6. On the Bookmarks menu that appears (see **Figure 10-10**), tap the bookmarked site you want to visit.

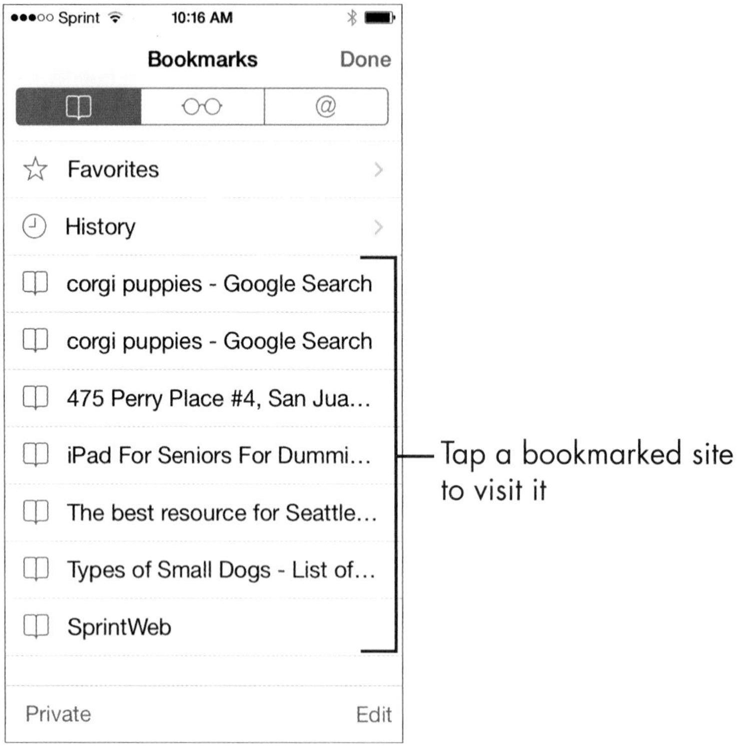

●●●○○ Sprint 📶 10:16 AM 🔋

Bookmarks Done

📖 🤓 @

☆ Favorites >

🕐 History >

📖 corgi puppies - Google Search

📖 corgi puppies - Google Search

📖 475 Perry Place #4, San Jua...

📖 iPad For Seniors For Dummi... — Tap a bookmarked site to visit it

📖 The best resource for Seattle...

📖 Types of Small Dogs - List of...

📖 SprintWeb

Private Edit

Figure 10-10

 If you want to sync your bookmarks on your iPhone browser to your computer, connect your iPhone to your computer and make sure that the Sync Safari Bookmarks setting on the Info tab of iTunes is activated. You can also go to Settings on iPhone and make sure iCloud is set to sync with Safari.

When you tap the Bookmarks button, you can tap Edit and then use the Bookmarks Bar New Folder option to create folders to organize your bookmarks.

When you next add a bookmark, you can then choose, from the dialog that appears, any folder to which you want to add the new bookmark.

Save Links and Web Pages to Safari Reading List

1. The Safari Reading List provides a way to save content that you want to read at a later time so you can easily call up that content again. You essentially save the content rather than a web page, which allows you to read the content even when you're offline. With the latest version of Safari, you can scroll from one item to the next easily. With a site you want to add to your Reading List displayed, tap the Menu button.

2. On the menu that appears (refer to **Figure 10-8**), tap the Add to Reading List link. The site is added to your Reading List.

3. To view your Reading List, tap the Bookmarks button and tap the Reading List tab (the middle tab near the top of the page).

4. On the Reading List that appears (see **Figure 10-11**), tap the content you want to revisit and resume reading.

If you want to see both the Reading List material you've read and the material you haven't read, tap the Show All tab in the Reading List pane (refer to **Figure 10-11**). To see just the material you haven't read, use the Show Unread button.

To save an image to your Reading List, tap and hold the image until a menu appears, and then tap Add to Reading list. To delete an item, with the Reading List displayed, swipe left or right on an item, and a Delete button appears. Tap this button to delete the item from the Reading List.

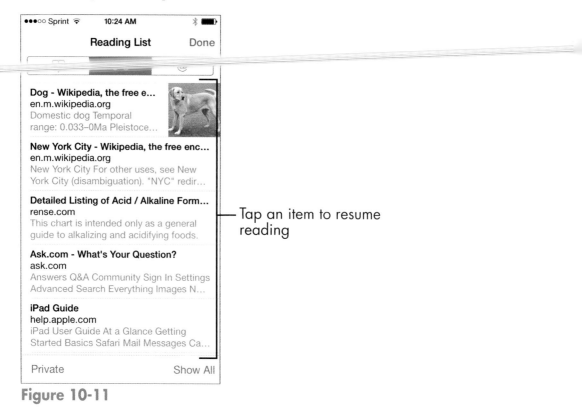

Tap an item to resume reading

Figure 10-11

Enjoy Reading More with Safari Reader

1. The Safari Reader feature gives you an e-reader type of experience right within your browser, removing other stories and links as well as those distracting advertisements. When you are on a site where you're reading content such as an article, Safari displays a Reader button on the left side of the Address field (see **Figure 10-12**). Tap the Reader button. The content appears in a reader format (see **Figure 10-13**).

Reader button

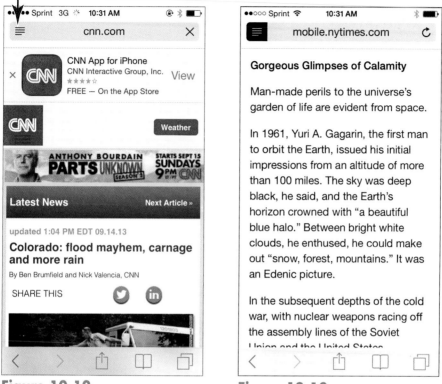

Figure 10-12

Figure 10-13

2. Scroll down the page. The entire content is contained in this one long page.

3. When you finish reading the material, just tap the Previous button to go back to its source.

Add Web Clips to the Home Screen

1. The Web Clips feature allows you to save a website as an icon on your Home screen so that you can go to the site at any time with one tap. With Safari open and displaying the site you want to add, tap the Menu button.

2. On the menu that appears (refer to **Figure 10-8**), tap Add to Home Screen.

3. In the Add to Home dialog that appears (see **Figure 10-14**), you can edit the name of the site to be more descriptive, if you'd like. To do so, tap the name of the site and use the onscreen keyboard to edit its name.

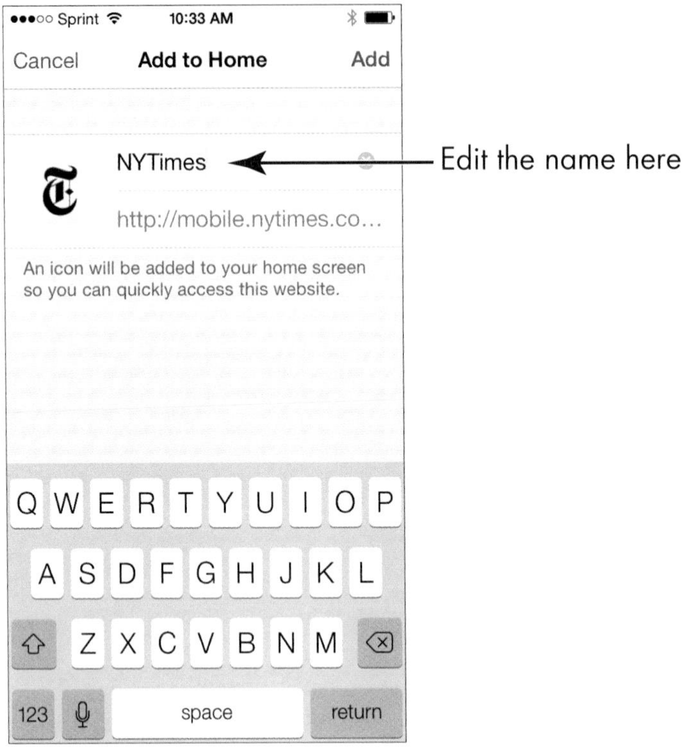

●●●○○ Sprint 📶 10:33 AM ⚹ ▬)	
Cancel **Add to Home** Add	
𝕿 NYTimes ⟵	— Edit the name here
http://mobile.nytimes.co…	
An icon will be added to your home screen so you can quickly access this website.	
Q W E R T Y U I O P	
A S D F G H J K L	
⇧ Z X C V B N M ⊗	
123 🎤 space return	

Figure 10-14

4. Tap the Add button. The site is added to your Home screen.

 Remember that you can have as many as 11 Home screens on your iPhone to accommodate all the web clips you create and apps you download (though there is a limit to how many will fit; however, you can place an unlimited number of apps in folders on Home screens). If you want to delete an item from a Home screen for any reason, press and hold the icon on the Home screen until all items on the screen start to jiggle and Delete badges appear on all items except preinstalled apps. Tap the Delete badge on each item you want to delete, and it's gone. (To get rid of the jiggle, press the Home button.)

Save an Image to Your Photo Library

1. Display a web page that contains an image you want to copy.

2. Press and hold the image. The menu shown in **Figure 10-15** appears.

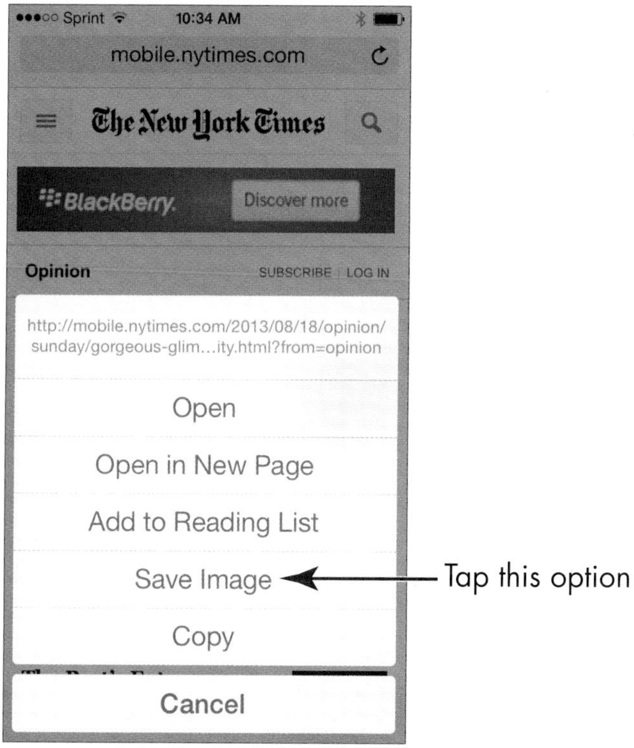

Figure 10-15

3. Tap the Save Image option (refer to **Figure 10-15**). The image is saved to your camera roll.

 Be careful about copying images from the Internet and using them for business or promotional activities. Most images are copyrighted, and you may violate the copyright even if you simply use an image in (say) a brochure for your association or a flyer for your community group. Note that some search engines' advanced search settings offer the option of browsing only for images that aren't copyrighted.

 Some websites are set up to prevent you from copying images on them, or display a pop-up stating that the contents on the site are copyrighted and should not be copied.

Post Photos from Safari

1. Before iOS 6, you had to post photos from within apps such as Photos. Now you can post photos to sites such as eBay, Craig's List, or Facebook from within Safari, rather than going through Photos or Videos. In this example, go to Facebook and sign in.

2. Tap a Photo or an Add Photo/Video or similar link, like the one shown in **Figure 10-16**.

3. In the case of Facebook you then tap a Choose File button, and a menu displays allowing you to take a photo or choose an existing one. Tap Choose Existing and then tap on a photo source such as Camera Roll or My Photo Stream and then tap the photo or video you want to post.

4. Tap the Post button.

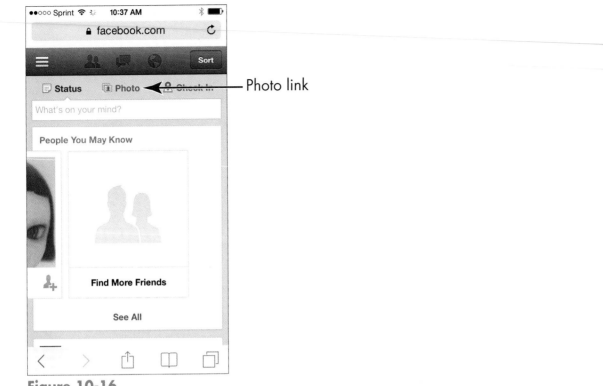

Figure 10-16

Send a Link

1. If you find a great site that you want to share, you can do so easily by sending a link in an e-mail. With Safari open and the site you want to share displayed, tap the Menu button.

2. On the menu that appears (refer to **Figure 10-8**), tap Mail.

3. On the message form that appears (see **Figure 10-17**), enter a recipient's e-mail address, a subject, and your message.

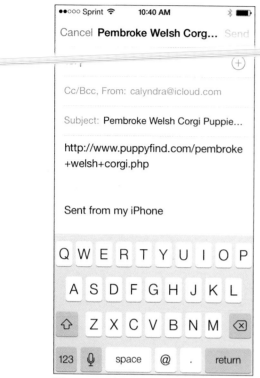
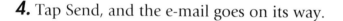

Figure 10-17

4. Tap Send, and the e-mail goes on its way.

 The e-mail is sent from the default e-mail account you have set up on iPhone. For more about setting up an e-mail account, see Chapter 11.

 To tweet the link using your Twitter account, in Step 2 of this task, choose Tweet, enter your tweet message in the form that appears, and then tap Send. For more about using Twitter with iPhone, see Chapter 9. You can also choose AirDrop in the same menu with any fifth-generation iPhone to share with someone in your immediate vicinity who has an AirDrop-enabled device.

Make Private Browsing and Cookie Settings

Apple has provided some privacy settings for Safari that you should consider using. Do Not Track automatically removes items from the download list, stops Safari from letting AutoFill save information used to complete your entries in the search or address fields as you type, and doesn't save some browsing history information. These features can keep your online activities more private. The Block Cookies setting allows you to stop the downloading of *cookies* (small files that document your browsing history so you can be recognized by a site the next time you go to or move within that site) to your iPhone.

You can control both settings by choosing Safari in the Settings window. Tap to turn on the Do Not Track feature (see **Figure 10-18**). Tap the arrow on Block Cookies and choose to always block cookies, never block cookies, or only block cookies from third parties and advertisers.

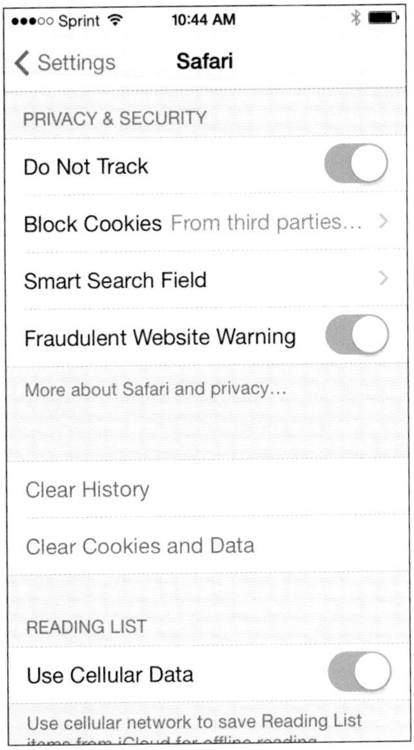

Figure 10-18

You can also tap the Clear History and the Clear Cookies and Data options (refer to **Figure 10-18**) to ~~manually clear your browsing~~ history, the saved cookies, and other data.

Print a Web Page

 1. If you have a wireless printer that supports Apple's AirPrint technology, you can print web content using a wireless connection. With Safari open and the site you want to print displayed, tap the Menu button.

2. On the menu that appears (refer to **Figure 10-8**), tap Print.

3. In the Printer Options dialog that appears (see **Figure 10-19**), tap Select Printer. In the list of printers that appears, tap the name of your wireless printer.

4. Tap either the plus or minus button in the Copy field to adjust the number of copies to print.

5. Tap Print to print the displayed page.

 The Mac applications Printopia and HandyPrint make any shared or network printer on your home network visible to your iPhone. Printopia has more features, but will cost you, whereas HandyPrint is free.

If you don't have an AirPrint–compatible wireless printer or don't wish to use an app to help you print wirelessly, just e-mail a link to the web page to yourself, open the link on your computer, and print from there.

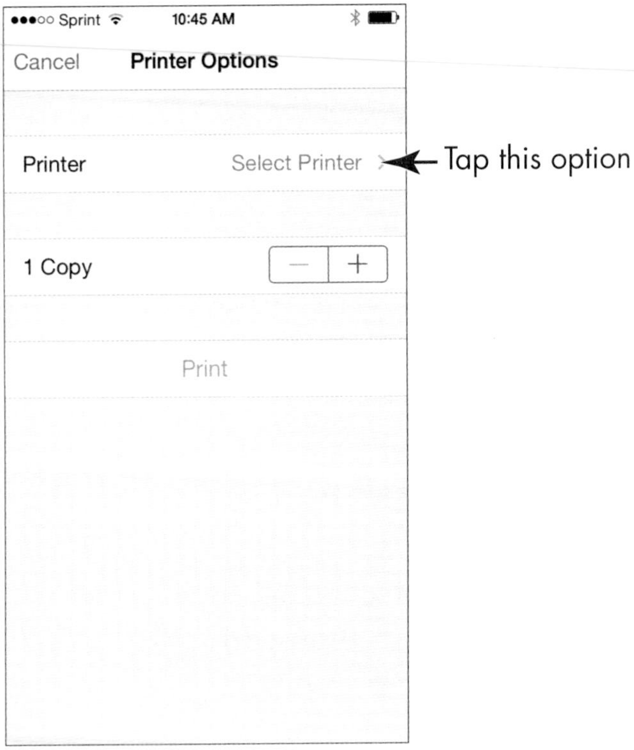

●●●○○ Sprint 🛜   10:45 AM   ＊ ▬▬▯

Cancel   **Printer Options**

Printer   Select Printer ＞ ◄── Tap this option

1 Copy   ⊟ ｜ ＋

Print

Figure 10-19

Understand iCloud Tabs

1. iCloud Tabs were new with iOS 6. This feature allows you to access all browsing history among your different devices from any device. If you begin to research a project on your iPad before you leave home, you can then pick up where you left off as you sit in a waiting room with your iPhone. First tap Settings on the Home screen and then tap Safari. Make sure that the Do Not Track setting is off so sharing can take place among devices.

2. Tap Settings and then tap iCloud to make sure both devices are using the same iCloud account.

3. Open Safari on another device and tap the Bookmarks button, and then tap iCloud Tabs to see a list similar to the one shown in Figure 10-20. All items in your iPhone's browsing history are displayed (in the case of Figure 10-20, the history is displayed on my iPad).

Figure 10-20

Working with E-mail in Mail

*S*taying in touch with others by using e-mail is a great way to use your iPhone. You can access an existing account using the handy Mail app supplied with your iPhone or sign in to your e-mail account using the Safari browser. Using Mail involves adding an existing e-mail account by way of iPhone Settings. Then you can use Mail to write, format, retrieve, and forward messages from that account.

Mail offers the capability to mark the messages you've read, delete messages, and organize your messages in a small set of folders, as well as using a handy search feature. New with iOS 6 came the ability to create a VIP list so that you're notified when that special person sends you an e-mail. In this chapter, you read all about Mail and its various features.

Add an iCloud, Gmail, Yahoo!, AOL, or Windows Live Hotmail Account

1. You can add one or more e-mail accounts, including the e-mail account associated with your iCloud account, using iPhone Settings. If you have an iCloud, Gmail, Yahoo!, AOL, or Outlook.com (this includes Microsoft accounts from Live, Hotmail, and so on) account, iPhone pretty much automates the setup. To set up iPhone to retrieve messages from your e-mail account at one of these popular providers, first tap the Settings icon on the Home screen.

2. In the Settings dialog, tap Mail, Contacts, Calendars. The settings shown in **Figure 11-1** appear.

3. Tap Add Account. The options shown in **Figure 11-2** appear.

Tap this option

Select your e-mail provider

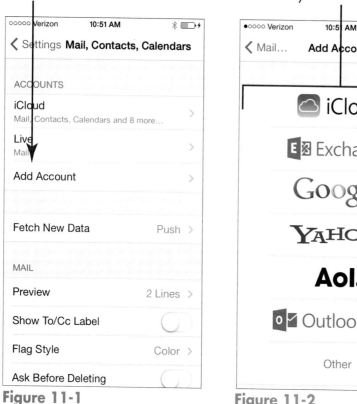

Figure 11-1

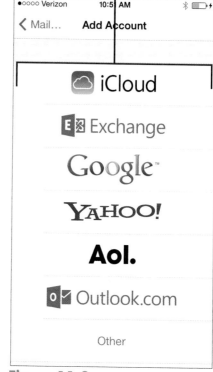

Figure 11-2

4. Tap iCloud, Gmail, Yahoo!, AOL, or Outlook.com. Enter your account information in the form that appears (see **Figure 11-3**).

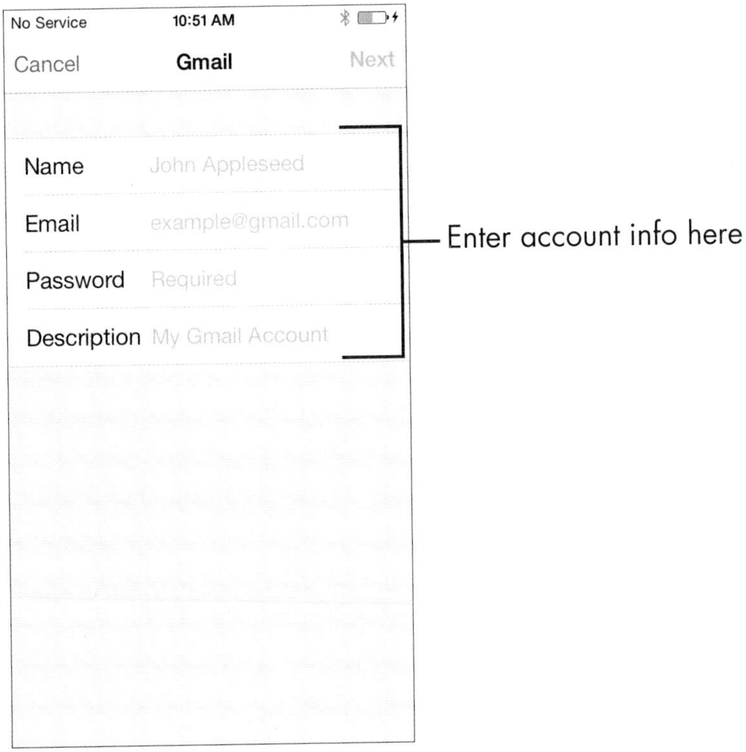

No Service	10:51 AM	
Cancel	**Gmail**	Next

Name	John Appleseed
Email	example@gmail.com
Password	Required
Description	My Gmail Account

— Enter account info here

Figure 11-3

5. After iPhone takes a moment to verify your account information, you can tap any On/Off button to have Mail, Contacts, Calendars, or Reminders from that account synced with iPhone.

6. When you're done, tap Save. The account is saved, and you can now open it using Mail.

Set Up a POP3 E-mail Account

1. You can also set up most popular e-mail accounts, such as those available through Earthlink or a cable provider's service, by obtaining the host name from the provider. To set up an existing account with a provider other than iCloud, Gmail, Yahoo!, AOL, or Outlook.com, you enter the account settings yourself. First, tap the Settings icon on the Home screen.

2. In Settings, tap Mail, Contacts, Calendars, and then tap the Add Account button (refer to **Figure 11-1**).

3. On the screen that appears (refer to **Figure 11-2**), scroll down and tap Other.

4. On the screen shown in **Figure 11-4**, tap Add Mail Account.

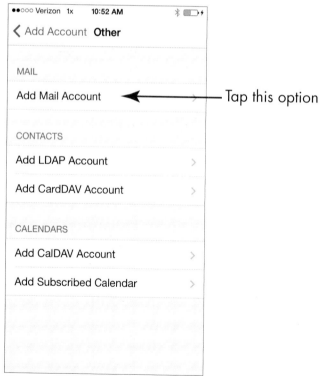

Figure 11-4

5. In the form that appears (refer to **Figure 11-3**), enter your name and an account address, password, and description, and then tap Next. iPhone takes a moment to verify your account and then returns you to the Mail, Contacts, Calendars page, with your new account displayed.

iPhone will probably add the outgoing mail server (SMTP) information for you, but if it doesn't, you may have to enter it yourself. If you have a less mainstream e-mail service, you may have to enter the mail server protocol (POP3 or IMAP — ask your provider for this information) and your password.

6. To make sure that the Account field is set to On for receiving e-mail, tap the account name. In the dialog that appears, tap the On/Off button for the Mail field and then tap the Mail button to return to Mail settings. You can now access the account through Mail.

If you turn on Calendars in the Mail account settings, any information you've put into your calendar in that e-mail account will be brought over into the Calendar app on your iPhone and reflected in the Notifications Center (discussed in more detail in Chapter 21).

Open Mail and Read Messages

1. Tap the Mail app icon, located in the Dock on the Home screen (see **Figure 11-5**). A red circle on the icon indicates the number of unread e-mails in your Inbox.

2. In the Mail app, (see **Figure 11-6**) tap the inbox whose contents you want to display.

The Mail app

Figure 11-5

Figure 11-6

3. Tap a message to read it. It opens (see **Figure 11-7**).

4. If you need to scroll to see the entire message, just place your finger on the screen and flick upward to scroll down. You can swipe right while reading a message to open the Inbox list of messages, and then swipe from the right to return to your list of mailboxes.

 You can tap the Next or Previous buttons (top-right corner of the message) to move to the next or previous message in the Inbox or tap Inbox in the top left corner to return to your inbox list of messages.

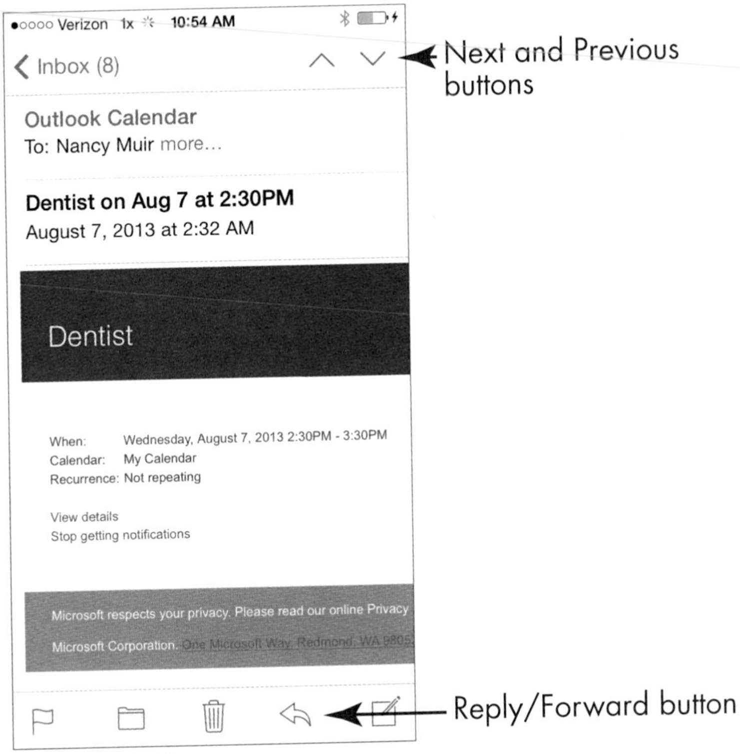

●oooo Verizon 1x ☼ 10:54 AM   ✳ ▭+

❮ Inbox (8)   ∧ ∨ ◄ Next and Previous
                              buttons

Outlook Calendar
To: Nancy Muir more...

Dentist on Aug 7 at 2:30PM
August 7, 2013 at 2:32 AM

Dentist

When: Wednesday, August 7, 2013 2:30PM - 3:30PM
Calendar: My Calendar
Recurrence: Not repeating

View details
Stop getting notifications

Microsoft respects your privacy. Please read our online Privacy

Microsoft Corporation. One Microsoft Way, Redmond, WA 980

⚐   ▭   🗑   ◁ ◄── ✎ ── Reply/Forward button

Figure 11-7

E-mail messages you haven't read are marked with a blue circle in your Inbox. After you read a message, the blue circle disappears. You can mark a read message as unread, to help remind you to read it again later. With a message open and details about it displayed, tap the Flag button in the bottom-left corner of the screen and then tap Mark as Unread. To flag a message, which places a little flag next to it in your inbox, helping you to spot items of more importance or to read again, tap Flag in this same menu.

To escape your e-mail now and then (or to avoid having messages retrieved while you're at a public Wi-Fi hotspot), you can stop retrieval of e-mail by using the Fetch New Data control of Mail in iPhone Mail, Contacts, Calendar Settings and using the Manual setting.

Reply To or Forward E-mail

1. With an e-mail message open (see the previous task), tap the Reply/Forward button which looks like a left-facing arrow (refer to **Figure 11-7**) and tap either Reply, Reply All (available if there are multiple recipients), or Forward in the menu that appears (see **Figure 11-8**).

2. In the form that appears (see **Figure 11-9**), tap in the To field and enter another addressee if you like (you have to do this if you're forwarding), and then tap in the message body and enter a message (see **Figure 11-10**).

Tap here to enter a recipient

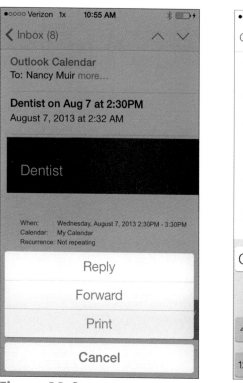

Figure 11-8

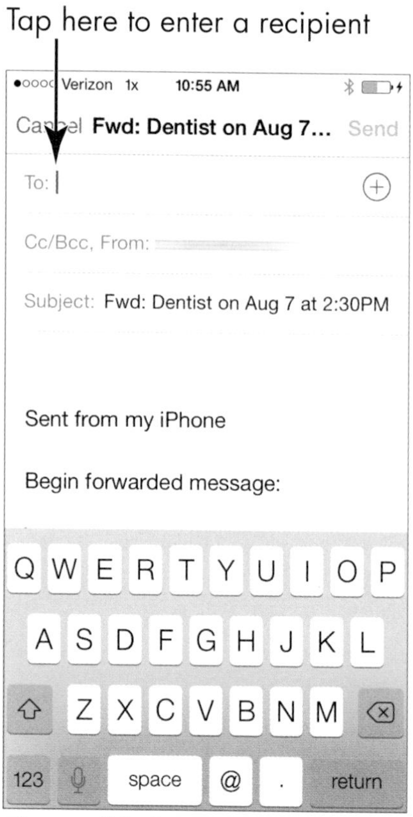

Figure 11-9

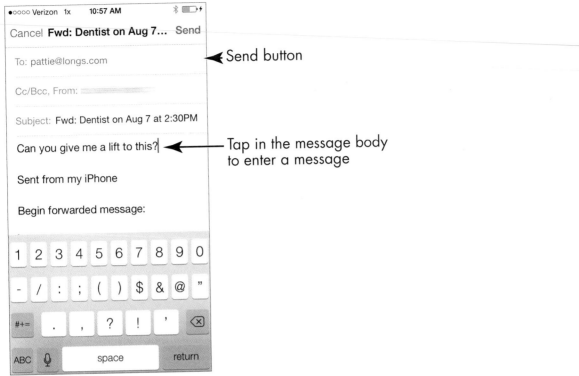

Send button

Tap in the message body to enter a message

Figure 11-10

3. Tap the Send button. The message goes on its way.

 If you want to move an address from the To field to the Cc or Bcc field, tap and hold the address and drag it to the other field.

 If you tap Forward to send the message to somebody else and the original message had an attachment, you're offered the option of including or not including the attachment when forwarding.

Create and Send a New Message

1. With Mail open, tap the New Message button in the bottom right hand corner (this looks like a page with a pen on it). A blank message form appears (see **Figure 11-11**).

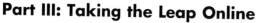

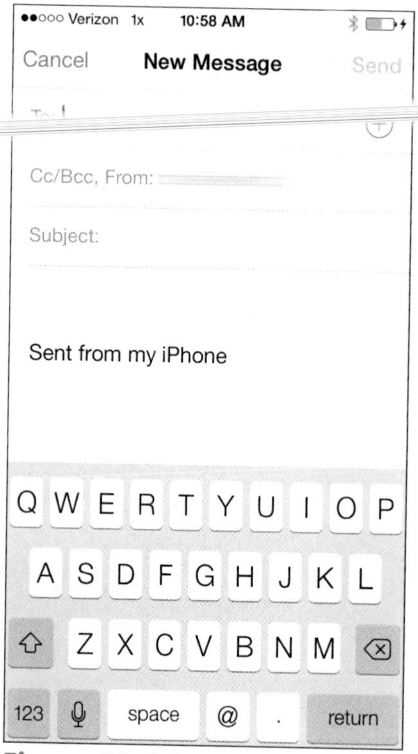

Figure 11-11

2. Enter a recipient's address in the To field. If you have saved addresses in Contacts, tap the plus sign (+) in the Address field to choose an addressee from the Contacts list that appears.

3. If you want to send a copy of the message to other people, enter their addresses in the Cc/Bcc field. If you want to send both carbon copies and *blind carbon copies* (copies you don't want other recipients to be aware of), note that when you tap the Cc/Bcc field, two fields are displayed; use the Bcc field to specify recipients of blind carbon copies.

4. Enter the subject of the message in the Subject field.

5. Tap in the message body and type your message.

6. Tap Send.

Format E-mail

1. A feature that arrived with iOS 5 is the capability to apply formatting to e-mail text. You can use bold, underline, and italic formats, and indent text using the Quote Level feature.

2. Tap the text in a message and choose Select or Select All to select a single word or all the words in the e-mail. Note that when you make a selection, handles appear that you can drag to add adjacent words to your selection.

3. Tap the arrow on the toolbar that appears to see more tools; to apply bold, italic, or underline formatting, tap the B*I*U button (see **Figure 11-12**).

4. In the toolbar that appears (see **Figure 11-13**), tap Bold, Italics, or Underline to apply formatting.

5. To change the indent level, tap and hold at the beginning of a line and then tap the arrow at the far end of the toolbar (refer to **Figure 11-12**). In the toolbar that appears, tap Quote Level.

6. Tap Increase to indent the text or Decrease to move indented text farther toward the left margin.

To use the Quote Level feature, make sure it's on using the iPad Settings. In Settings, tap Mail, Contacts, Calendars, and then tap the Increase Quote Level On/Off button.

Tap this option   Make your selection here

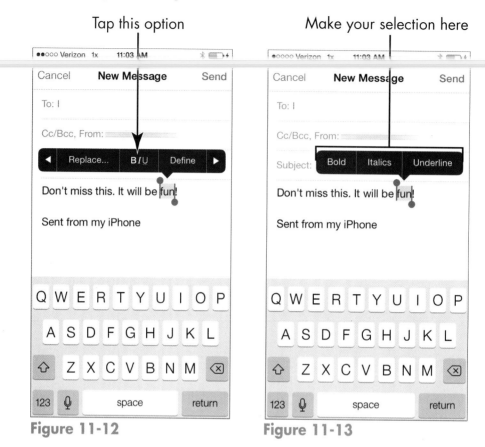

Figure 11-12   **Figure 11-13**

Search E-mail

1. What do you do if you want to find all messages from a certain person or containing a certain word in the Subject field? You can use Mail's handy Search feature to find these e-mails (though you can't search message contents). With Mail open, tap an account to display its Inbox.

2. In the Inbox, tap in the Search field. The onscreen keyboard appears.

3. Enter a search term or name as shown in **Figure 11-14**. Matching e-mails are listed in the results (refer to **Figure 11-14**).

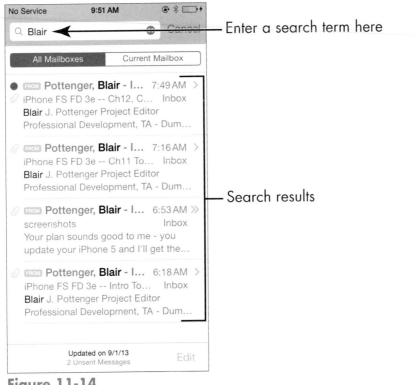

Enter a search term here

Search results

Figure 11-14

4. Swipe down on the screen and tap the All Mailboxes tab to view messages that contain the search term in one of those fields in any mailbox, or tap the Current Mailbox tab to see only matches within the current mailbox (refer to **Figure 11-14**).

 You can also use the Spotlight Search feature covered in Chapter 2 to search for terms in the To, From, or Subject lines of mail messages.

 To start a new search or go back to the full Inbox, tap the Delete icon (the circled X) on the far-right end of the Search field to delete the term or just tap the Cancel button.

Delete E-mail

1. When you no longer want an e-mail cluttering your Inbox, you can delete it. With the Inbox displayed, tap the Edit button. Circular check boxes are displayed to the left of each message (see **Figure 11-15**).

— Tap to select the message

— Selected messages

Figure 11-15

2. Tap the circle next to the message you want to delete. (You can tap multiple items if you have several e-mails to delete.) A message marked for deletion shows a check mark in the circular check button (refer to **Figure 11-15**).

3. Tap the Trash button at the bottom of the Inbox dialog. The message is moved to the Trash folder.

 You can also delete an open e-mail by tapping the trashcan icon on the toolbar that runs across the bottom of the screen, or swiping left or right on a message displayed in an inbox and tapping the Trash button that appears.

Organize E-mail

1. You can move messages into any of several predefined folders in Mail (these will vary depending on your e-mail provider and the folders you've created on your provider's server). After displaying the folder containing the message you want to move (for example, Trash or Inbox), tap the Edit button. Circular check boxes are displayed to the left of each message (refer to **Figure 11-15**).

2. Tap the circle next to the message you want to move.

3. Tap the Move button.

4. In the Mailboxes list that appears (see **Figure 11-16**), tap the folder where you want to store the message. The message is moved.

 If you receive a junk e-mail, you might want to move it to the Spam or Junk folder if your e-mail account provides one. Then any future mail from the same sender is automatically placed in the Spam or Junk folder.

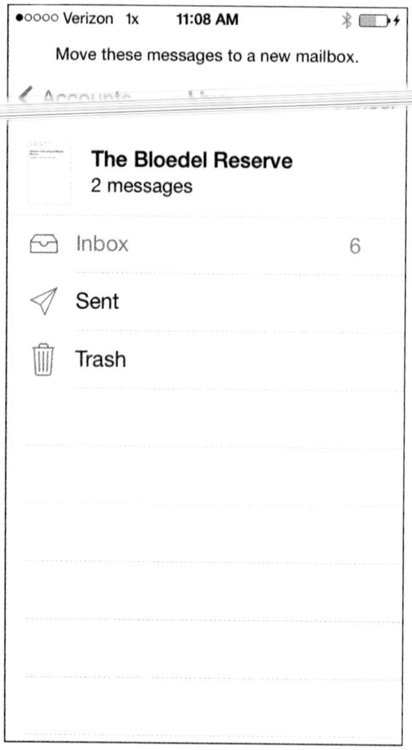

●oooo Verizon 1x   11:08 AM   ∗ ▭◗+

Move these messages to a new mailbox.

❮ Accounts

The Bloedel Reserve
2 messages

▱ Inbox   6

◁ Sent

🗑 Trash

Figure 11-16

Create a VIP List

1. iOS 6 brought a new feature to Mail called VIP List. This is a way to create a list of senders. When any of these senders sends you an e-mail, you'll be notified of it through the Notifications feature of iPhone. In the list of all Mailboxes, tap the arrow to the right of VIP (see **Figure 11-17**).

2. Tap Add VIP (see **Figure 11-18**), and your Contacts list appears. Tap a contact to add that person to the VIP list.

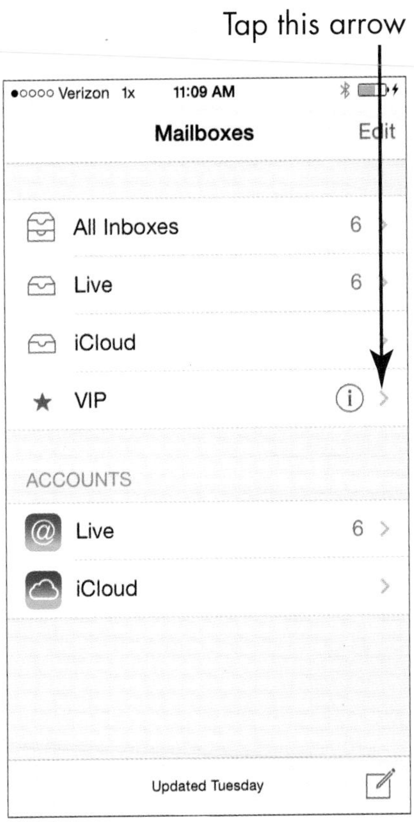

Tap this arrow   Tap this option

Figure 11-17

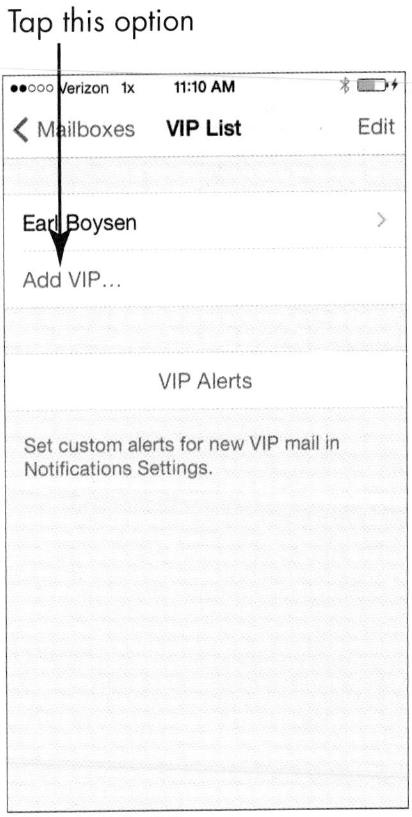

Figure 11-18

3. Press the Home button and then tap Settings.

4. Tap Notification Center and then tap Mail. In the settings that appear, shown in **Figure 11-19**, tap VIP.

5. Tap the Notification Center On/Off button to turn on notifications for VIP mail.

6. Tap an alert style and choose whether a badge icon or sound should occur. You can also choose to have the notification displayed on your Lock Screen (see **Figure 11-20**).

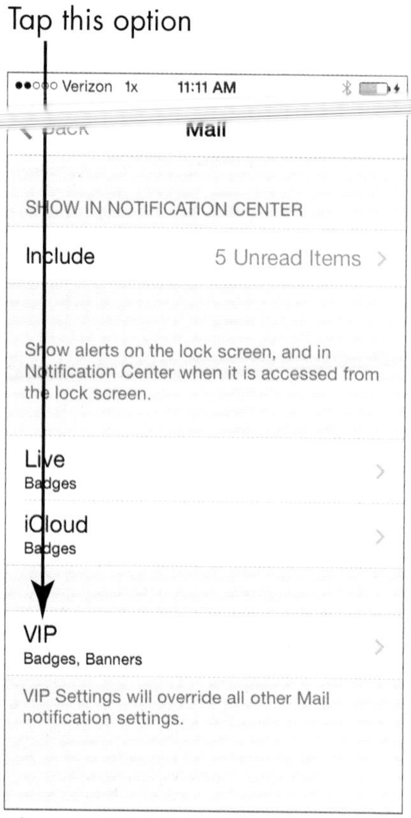

Tap this option

Figure 11-19

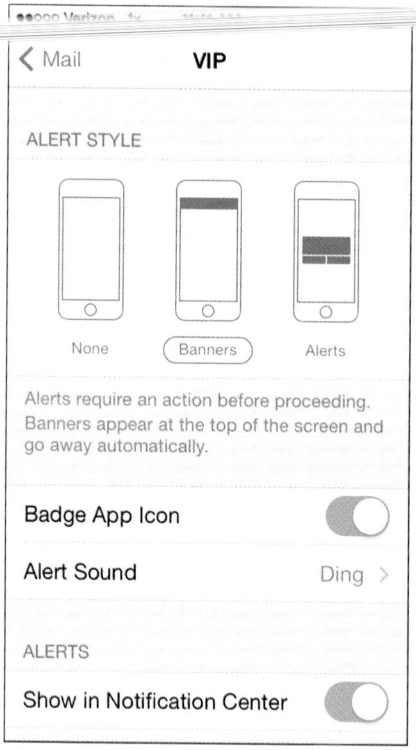

Figure 11-20

7. Press the Home button to close Settings. New mail from your VIPs should now appear in Notifications when you swipe down from the top of the screen, and depending on the settings you chose, may cause a sound to play or a note to appear on your Lock Screen, or a blue star icon to appear to the left of these messages in the inbox in Mail.

Shopping the iTunes Store

Chapter 12

The iTunes Store app that comes preinstalled in iPhone lets you easily shop for music, movies, TV shows, and audiobooks. If you've downloaded the free iTunes U, you can even install online classes.

In this chapter, you discover how to find content in the iTunes Store. You can download the content directly to your iPhone or to another device and then sync it to your iPhone. In addition, I cover a few options for buying content from other online stores.

Note that I cover opening an iTunes account and downloading iTunes software to your computer in Chapter 3. If you need to, read Chapter 3 to see how to handle these two tasks before digging into this chapter.

Explore the iTunes Store

1. Visiting the iTunes Store from your iPhone is easy with the built-in iTunes Store app. Tap the iTunes Store icon on the Home screen.

2. If you're not already signed in to iTunes, the dialog
   shown in **Figure 12-1** appears, asking for your iTunes
   ~~password. Enter your password and tap OK.~~

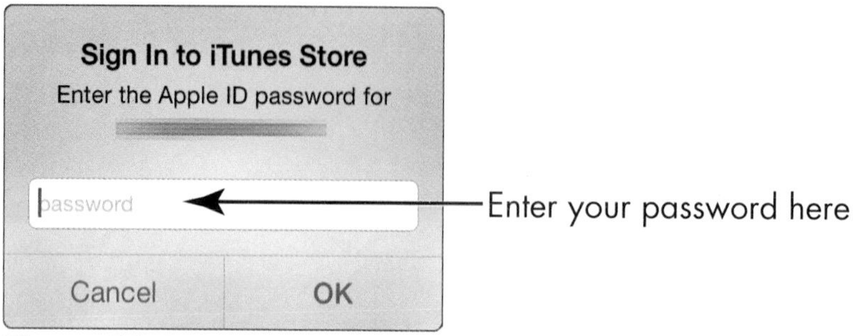

Sign In to iTunes Store
Enter the Apple ID password for

password   ←————— Enter your password here

Cancel   OK

Figure 12-1

3. Tap the Music button (if it isn't already selected) in the
   row of buttons at the bottom of the screen. You see several rows of categories of selections such as New Releases,
   Recent Releases, and Singles.

4. Flick your finger up to scroll through the featured selections or tap the See All button to see more selections in
   any category, as shown in **Figure 12-2**.

5. Tap the Genres or Charts tab at the top of the screen. The
   first displays a list of genres you can tap on to narrow
   your selections, while Charts contains lists of best-selling
   songs and albums in the iTunes Store.

6. Tap any listed item to see more detail about it, as shown
   in **Figure 12-3,** and hear a brief preview when you tap on
   the number to the left of a song.

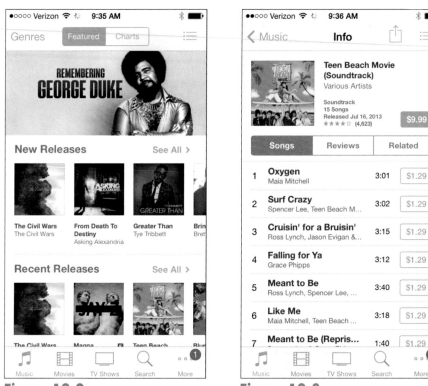

Figure 12-2

Figure 12-3

 The navigation techniques in these steps work essentially the same in any of the content categories (the buttons at the bottom of the screen), which include Music, Movies, and TV Shows, Audiobooks, and Tones (the last two are accessed through the More button at the bottom of the iTunes screen). Just tap one to explore it.

 If you want to use the Genius playlist feature, which recommends additional purchases based on the contents of your library in the iTunes app on your iPhone, tap the More button at the bottom of the screen and then tap Genius. If you've made enough purchases in iTunes, song and album recommendations appear based on those purchases as well as the content in your iTunes Match library, if you have one.

To use Podcasts and iTunes U courses you have to install separate apps. Go to the App Store on your iPhone and search for Podcasts or iTunes U and install these free apps to get access to this additional content.

Find a Selection

You can look for a selection in the iTunes Store in several ways. You can use the Search feature, search by genre or category, or view artists' pages. Here's how these work:

➟ Tap the Search button at the bottom of the screen and the search screen shown in **Figure 12-4** appears. Enter a search term using the onscreen keyboard. Tap the Search button on the keyboard or, if a suggestion in the list of search results appeals to you, just tap that suggestion.

➟ Tap an item such as Music at the bottom of the screen, and then tap the Genres button at the top of the screen. A list of genres like the one shown in **Figure 12-5** appears.

➟ On a description page that appears when you tap a selection, you can find more offerings by the people involved with that particular work. For example, for a music selection, tap the Reviews tab at the middle of the page to see all reviews of the album (see **Figure 12-6**). For a movie (tap Movies at the bottom of the iTunes Store home page), tap Reviews, or tap the Related tab to see what those who bought this movie also purchased.

Enter a search term here

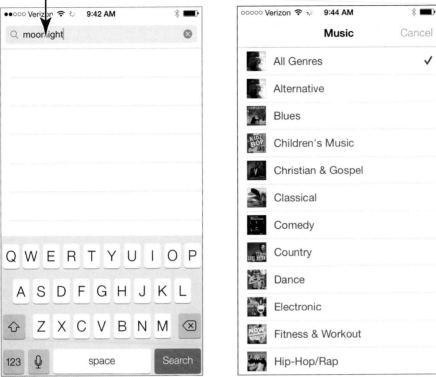

Figure 12-4

Figure 12-5

 If you find a selection you like, tap the Share button on its description page to share your discovery with a friend via AirDrop, Mail, Message, Twitter, or Facebook. A message form appears with a link your friend can tap to view information about the selection. Note that you must have set up an associated account (such as Twitter) using the iPhone Settings before you can use this service.

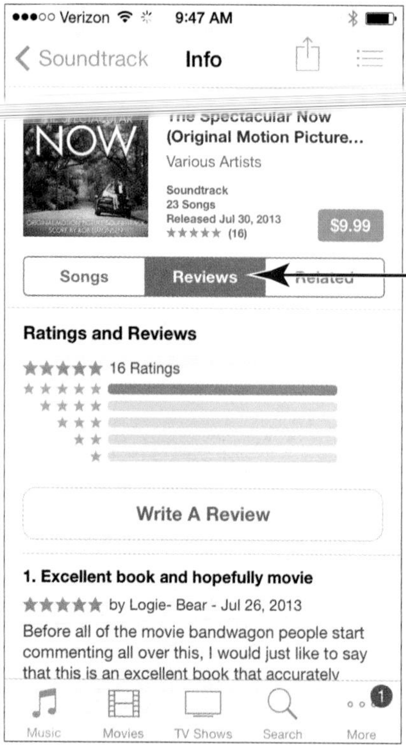

Reviews tab

Figure 12-6

Preview Music, a Video, or an Audiobook

1. Because you've already set up an iTunes account (if you haven't done so yet, refer to Chapter 3), when you choose to buy an item, it's automatically charged to the credit card you have on record, to your PayPal account, or against any allowance you have outstanding from an iTunes gift card. You might want to preview an item before you buy it. If you like it, buying and downloading are then easy and quick. Open iTunes and use any method outlined in earlier tasks to locate a selection you might want to buy.

2. Tap the item to see detailed information about it, as shown in **Figure 12-7**.

3. For audiobooks, tap the Preview button to play a preview. For a TV show, tap an episode to get further information (refer to **Figure 12-7**). If you're looking at a music selection, tap the track number or name of a selection to play a preview. For a movie or audiobook selection, tap the Trailers Play button (movies) shown in **Figure 12-8,** or the Preview button (audiobooks).

Figure 12-7

Figure 12-8

Buy a Selection

1. When you find an item ~~you want to buy, tap the button~~ that shows either the price (if it's a selection available for purchase; see **Figure 12-9**) or the button with the word *Free* on it (if it's a selection available for free).

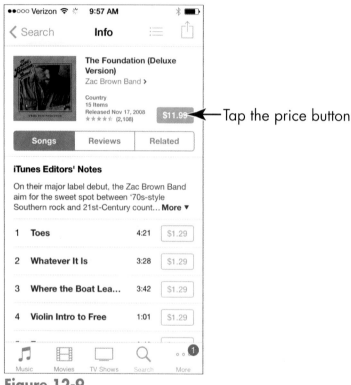

Tap the price button

Figure 12-9

The button label changes to Buy X, where X is the type of content, such as a song or album, you're buying. If the item is free, the label changes to Install.

2. Tap the Buy X button. The iTunes Password dialog appears (refer to **Figure 12-1**).

3. Enter your password and tap OK. The item begins downloading, and the cost, if any, is automatically charged against your account. When the download finishes, you can view the content using the Music or Video app, depending on the type of content.

 If you want to buy music, you can open the description page for an album and tap the album price, or buy individual songs rather than the entire album. Tap the price for a song and then proceed to purchase it.

 Note the Redeem button on some iTunes screens. Tap this button to redeem any iTunes gift certificates you might get from your generous friends, or from yourself.

 If you don't want to allow purchases from within apps (for example Music or Videos) but rather want to allow purchases only through the iTunes Store, you can go to Settings, General, tap Restrictions, and then tap Enable Restrictions and enter a passcode. After you've set a passcode, you can tap individual apps to turn on restrictions for them, as well as for actions such as sharing via AirDrop, deleting apps, or using Siri.

 You can allow content to be downloaded over your 3G/4G cellular network if you're not near a Wi-Fi hotspot. Be aware, however, that you could incur hefty data charges with your provider if you run over your allotted data. However, if you aren't near a Wi-Fi hotspot, this might be your only option. Go to Settings, iTunes & App Stores, and tap the On/Off button for the Use Cellular Data setting.

Rent Movies

1. In the case of movies, you can either rent or buy content.
If you rent, which is less expensive but a one-time deal,
you have 30 days from the time you rent the item to
begin to watch it. After you have begun to watch it, you
have 24 hours from that time left to watch it on the same
device, as many times as you like. With iTunes open, tap
the Movies button.

2. Locate the movie you want to rent and tap it, as shown
in **Figure 12-10**.

3. In the detailed description of the movie that appears, tap the
Rent button (if it's available for rental); see **Figure 12-11**.

Rent button

Figure 12-10   **Figure 12-11**

4. The gray Rent button changes to a green Rent Movie button; tap it to confirm the rental. The movie begins to download to your iPhone immediately, and your account is charged the rental fee.

5. To check the status of your download, tap the More button and then tap Downloads. The progress of your download is displayed. After the download is complete, you can use the Videos app to watch it. (See Chapter 17 to read about how this app works.)

Some movies are offered in high-definition versions. These HD movies look pretty good on that crisp, colorful iPhone screen.

You can also download content to your computer and sync it to your iPhone. Refer to Chapter 3 for more about this process.

Shop Anywhere Else

One feature that's missing from the iPhone is support for Flash, a format of video playback that many online video-on-demand services and interactive games use. However, many online stores that sell content such as movies and music are hurriedly adding iPhone-friendly videos to their collections, so you do have alternatives to iTunes for your choice of movies and TV shows. You can also shop for music from sources other than iTunes, such as Amazon.com.

You can open accounts at one of these stores by using your computer or your iPhone's Safari browser and then following the store's instructions for purchasing and downloading content.

These content providers offer iPhone-compatible video content, and more are opening all the time:

⟹ **ABC:** http://abc.go.com

⟹ **CBS News:** www.cbsnews.com

➡ **Clicker:** www.clicker.com

➡ Netflix: www.netflix.com

➡ **Ustream:** www.ustream.tv

➡ **iMP4Movies:** www.imp4movies.com

For non–iPhone-friendly formats, you can download the content on your computer and stream it to your iPhone using Air Video ($2.99) on the iPhone and Air Video Server (which is free) using your Mac or Windows computer. For more information go to www.inmethod.com/air-video/index.html.

Enable Auto Downloads of Purchases from Other Devices

1. With iCloud, you can make a purchase or download free content on any of your Apple devices, and iCloud automatically shares those purchases with all your Apple devices. To enable this auto-download feature on iPhone, start by tapping Settings on the Home screen.

To use iCloud, first set up an iCloud account. See Chapter 3 for detailed coverage of iCloud, including setting up your account.

2. Tap iTunes & App Stores.

3. In the options that appear, scroll down and then tap the On/Off button for any category of purchases you want to auto-download to your iPhone from other Apple devices: Music, Apps, or Books (see **Figure 12-12**).

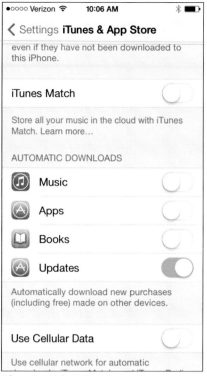

Figure 12-12

 At this point, Apple doesn't offer an option of auto-downloading video content using these settings, probably because video is such a memory and bandwidth hog. You are probably better off downloading video using the iTunes app and then using iTunes to get the content onto your iPhone.

Expanding Your iPhone Horizons with Apps

*S*ome *apps* (short for *applications*) come pre-installed on your iPhone, such as Contacts and Videos. But you can choose from a world of other apps out there for your iPhone, some for free (such as iBooks) and some for a price (typically, from 99 cents to about $10, though some can top out at $90 or more).

Apps range from games to financial tools like loan calculators to apps that help you when you are planning or taking a trip.

In this chapter, I suggest some apps you might want to check out and explain how to use the App Store feature of iPhone to find, purchase, and download apps.

Explore Senior-Recommended Apps

As I write this book, new iPhone apps are in development, so even more apps that could fit your needs will be available. Still, to get you exploring what's available, I want to provide a quick list of apps that might whet your appetite.

Access the App Store by tapping the App Store icon on the Home screen. Then tap the Search button at the bottom of the screen and enter an app name or other descriptive text. Suggested matches are listed. Tap one to see more information about it.

Here are some interesting apps to explore:

➡ **Sudoku2 (free):** If you like this mental logic puzzle in print, try it out on your iPhone (see **Figure 13-1**). It has three lessons and several levels ranging from easiest to nightmare, making it a great way to make time fly by in a doctor's or dentist's waiting room.

Figure 13-1

➟ **StockWatch Portfolio Tracking ($1.99):** Even though there's a Stocks app on the iPhone Home screen, this app will help you keep track of your investments in a portfolio format. You can use the app to create a watch list and record your stock performance.

➟ **Flickr (free):** If you use the Flickr photo-sharing service on your computer, why not bring the same features to your iPhone? This app is useful for sharing images with family and friends.

➟ **Paint Studio ($3.99):** Get creative! You can use this powerful app to draw, add color, and even create special effects. If you don't need all these features, try Paint Studio Jr.

➟ **Virtuoso Piano Free 3 (free):** If you love to make music, you'll love this app, which gives you a virtual piano keyboard to play and compose on the fly.

➟ **iPhoto ($4.99):** This is an Apple app that provides all kinds of tools for editing those great photos you can grab with your iOS 7-based iPhone.

➟ **Travelzoo (free):** Get great deals on hotels, airfare, rental cars, entertainment, and more. This app also offers tips from travel experts.

➟ **Nike Training Club (free):** Use this handy utility to help design personalized workouts, see step-by-step instructions to help you learn new exercises, and watch video demonstrations. The reward system in this app may just keep you going toward your workout goals.

 iBooks is the outstanding, free e-reader app that opens up a world of reading on your iPhone. See Chapter 14 for details about using iBooks.

Search the App Store

1. Tap the App Store icon on the Home screen. The site shown in **Figure 13-2** appears.

2. At this point, you have several options for finding apps:

- Scroll downward to view various categories of Featured apps such as New and Noteworthy and What's Hot.

- Tap the Top Charts or Near Me tab at the bottom of the screen to see that category of apps. The Near Me option, new with iOS 7, displays apps that are popular among people in or near your location (this may or may not produce useful results depending on where you are!).

- Tap the Search button at the bottom of the screen and then tap in the Search field, enter a search term, and tap the result you want to view.

- Tap the Categories button in the top-left corner of the screen on the Featured and Top Charts views to browse by type of app such as Education or Entertainment, as shown in **Figure 13-3**.

- Tap the See All button in any category to view all the items in that category.

- In the Top Charts view use the Paid, Free, and Top Grossing tabs to narrow down your search.

Figure 13-2   **Figure 13-3**

Get Applications from the App Store

1. Buying or getting free apps requires that you have an iTunes account, which I cover in Chapter 3. After you have an account, you can use the saved payment information there to buy apps or download free apps with a few simple steps. I strongly recommend that you install the free iBooks app, so in this task, I walk you through the steps for getting it. With the App Store open, tap the Search button, enter iBooks in the Search field, and then tap the name of the app when it appears in the results list and the app information appears, as shown in **Figure 13-4**.

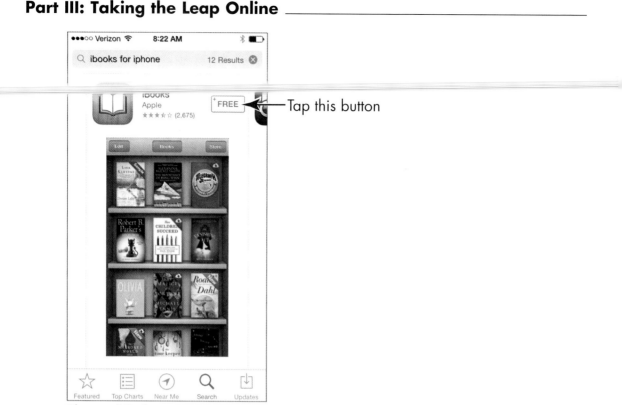

Tap this button

Figure 13-4

2. Tap the Free button for iBooks in the results that appear. (To get a *paid* app, you tap the same button, which is now labeled with a price.)

3. The Free button changes to read *Install App* (or, in the case of a paid app, the button changes to read *Buy*). Tap the button and the button changes to read *Installing*. You may be asked to enter your iTunes password; tap the OK button to proceed.

4. The app downloads; if you purchase an app that isn't free, at this point, your credit card or gift card balance is charged for the purchase price.

 Out of the box, only preinstalled apps are located on the first iPhone Home screen. Apps you download are placed on available Home screens, and you have to scroll to view and use them; this procedure is

covered later in this chapter. See the next task for
help in finding your newly downloaded apps using
multiple Home screens.

 If you've opened an iCloud account, you can set it up
so that anything you purchase on your iPhone is
automatically pushed to other Apple iOS devices and
your iTunes Library and vice versa. See Chapter 3 for
more about iCloud.

 If you're starting fresh with your iPhone with iOS 7
and haven't downloaded any apps yet, when you go
to the App Store you will be presented with a set of
free apps to download together, including iBooks,
iMovie, Twitter, and a couple more. You can choose
this group download to get iBooks on your iPhone, if
you like.

Organize Your Applications on Home Screens

1. iPhone can display up to 15 Home screens. By default,
the first contains preinstalled apps, and the second Home
screen contains a few more preinstalled apps in the
Utilities folder. Other screens are created to contain any
apps you download or sync to your iPhone. At the bottom of any iPhone Home screen (just above the Dock),
dots indicate the number of Home screens you've filled
with apps; a solid dot specifies which Home screen
you're on now, as shown in **Figure 13-5**. Press the Home
button to open the last displayed Home screen.

2. Flick your finger from right to left to move to the next
Home screen. To move back, flick from left to right.

3. To reorganize apps on a Home screen, press and hold
any app on that page. The app icons begin to jiggle (see
Figure 13-6), and any apps you installed will sport a
Delete button (a black circle with a white X on it).

Screen you're on   A Delete button

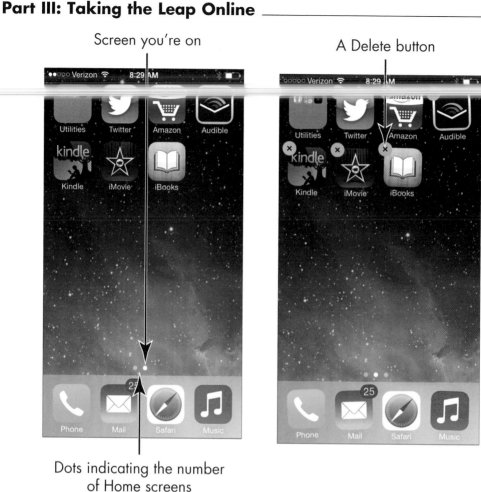

Dots indicating the number
of Home screens

Figure 13-5   Figure 13-6

4. Press, hold, and drag an app icon to another location on the screen to move it.

5. Press the Home button to stop all those icons from jiggling!

 To move an app from one page to another, while the apps are jiggling, you can press, hold, and drag an app to the left or right to move it to the next Home screen. You can also manage what app resides on what Home screen and change the order of the Home screens from iTunes when you've connected iPhone to iTunes via a cable or wireless sync.

With iOS 7 comes some new multitasking features for switching between apps easily. Press the Home button twice and you get a preview of open apps. Scroll among them and tap the one you want to go to. You can also swipe an app upward from this preview list and it closes.

Organize Apps in Folders

iPhone lets you organize apps in folders so you can find them more easily. The process is simple:

1. Tap and hold an app until all apps do their jiggle dance.

2. Drag an app on top of another app. The two apps appear in a box with a placeholder name in a strip above them (see **Figure 13-7**).

Figure 13-7

3. To change the name, tap in the field at the end of the placeholder name, and the keyboard appears.

4. Tap the Delete key to delete the placeholder name and type one of your own.

5. Tap Done, and then tap anywhere outside the box to close it.

6. Press the Home button to stop the icons from dancing around, and you'll see your folder appears on the Home screen where you began this process.

Delete Applications You No Longer Need

1. When you no longer need an app you have installed, it's time to get rid of it. (You can't delete apps that are prein-stalled on the iPhone.) If you use iCloud to push content across all Apple iOS devices, note that deleting an app on your iPhone won't affect that app on other devices. Display the Home screen that contains the app you want to delete.

2. Press and hold the app until all apps begin to jiggle.

3. Tap the Delete button for the app you want to delete (refer to **Figure 13-6**).

4. A confirmation like the one shown in **Figure 13-8** appears. Tap Delete to proceed with the deletion.

Delete "Audible"

Deleting "Audible" will also delete all of its data.

Delete ◄──────── Cancel ──────Tap this button

Figure 13-8

 Don't worry about wiping out several apps at once by deleting a folder. When you delete a folder, the apps that were contained within the folder are placed back on a Home screen if space is available, and you can still find the apps using the Spotlight search feature.

Update Apps

1. App developers update their apps all the time, so you might want to check for those updates. The App Store icon on the Home screen will display the number of available updates in a red circle. Tap the App Store icon on the Home Screen.

2. Tap the Updates button to access the Updates screen and then tap any item you want to update. To update all, tap the Update All button.

3. On the app screen that appears, tap Update. You may be asked to confirm that you want to update, or to enter your Apple ID; tap OK to proceed. You may also be asked to confirm that you are over a certain age or agree to terms and conditions; if so, scroll down the terms dialog and, at the bottom, tap Agree. The download progress is displayed.

 In iOS 5, Apple introduced the capability to download multiple apps at once. If you choose more than one app to update instead of downloading them sequentially as in previous versions of the iOS, several items will download simultaneously. As of iOS 6 you no longer have to exit to Home screens; you can keep working in the Store after you've downloaded an item.

If you have an iCloud account that you have activated on several devices and update an app on your iPhone, any other Apple iOS devices are also updated automatically and vice versa.

iOS 7 performs what Apple calls "intelligently scheduled updates," meaning that updates to apps and the iOS happen at times when your iPhone isn't using much power, for example when you're connecting to the Internet via Wi-Fi. And speaking of updating, iOS 7 also studies your habits and can update apps that require updated content, such as Facebook or Stocks, around the time you usually check them so you have instant access to current information.

Part IV

Having Fun and Consuming Media

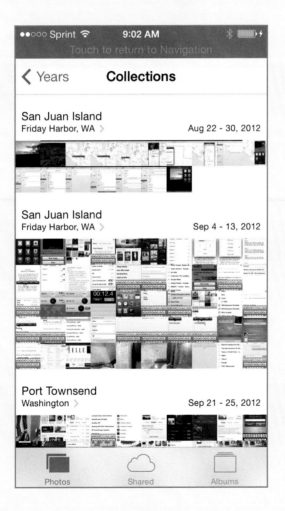

Using Your iPhone as an E-reader

A traditional *e-reader* is a device that's used primarily to read the electronic version of books, magazines, and newspapers. If you're happy reading on your smaller iPhone screen, your phone can be a great e-reader, although it isn't a traditional e-reader device like the Barnes & Noble Nook because it gets its functionality from an e-reader app.

Apple's free, downloadable app that turns your iPhone into an e-reader is *iBooks*, which also enables you to buy and download books from Apple's iBookstore. You can also use one of several other free e-reader apps — for example Kindle, Stanza, or Nook — to download books to your iPhone from a variety of online sources such as Amazon and Google so you can read to your heart's content.

An app that arrived with iOS 5 is Newsstand, covered later in this chapter. Newsstand provides access to another reading experience, but its focus is on subscribing to and reading magazines, newspapers, and other periodicals. With iOS 7 comes a drastic revision to the appearance of Newsstand, which now boasts a contemporary background replacing the wooden shelf look of yore.

In this chapter, you discover the options available for reading material and how to buy books and subscribe to publications. You also learn how to get around electronic publications: how to navigate a book or periodical and adjust the brightness and type, as well as how to search books and organize your iBooks and Newsstand libraries.

Discover E-reading

An *e-reader* is any electronic device that enables you to download and read books, magazines, pdf files, or newspapers. These devices are typically portable and dedicated only to reading the electronic version of published materials. Many e-readers use E Ink technology to create a paperlike reading experience.

The iPhone is a bit different. It isn't only for reading books, and you have to download an app to enable it as an e-reader (though the apps are usually free). Also, the iPhone doesn't offer the paperlike reading experience — you read from a phone screen (though you can adjust the brightness and background color of the screen).

When you buy a book online (or get one of many free publications), it downloads to your iPhone in a few seconds using a Wi-Fi or 3G/4G connection. The iPhone offers several navigation tools to move around a book, which you explore in this chapter.

Find Books with iBooks

1. In Chapter 13, I walk you through the process of downloading the iBooks application in the "Get Applications from the App Store" task, so you should do that first, if you haven't already. To shop using iBooks, tap the iBooks application icon to open it. (It's probably on your second or third Home screen, so you may have to swipe your finger to the left on the screen to locate it.)

2. In the iBooks library that opens (see **Figure 14-1**), you see a bookshelf; yours probably has only one free book already downloaded to it. (If you don't see the bookshelf,

tap the Library button to go there.) Tap the Store button, and the shelf pivots 180 degrees.

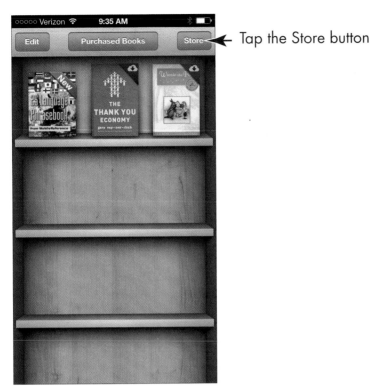

← Tap the Store button

Figure 14-1

3. In the iBookstore, shown in **Figure 14-2,** featured titles are shown by default. You can do any of the following to find a book:

- Tap in the Search field at the top of the screen and type a search word or phrase in the search field that appears, using the onscreen keyboard.

- Tap the More button along the top of the screen and scroll down to Browse Categories to see links to popular categories of books, as shown in **Figure 14-3.** Tap a category to view those selections.

- Press your finger on the screen and flick up to scroll to more suggested titles on a page.

- Tap the appropriate button at the bottom of the screen to view particular categories: Featured books, NY Times or Top Charts to see books listed on top bestseller lists, browse worthy lists or Top Authors, or only titles you've already purchased on any Apple device connected via iCloud.

 Scroll to the bottom of any screen to access Quick Links, which include shortcuts to Best of the Month, Free Books, and Textbooks.

- Tap a suggested selection or featured book to read more information about it.

Categories   Library

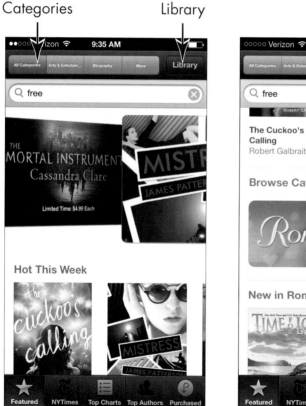

Figure 14-2

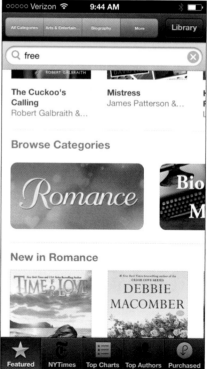

Figure 14-3

Download free samples before you buy. You get to read several pages of the book to see whether it appeals to you, and it doesn't cost you a dime! Look for the Get Sample button when you view details about a book.

Explore Other E-book Sources

The iPhone is capable of using iBooks and other e-reader apps to read book content from other bookstores. To do so, first download another e-reader application such as Kindle from Amazon or the Barnes & Noble Nook reader from the iPhone App Store (see Chapter 13 for how to download apps). You can also download a non-vendor-specific app such as Bluefire Reader, which handles ePub and PDF format, as well as the format that most public libraries use (protected PDF). Then use their features to search for, purchase, and download content.

The Kindle e-reader application is shown in **Figure 14-4**. After downloading the free app from the App Store, you just enter the e-mail address associated with your Amazon account and password. Any content you've already bought from the Amazon.com Kindle Store is archived online and can be placed on your Kindle Home page on the iPhone for you to read anytime you like. Tap the Device tab to see titles stored on iPhone rather than in Amazon's Cloud library. Use features to enhance your reading experience such as changing the background to a sepia tone or changing font. To delete a book from this reader, press the title with your finger, and the Remove from Device button appears.

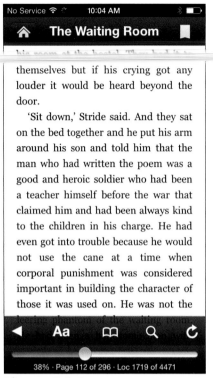

Figure 14-4

 e-Books are everywhere! You can also get content from a variety of other sources: Project Gutenberg, Google, some publishers like Baen, and so on. Get the content using your computer if you like and then just add the items to Books in iTunes and sync them to your iPhone. Just be aware that your iPhone won't work with formats other than epub or PDF (such as mobi and azw). You can also make settings to iCloud so that books are pushed across your Apple devices or place them in an online storage service such as Dropbox and access them from there.

Buy Books

1. If you've set up an account with iTunes, you can buy books at the iBookstore using the iBooks app. (See

Chapter 3 for more about iTunes.) Open iBooks and tap Store. When you find a book in the iBookstore that you want to buy, tap it, and then tap the Price button. The button changes to the Buy Book button, as shown in **Figure 14-5.** (If the book is free, these buttons are labeled Free and Get Book, respectively.)

2. Tap the Buy Book or Get Book button. If you haven't already signed in, the iTunes Password dialog, shown in **Figure 14-6,** appears.

 If you have signed in, your purchase is accepted immediately — no returns are allowed, so tap carefully!

Buy Book button

Figure 14-5

iTunes Password

ipadsenior@gmail.com

Password

Cancel   OK

Figure 14-6

3. Enter your password and tap OK.

4. The book appears on your bookshelf, and the cost is charged to whichever credit card you specified when you opened your iTunes account.

 You can also sync books you've downloaded to your computer to your iPhone by using the Lightning to USB Cable and your iTunes account or by using the wireless iTunes Wi-Fi Sync setting on the General Settings menu. Using this method, you can find lots of free books from various sources online and share them online with a service such as Dropbox, or drag them into your iTunes Book library; then simply sync them to your iPhone. See Chapter 3 for more about syncing.

Navigate a Book

1. Tap iBooks and, if your Library (the bookshelf) isn't already displayed, tap the Library button.

2. Tap a book to open it. The book opens to its title page or the last spot you read on any compatible device, as shown in **Figure 14-7.**

3. Take any of these actions to navigate the book:

- **To go to the book's Table of Contents:** Tap the Table of Contents button at the top of the page (refer to **Figure 14-7**) and then tap the name of a chapter to go to it (see **Figure 14-8**).

Table of Contents button

Tap any chapter to go to it

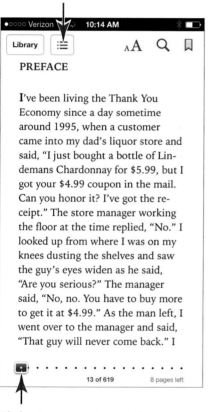

Slider to move to another page

Figure 14-7

Figure 14-8

- **To turn to the next page:** Place your finger any-where along the right edge of the page and flick to the left.

- **To turn to the preceding page:** Place your finger anywhere on the left edge of a page and flick to the right.

- **To move to another page in the book:** Tap and drag the slider at the bottom of the page (refer to **Figure 14-7**) to the right or left.

 To return to the Library to view another book at any time, tap the Library button. If the button isn't visi-ble, tap anywhere on the page, and the button and other tools appear.

Adjust Brightness in iBooks

1. iBooks offers an adjustable brightness setting that you can use to make your book pages comfortable to read. With a book open, tap the Font button, shown in **Figure 14-9**.

2. On the Brightness setting that appears (refer to **Figure 14-9**), tap and drag the slider to the right to make the screen brighter, or to the left to dim it.

3. Tap anywhere on the page to close the Font dialog.

 Experiment with the brightness level that works for you, or try out the Sepia setting, which you find by tapping Themes in the Fonts dialog. Bright white screens are commonly thought to be hard on the eyes, so setting the brightness halfway relative to its default setting or less is probably a good idea (and saves on battery life).

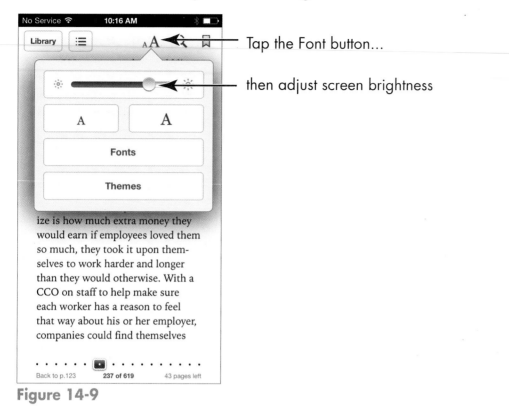

Tap the Font button...

then adjust screen brightness

Figure 14-9

Change the Font Size and Type

1. If the type on your screen is a bit small for your taste, you can change to a larger font size or choose a different font for readability. With a book open, tap the Font button (it sports a small letter *a* and a large capital *A*, as shown in **Figure 14-10**).

2. In the Font dialog that appears (refer to **Figure 14-10**), tap the button with a small A on the left to use smaller text, or the button with the large A on the right to use larger text.

3. Tap the Fonts button. The list of fonts shown in **Figure 14-11** appears.

Tap the Font button

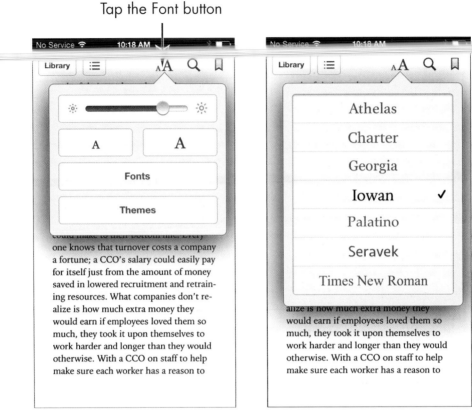

Figure 14-10   Figure 14-11

4. Tap a font name to select it. The font changes on the book page.

5. If you want a sepia tint on the pages, which can be easier on the eye, tap the Font button twice to redisplay the dialog, and then tap Themes. Tap on the Normal, Sepia, or Night setting to activate it.

6. Tap outside the Fonts dialog to return to your book.

 Some fonts appear a bit larger on your screen than others because of their design. If you want the largest font, use Iowan.

Search in Your Book

1. You may want to find a certain sentence or reference in your book. To do so, with the book displayed, tap the Search button shown in **Figure 14-12.** The onscreen keyboard appears.

2. Enter a search term and then tap the Search key on the keyboard. iBooks searches for any matching entries.

3. Use your finger to scroll down the entries (see **Figure 14-13**).

Search button

Scroll through the entries

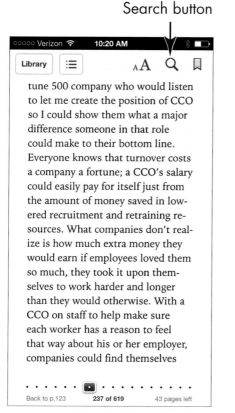

Figure 14-12

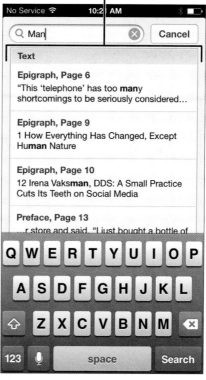

Figure 14-13

4. Tap outside the keyboard to close it and you can use either the Search Web or Search Wikipedia button at the bottom of the Search dialog if you want to search for information about the search term online.

 You can also search for other instances of a particular word while in the book pages by pressing your finger on the word and tapping the right facing arrow and then Search on the toolbar that appears.

Use Bookmarks and Highlights

1. Bookmarks and highlights in your e-books are like favorite sites you save in your web browser: They enable you to revisit a favorite passage or refresh your memory about a character or plot point. To bookmark a page, with that page displayed, just tap the Bookmark button in the top-right corner (see **Figure 14-14**).

2. To highlight a word or phrase, press a word until the toolbar shown in **Figure 14-15** appears.

3. Tap the Highlight button. A colored highlight is placed on the word.

4. To change the color of the highlight, add a note, or remove the highlight, tap the highlighted word. The toolbar shown in **Figure 14-16** appears.

5. Tap one of these four buttons (from left to right):

   • *Colors:* Displays a menu of colors you can tap to change the highlight color as well as an underline option.

   • *Remove Highlight:* Removes the highlight.

- *Note:* Lets you add a note to the item.

- *Share:* Allows you to share the highlighted text with others via AirDrop, Message, Mail, Twitter, or Facebook, or to copy the text.

6. You can also tap the button at the right side of the toolbar to access Copy, Define, and Search tools. Tap outside the highlighted text to close the toolbar.

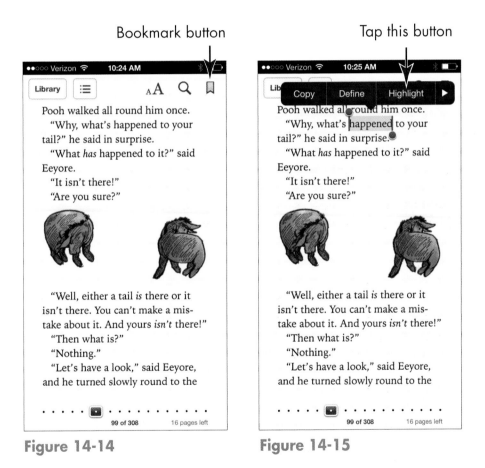

Figure 14-14

Figure 14-15

7. To go to a list of bookmarks and highlights, tap the page and then tap the Table of Contents button that appears (refer to Figure 14-7).

8. In the Table of Contents, tap the Bookmarks tab. As shown in **Figure 14-17,** all bookmarks are displayed. If you wish to see highlighted text and associated notes, you display the Notes tab.

9. Tap a bookmark in the bookmark list to go to that location in the book.

Bookmarks tab

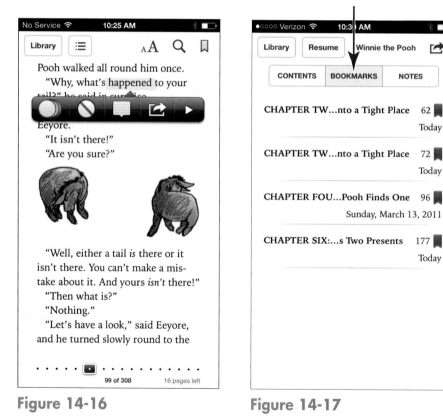

Figure 14-16

Figure 14-17

iPhone automatically bookmarks where you left off reading in a book so you don't have to mark your place manually. If you use any other device registered to your account, you also pick up where you left off reading.

Check Words in the Dictionary

1. As you read a book, you may come across unfamiliar words. Don't skip over them — take the opportunity to learn a new word! With a book open, press your finger on a word and hold it until the toolbar shown in **Figure 14-18** appears.

2. Tap the Define button. A definition dialog appears, as shown in **Figure 14-19**.

Tap this option

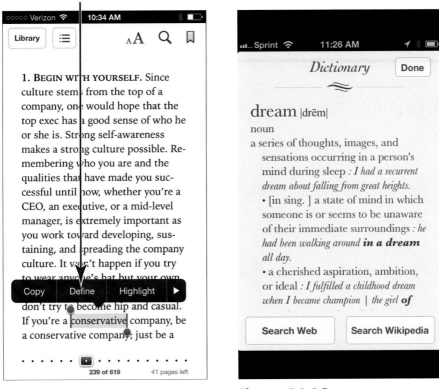

Figure 14-18

Figure 14-19

3. Tap the definition and scroll down to view more.

4. When you finish reviewing the definition, tap Done, and the definition disappears.

 You can also tap the Search Web or Search Wikipedia buttons to look for information about a word from those sources, and tap the Manage button to choose which dictionary your definitions come from.

Organize Books in Collections

1. iBooks lets you create collections of books to help you organize them by your own logic, such as Tear Jerkers, Work-Related, and Great Recipes. You can place a book in only one collection, however. To create a collection from the Library bookshelf, tap Edit.

2. On the screen that appears, tap a book and then tap Move. In the Collections screen shown in **Figure 14-20,** tap New. On the blank line that appears, type a name.

3. Tap Done, which closes the dialog and returns you to the Collection. To add a book to a collection from the Library, tap Edit.

4. Tap a book and then tap the Move button that appears in the top of the screen (see **Figure 14-21**). In the dialog that appears, tap the collection to which you'd like to move the book, and the book now appears on the book-shelf in that collection. To change which collection you're viewing, tap the button with the current collec-tion's name to display other collections, tap the one you want, and then tap Done.

Tap this button   Tap this button

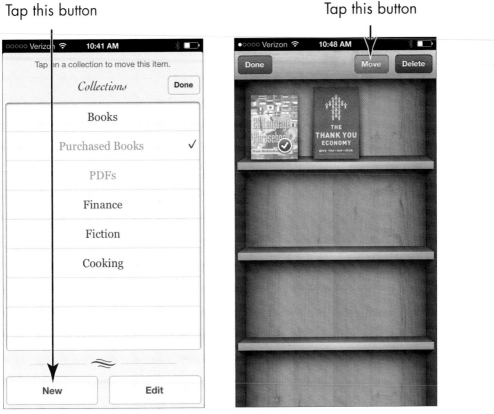

Figure 14-20   **Figure 14-21**

5. To delete a book from a collection with the collection displayed, tap Edit, tap the book, and then tap Delete.

 To delete a collection with the Collections dialog displayed, select the collection you want to delete and then tap Edit. Tap the minus sign to the left of the collection and then tap Delete to get rid of it. A message appears, asking you to tap Remove to remove the contents of the collection from your iPhone or Don't Remove. Note that if you choose Don't Remove, all titles within a deleted collection are returned to their original collections in your library, the default one being Books.

Download Magazine Apps to Newsstand

1. Newsstand is an interface that allows you to access a collection of apps that allow you to subscribe to and read magazines, newspapers, and periodicals other than books. Newsstand comes pre-installed on iPhone and has a brand new look with iOS 7. When you download a free publication, you're actually downloading an app to Newsstand. You can then tap that app to buy individual issues, as covered in the next section. Tap the Newsstand icon on the Home screen to open Newsstand (see **Figure 14-22**).

2. Tap the Store button (refer to **Figure 14-22**). The store opens, displaying Featured periodicals. There are also Top Charts and Near Me tabs along the bottom of the screen that take you to other kinds of apps (see **Figure 14-23**).

3. Tap any of the items displayed, scroll down the screen to view other choices, or tap the Search button on the bottom of the screen and enter a search term to locate a publication you're interested in.

 If you tap other icons at the bottom of the screen, such as Near Me or Top Charts, you're taken to other types of content than periodicals. Also, if you tap the Featured icon again after tapping one of these icons, you're taken to other kinds of apps than periodicals. If you're focused on finding only periodicals, your best bet is to stay on the Store screen that displays when you tap the Store button in Newsstand.

Tap this button

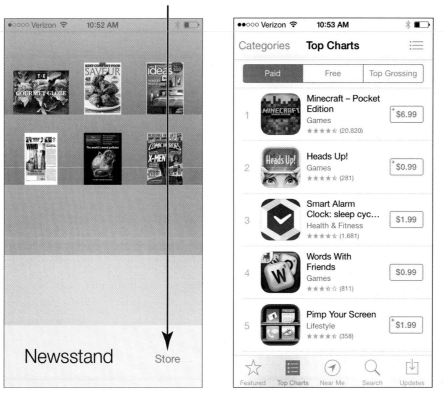

Figure 14-22

Figure 14-23

4. When you find an item, tap it to view a detailed description (see **Figure** 14-24).

5. Tap the Free button and then tap Install. The app downloads to Newsstand.

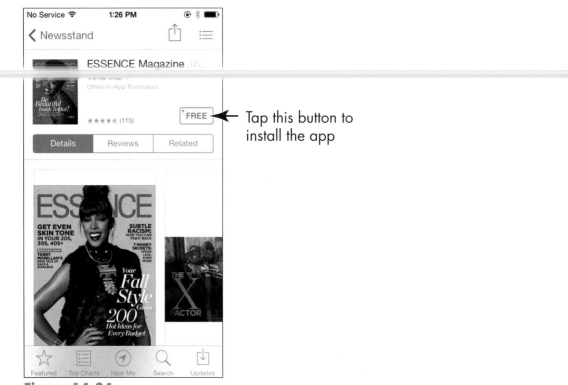

No Service 🛜   1:26 PM   🅒 ⚹ 🔋

< Newsstand   ⬆   ☰

ESSENCE Magazine

Offers In-App Purchases

★★★★☆ (115)   FREE ◄— Tap this button to install the app

Details | Reviews | Related

GET EVEN SKIN TONE IN YOUR 20S, 30S, 40S+

SUBTLE RACISM: HOW YOU CAN FIGHT BACK

7 MONEY SECRETS: SPEND LESS, EARN MORE

Your *Fall Style* Guide *200 Hot Ideas for Every Budget*

☆ Featured | ☷ Top Charts | ◉ Near Me | 🔍 Search | ⬇ Updates

Figure 14-24

Preview and Buy Issues of Periodicals Through Newsstand

1. Tap a periodical app that you've added to Newsstand. The message shown in **Figure 14-25** appears, asking if you'd like to be informed of new issues. Tap OK if you want to be informed.

2. Tap the Preview Issue button to take a look at a description of its content, or tap the Buy button (or, in the case of a free publication, the Download button).

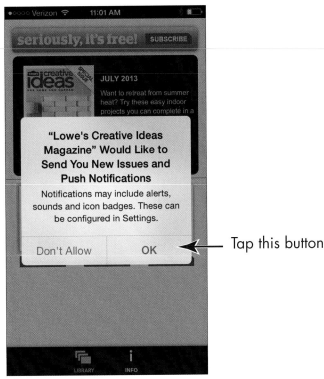

— Tap this button

Figure 14-25

3. In the purchase confirmation dialog that appears, tap Buy. The issue is charged to your iTunes account.

 Note that different stores offer different options for subscribing, buying issues, and organizing issues. Think of Newsstand as a central collection point for apps that allow you to preview and buy content in each publication's store.

Read Periodicals in Your Newsstand Apps

1. If you buy a periodical or you've downloaded a free subscription preview, such as *The New Yorker* shown in **Figure 14-26,** you can tap the publication in Newsstand to view it.

2. In the publication that appears, use your finger to swipe left, right, up, and down to view more of the pages (see Figure 14-27).

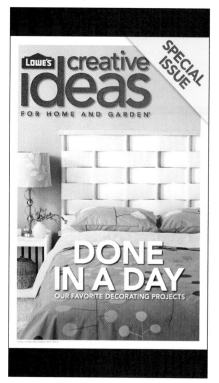

Figure 14-26

Figure 14-27

 Note that different publications offer different options for subscribing, buying issues, navigating, and organizing issues.

Playing with Music on iPhone

*i*Phone includes an iPod-like app called Music that allows you to take advantage of its amazing little sound system to play your favorite music or podcasts and audiobooks.

In this chapter, you get acquainted with the Music app and its features that allow you to sort and find music and control playback. You also get an overview of AirPlay for accessing and playing your music over a home network. Finally, I introduce you to iTunes Radio, coming to iPhone with iOS 7.

View the Library Contents

1. Tap the Music app icon, located in the Dock on the Home screen. The Music library appears (the Artists view is shown **Figure 15-1**).

2. Tap the Playlists, Artists, or Songs buttons at the bottom of the library to view your music according to these criteria (refer to **Figure 15-1**).

3. Tap the More button (see **Figure 15-2**) to view music by album, genre, or composer, or to view any audiobooks you've acquired.

Tap a criteria to use   Tap this button

Figure 15-1   Figure 15-2

 iTunes has several free items you can download and use to play around with the features in Music. You can also sync content, such as iTunes Smart Playlists stored on your computer or other Apple devices to your iPhone, and play it using the Music app. (See Chapter 3 for more about syncing and Chapter 12 for more about getting content from iTunes.)

Apple offers a service called iTunes Match (visit www. apple.com/itunes/ for more information). You pay $24.99 per year for the capability to match the music you've bought from other providers (and stored on your computer) to what's in the iTunes library. If there's a match (and there usually is), that content is added to your iTunes library on iCloud. Then, using iCloud, you can sync the content among all your Apple devices.

Create Playlists

1. You can create your own playlists to put tracks from various sources into collections of your choosing. Tap the Playlists button at the bottom of the iPhone screen.

2. Tap New Playlist. In the dialog that appears, enter a name for the playlist and tap Save.

3. In the list of selections that appears (see **Figure 15-3**), tap the plus sign next to each item you want to include.

4. Tap the Done button, and then tap the Playlists button to return to the Playlists screen.

5. Your playlist appears in the list, and you can now play it by tapping the list name and then tapping a track to play it.

 To search for a song in your music libraries, use the Spotlight Search feature. From your first Home screen, you can swipe down from any app icon outside of the Dock and enter the name of the song. It should appear in a list of search results.

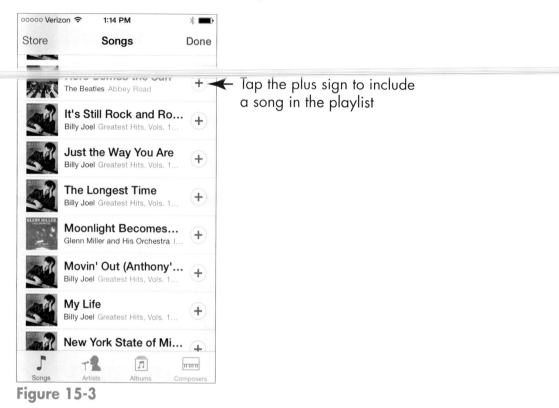

Tap the plus sign to include a song in the playlist

Figure 15-3

Search for Audio

1. You can search for an item in your Music library by using the Search feature. With Music open, tap the Search field (see **Figure 15-4**). The onscreen keyboard appears.

2. Enter a search term in the Search field. Results are displayed, narrowing as you type, as shown in **Figure 15-5**.

3. Tap an item to play it.

 You can enter an artist's name, a lyricist's or a composer's name, or a word from the item's title in the Search field to find what you're looking for.

Tap here to search for audio   Results display here

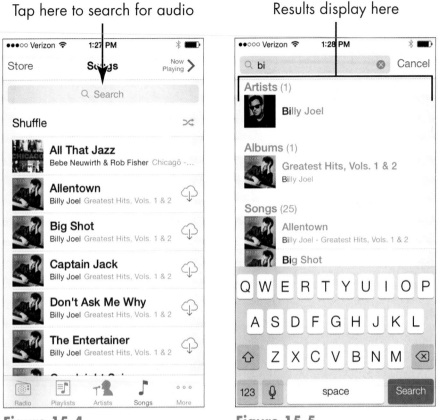

Figure 15-4   **Figure 15-5**

Play Music and Other Audio

1. Locate the song or audiobook you want to play using the methods described in previous tasks in this chapter.

2. Tap the item you want to play. Note that if you're displaying the Songs tab, you don't have to tap an album to open a song; you need only tap a song to play it. If you're using any other tab, you have to tap items such as albums (or multiple songs from one artist) to find the song you want to hear.

3. Tap the item you want to play from the list that appears; it begins to play (see **Figure 15-6**).

4. Use the Previous and Next buttons at the bottom of the screen shown in **Figure 15-7** to navigate the audio file that's playing. The Previous button takes you back to the beginning of the item that's playing; the Next button takes you to the next item. Use the Volume slider on the bottom of the screen (or the Volume buttons on the side of your iPhone) to increase or decrease the volume.

Progress bar

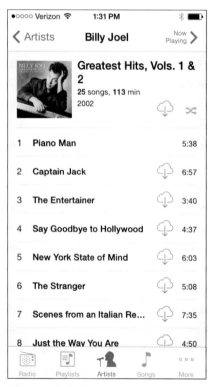

Figure 15-6

Previous Pause Volume Next
slider

Figure 15-7

5. Tap the Pause button to pause playback. Tap the button again to resume playing.

6. Tap and drag the slider that indicates the current playback location on the Progress bar to the left or right to "scrub" to another location in the song. If the slider isn't visible, tap the image of the album cover, and the Progress bar appears.

7. If you don't like what's playing, here's how to make another selection: Tap the Back to Library arrow in the top-left corner to return to the Library view or tap the Album List button in the top-right corner to show other selections in the album that's playing.

 You can use Siri to play music handsfree. Just press and hold the Home button, and when Siri appears, say something like "Play Take the A Train" or "Play The White Album."

 Home Sharing is a feature of iTunes you can use to share music among up to five devices that have Home Sharing turned on. To use the feature, each device has to have the same Apple ID on your network. Once Home Sharing is set up via iTunes, any of your devices can stream music and videos to other devices, and you can even click and drag content between devices using iTunes. For more about Home Sharing, visit this site: `www.apple.com/support/homesharing`.

Shuffle Music

1. If you want to play a random selection of the music in an album on your iPhone, you can use the Shuffle feature. Tap Music on the Home screen, tap the albums tab, and then tap an album.

2. With an album open, tap the Shuffle button which looks like two lines crossing to form an X (see **Figure** 15-8). Your content plays in random order.

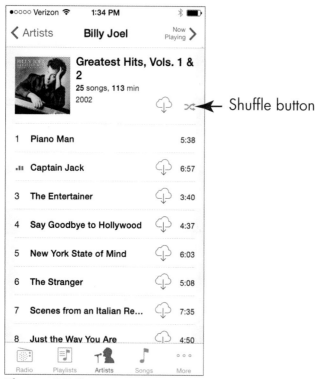

Figure 15-8

 If you're playing music and have set the Volume slider as high as it goes and you're still having trouble hearing, consider getting a headset. It cuts out extraneous noises and may improve the sound quality of what you're listening to, as well as adding stereo to iPhone's mono speaker. Preferably, you should use a 3.5mm stereo headphone; insert it in the headphone jack at the bottom of your iPhone.

Use AirPlay

The AirPlay streaming technology is built into the iPhone, iPod touch, Macs and PCs running iTunes, and iPad. *Streaming* technology allows you to send media files from one device to be played on another. You can send (say) a movie you've purchased on your iPhone or a slideshow of your photos to be played on your Apple TV — and control the TV playback from your iPhone. You can also send music to be played over speakers. You can check out the Apple Remote app which you can use to control your Apple TV.

You can take advantage of AirPlay in a few ways:

➡ Purchase Apple TV and stream video, photos, and music to the TV.

➡ Purchase AirPort Express and attach it to your speakers to play music.

➡ If you buy AirPort Express, you can stream audio directly to your wireless speakers. Because this combination of equipment varies, my advice — if you're interested in using AirPlay — is to visit your nearest Apple Store and find out which hardware combination will work best for you.

➡ Get AirPlay-compatible speakers. With these you don't need AirPort Express at all because you can AirPlay to the speakers directly.

 If you get a bit antsy watching a long movie, one of the beauties of AirPlay is that you can still use your iPhone to check e-mail, browse photos or the Internet, or check your calendar while the media file is playing.

Play Music with iTunes Radio

1. You can access iTunes Radio with any Apple device that has iOS 7. Begin by tapping the Music icon on the Home screen.

2. On the screen that appears, tap the Radio button at the bottom of the screen.

3. Tap on a Featured Station; a featured song begins to play (see **Figure** 15-9).

4. Use the tools at the bottom of the screen (refer to **Figure** 15-9) to control playback.

Figure 15-9

Figure 15-10

5. Tap the star-shaped Favorites button at the bottom of the screen to display the options shown in **Figure 15-10**. Here you can choose to Play More Like This, Never Play This Song, or Add to iTunes Wish List. By using these settings, you help iTunes understand your musical suggestions and can even build custom radio stations.

Add Stations to iTunes Radio

You aren't just limited to playing featured stations. You can add a station to My Stations in a couple of ways. You can play a featured station and tap the Information icon (the circled "i" in the top-middle of the screen), and choose New Station from Artist or New Station from Song. You can also create a New Station of your own.

1. Tap the Music icon in the Dock.

2. Tap Radio.

3. From the iTunes Radio home page, tap the New Station button (see **Figure 15-11**).

4. Tap on a category of music such as Jazz or Latin Hits (see **Figure 15-12**). If sub-categories are then offered, tap on the one you prefer and then tap the Add New button that appears to the right of the category. The category is added to your stations.

Tap this button   Select a category here

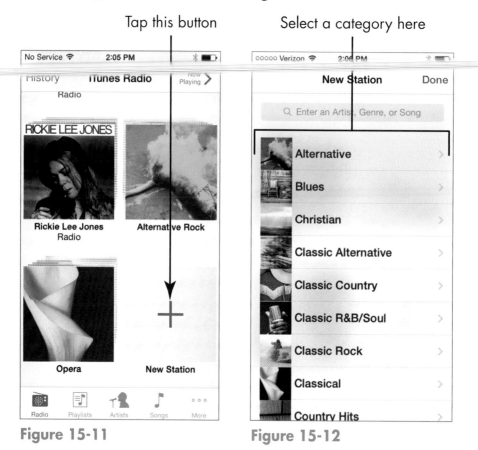

Figure 15-11   Figure 15-12

View Your iTunes Radio History

iTunes Radio offers a great way to see where you've been and where you're going, musically speaking, with its History and Wish List features.

1. Tap the Music icon in the Dock.

2. In the screen that appears (see **Figure 15-13**), tap History in the top-left corner.

3. Tap the Played tab to see the music you've listened to.

4. Tap the Wish List tab (see **Figure 15-14**) to see items you've added to your Wish List (see the earlier task, "Play Music with iTunes Radio," to discover how to add a selection to your Wish List).

 When a song is playing, tap the Information button and then tap Share Station to share a song via AirDrop, Message, Mail, Twitter, or Facebook.

Tap this option   Wish List tab

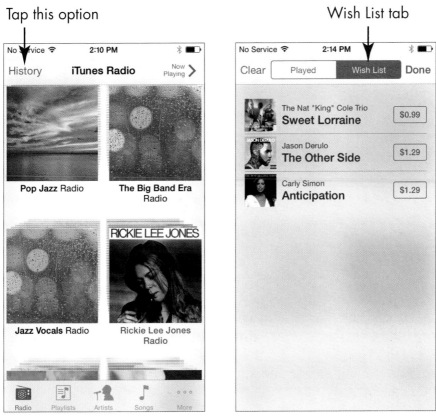

Figure 15-13   **Figure 15-14**

Playing with Photos

Chapter 16

With its gorgeous screen, the iPhone is a natural for taking and viewing photos. It supports most common photo formats, such as JPEG, TIFF, and PNG. You can shoot your photos by using the built-in cameras in iPhone with built-in square or panorama modes. If you have an iPhone 5 or later, you can edit your images using filters that are new with the Camera app that comes with iOS 7. You can also sync photos from your computer, save images you find online to your iPhone, or receive them by e-mail, MMS, or iMessage.

The Photo Streams feature lets you share groups of photos with people using iCloud on an iOS 7 device or on a Mac or Windows computer with iCloud access.

When you have photos to play with, the Photos app lets you organize photos from the Camera Roll or view photos in albums one by one or in a slideshow. A new feature lets you view photos by years they were taken, with images divided into collections by the location or time you took the them. You can also AirDrop (iPhone 5 and later), e-mail, message, or tweet a photo to a friend, print it, or post it to Facebook. You can read about all these features in this chapter.

Get ready to . . .

Take Pictures with the iPhone Cameras

1. The cameras in the iPhone 4, 4S, 5, 5S, and 5C are just begging to be used, so no matter which phone model you have, let's get started! Tap the Camera app icon on the Home screen to open the app.

2. If the camera type options at the bottom of the screen (see **Figure 16-1**) is set at Video, slide it to the left to choose Photo (the still camera) rather than Video.

> iPhone's front- and rear-facing cameras allow you to capture photos and video (see Chapter 17 for more about the video features) and share them with family and friends. The rear-facing cameras on the iPhone 4S, 5, 5S, and 5C sport 8mp and 1080p cameras; the iPhone 4's rear-facing camera provides a 5mp and 720p camera.

3. You can set the Pano (for panorama) and Square options using the slider control above the Capture button on the iPhone 5S and 5C. These controls let you create square images like those you see on the popular Instagram site. With Pano selected, tap to begin to take a picture, pan across a view, and then tap Done to capture a panoramic display.

4. Tap the Flash button in the top-left corner of the screen when using the rear camera and tap On if your lighting is dim enough to require a flash, Off if you don't want iPhone to use a flash, or Auto if you want to let iPhone decide for you.

5. Move the camera around until you find a pleasing image. You can do a couple of things at this point to help you take your photo:

- Tap the area of the grid where you want the camera to autofocus.

- Pinch the screen to display a digital zoom control; drag the circle in the zoom bar to the right or left to zoom in or out on the image.

6. Tap the Capture button at the bottom center of the screen and release. You've just taken a picture, and it's stored in the Photos app gallery automatically.

 You can also use the Volume button with the plus sign on it (located on the left side of your iPhone) to capture a picture or start or stop video camera recording.

7. Tap the Switch Camera button in the top-right corner to switch between the front camera and rear camera. You can then take pictures of yourself, so go ahead and tap the Capture button to take another picture.

8. To view the last photo taken, swipe to the left or tap the thumbnail of the latest image in the bottom-left corner of the screen; the Photos app opens and displays the photo.

9. Tap the Menu button (it's the box with an arrow coming out of it, located in the bottom-left corner of the screen) to display a menu that allows you to AirDrop, e-mail, or instant message the photo, assign it to a contact, use it as iPhone wallpaper, tweet it, post it to Facebook, share via Photo Stream, or print it (see **Figure 16-2**).

10. To delete the image, with it displayed, tap the Trash Can button in the bottom-right corner of the screen.

11. Tap Delete Photo in the confirming menu that appears.

 To go to the camera with the Lock screen displayed, swipe the camera icon up to go directly to the Camera app.

Flash HDR Switch Camera

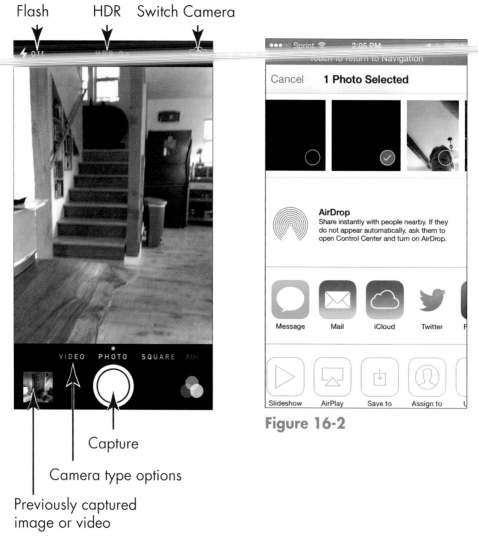

Figure 16-2

Capture

Camera type options

Previously captured
image or video

Figure 16-1

 You can use the Photo Stream feature to automatically upload photos to iCloud. The photos are then downloaded to other iOS devices that are set up to download photos. Turn on Photo Stream in iPhone Settings for Photos & Camera.

Save Photos from the Web

1. The web offers a wealth of images you can download to your Photo Library. Open Safari and navigate to the web page containing the image you want.

2. Press and hold the image; a menu appears, as shown in **Figure 16-3**.

3. Tap Save Image. The image is saved to your Camera Roll folder in the Photos app, as shown in **Figure 16-4**.

Tap this option

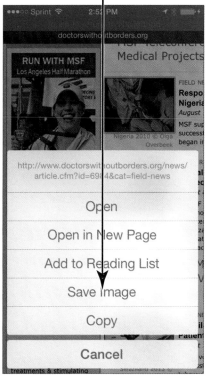

Figure 16-3   Figure 16-4

For more about how to use Safari to navigate to or search for web content, see Chapter 10.

A number of sites protect their photos from being copied by applying an invisible overlay. This blank overlay image ensures that you don't actually get the image you think you're tapping. Even if a site doesn't take these precautions, be sure that you don't save images from the web and use them in ways that violate the rights of the person or entity that owns them.

If you want to capture your iPhone screen the process is simple. Press the power button and Home button simultaneously. The screen capture is saved in PNG format to your Camera Roll. To save a picture sent as an e-mail attachment in Mail, tap on the attachment icon and the picture opens. Press on the screen until a menu appears and then tap Save.

View an Album

1. The Photos app organizes your pictures into albums, using such criteria as the folder or album on your computer from which you synced the photos or photos captured using the iPhone camera (the Camera Roll). You may also have albums for images you synced from other devices through iTunes or your iCloud Photo Stream. To view your albums, start by tapping the Photos app icon on the Home screen.

2. If the Places tab is selected when the Photos app opens, tap the Albums tab to display your albums, as shown in **Figure 16-5**.

3. Tap an album. The photos in it are displayed.

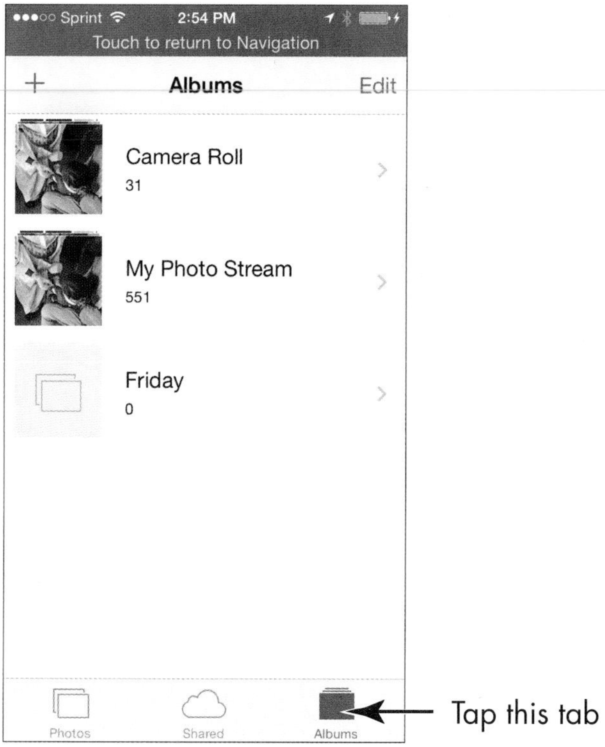

Tap this tab

Figure 16-5

View Individual Photos

1. Tap the Photos app icon on the Home screen.

2. Tap Albums (refer to **Figure 16-5**).

3. Tap an album to open it, and then, to view a photo, tap it. The picture expands, as shown in **Figure 16-6**.

Figure 16-6

4. Flick your finger to the left or right to scroll through the album to look at the individual photos in it.

5. You can tap the Albums button (which may display the name of the currently opened album) to return to the Album view.

You can place a photo on a person's information page in Contacts. For more about how to do so, see Chapter 5.

You can associate photos with faces and events; when you do, additional tabs appear at the bottom of the screen when you display an album containing such photos.

Edit Photos

1. A feature that arrived with iOS 5 is the ability to edit photos. Tap the Photos app on the Home screen to open it.

2. Using methods previously described in this chapter, locate a photo you want to edit.

3. Tap the Edit button; the Edit Photo screen shown in **Figure** 16-7 appears.

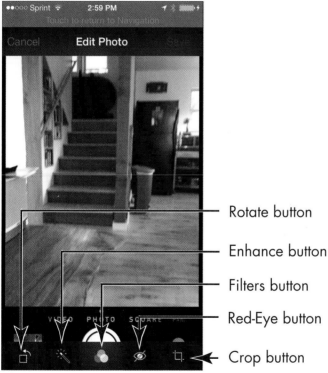

Rotate button

Enhance button

Filters button

Red-Eye button

← Crop button

Figure 16-7

4. At this point, you can take four possible actions with these tools:

- *Rotate:* Tap the Rotate button to rotate the image 90 degrees at a time. Continue to tap the button to move another 90 degrees.

- *Enhance:* Tap Enhance to turn Auto-Enhance on or off. This feature optimizes the crispness of the image.

- *Filters:* Apply any of nine filters such as Fade, Mono, or Noir to change the feel of your image. These effects adjust the brightness of your image or apply a black and white tone to your color photos. Tap the Filters button in the middle of the tools at the bottom of the screen and scroll to view available filters. Tap one and then tap Apply to apply the effect to your image.

- *Red-Eye:* Tap Red-Eye if a person in a photo has that dreaded red-eye effect. When you activate this feature, simply tap each eye that needs clearing up.

- *Crop:* To crop the photo to a portion of its original area, tap the Crop button. You can then tap any corner of the image and drag inward or outward to remove areas of the photo. Tap Crop and then Save to apply your changes.

5. If you're pleased with your edits, tap the Save button, and a copy of the edited photo is saved.

 Each of the four editing features has a Cancel button. If you don't like the changes you made, tap this button to stop making changes before you save the image.

Organize Photos in Camera Roll

1. If you want to create your own album, display the Camera Roll album.

2. Tap the Select button in the top-right corner, and then tap individual photos to select them. Small check marks appear on the selected photos (see **Figure** 16-8).

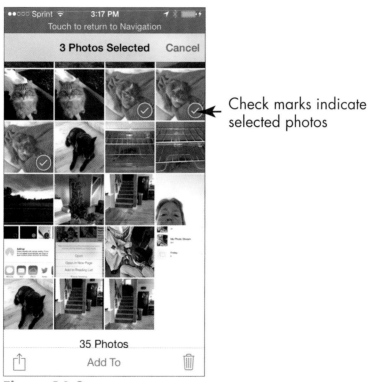

Check marks indicate selected photos

Figure 16-8

3. Tap the Add To button and then tap New Album. (*Note:* If you've already created albums, you can choose to add the photo to an existing album at this point.)

4. Enter a name for a new album and then tap Save. If you created a new album, it now appears in the Photos main screen with the other Albums that are displayed.

 You can also choose the Share or Delete buttons when you've selected photos in Step 2 of this task. This allows you to share or delete multiple photos at a time.

View Photos by Years and Location

 1. New with Photos and iOS 7 comes the ability to view your photos in logical categories such as Years and Moments. These so-called smart groupings let you, for example, view all photos taken this year or all the photos from your summer vacation. Tap Photos on the Home screen to open it.

2. Tap Photos at the bottom of the screen. The display of photos by year appears (see **Figure 16-9**).

3. Tap the yearly photos and you see collections of photos by location and date (see **Figure 16-10**).

4. Tap a collection and you can view the individual "moments" in that collection broken down day by day.

 To go back to larger groupings, such as from a moment in a collection to the larger collection to the entire last year, just keep tapping the back button at the top left of the screen (which will be named after the next collection up in the grouping hierarchy such as Collections or Years).

Figure 16-9   **Figure 16-10**

Share Photos with Mail, Twitter, or Facebook

1. You can easily share photos stored on your iPhone by sending them as e-mail attachments, via iMessage or MMS (text message), by posting them to Facebook, or as tweets via Twitter. You have to go to Facebook or Twitter using a browser and set up an account before you can use this feature. First, tap the Photos app icon on the Home screen.

2. Tap the Photos or Album tab and locate the photo you want to share.

3. Tap the photo to select it and then tap the Menu button. (It looks like a box with an arrow jumping out of it.) The menu shown in **Figure 16-11** appears.

Figure 16-11

4. Tap the Mail, Message, Twitter, or Facebook option.

5. In the message form that appears, make any modifications you want in the To, Cc/Bcc, or Subject fields and then type a message for e-mail or enter your Facebook posting or tweet text.

6. Tap the Send button, and the message and photo go on their way.

 You can also copy and paste a photo into documents such as those created in the Pages word-processor application. To do this, press and hold a photo in Photos until the Copy command appears. Tap Copy and then, in the destination application, press and hold the screen and tap Paste.

Share a Photo Using AirDrop

 AirDrop, available to users of iPhone 5 and later, provides a way to share content such as photos with others who are nearby and have an AirDrop-enabled device. Follow the steps in the previous task to locate a photo you want to share; once you've located the photo you want to share, follow these steps:

1. Tap the Menu button.

2. If an AirDrop-enabled device is in your immediate vicinity (like within 30 feet or so), you see the device listed at the top of the Share window (see **Figure 16-12**). Tap the device name and your photo is sent to the other device.

 Note that the other device has to have AirDrop enabled. To do that you open the Control Center (swipe up from the bottom of any screen) and tap AirDrop. Choose Contacts or Everyone to specify who you can use AirDrop with.

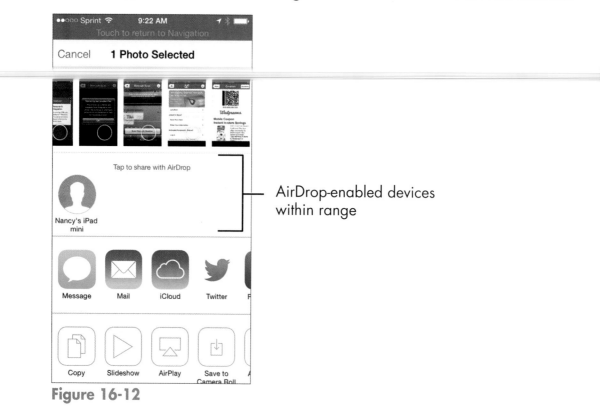

AirDrop-enabled devices within range

Figure 16-12

Share Photos Using Photo Stream

1. Photo Stream allows you to automatically send copies of any new photos to any iCloud devices, and to share photo streams with others. You can also subscribe to another person's photo stream if they share it with you. First, set up Photo Stream. Tap Settings, Photos & Camera, and then tap the On button for My Photo Stream to share among your devices and Photo Sharing to share with others.

2. To share a Photo Stream with somebody else, return to the Home screen and tap Photos. Locate a photo you want to share, tap the iCloud tab, and then tap New Shared Stream.

3. In the form that appears (see **Figure 16-13**), enter a Stream name and tap Next.

4. In the next form, enter the e-mail address of somebody you want to share the stream with. A list of matches from your contacts appears; tap the one you want. If you want to add more people to share with, tap the Add button (shaped like a plus sign) and choose another contact, and so on.

Figure 16-13

5. Tap Create and the stream is created. Your contact receives an e-mail message with a link to join your photo stream.

Print Photos

1. If you have a wireless printer that's compatible with Apple's AirPrint technology, you can print photos. With Photos open, locate the photo you want to print and tap it to maximize it.

2. Tap the Menu button and on the menu that appears (refer to **Figure 16-11**), scroll in the bottom row of buttons to the far right and then tap Print.

3. In the Printer Options dialog that appears (see **Figure 16-14**), tap Select Printer. iPhone presents you with a list of any compatible wireless printers on your local network.

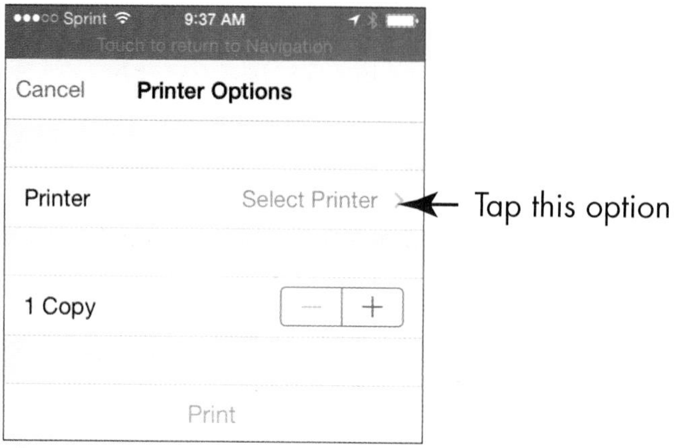

Figure 16-14

4. Tap the plus or minus symbols in the Copy field to set the number of copies to print.

5. Tap the Print button, and your photo is sent to the printer.

Run a Slideshow

1. You can run a slideshow of your images in Photos and even play music and choose transition effects for the show. Tap the Photos app on the Home screen.

2. Display an individual photo in an album that contains more than one photo.

3. Tap the Menu button and then tap Slideshow to see the Slideshow Options menu, shown in **Figure 16-15.**

4. If you want to play music along with the slideshow, tap the On/Off button on the Play Music field.

5. To choose music to play along with the slideshow, tap Music and, in the list that appears (see **Figure 16-16**), tap any selection from your Music library.

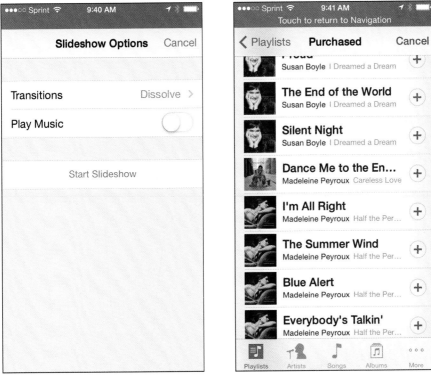

Figure 16-15   **Figure 16-16**

6. In the Slideshow Options dialog, tap Transitions and then tap the transition effect you want to use for your slideshow.

7. Tap the Start Slideshow button. The slideshow begins. Tap the screen to stop the slideshow at any time.

 To run a slideshow that includes only the photos contained in a particular album, tap the Albums tab, tap an album to open it, and then tap the Slideshow button to make settings and run a slideshow.

Delete Photos

1. You might find that it's time to get rid of some of those old photos of the family reunion or the last community center project. If the photos weren't transferred from your computer, but instead were taken, downloaded, or captured as screenshots on the iPhone, you can delete them. Tap the Photos app icon on the Home screen.

2. Tap the Albums or Photos tab and then if you've opened the Albums tab, tap an album to open it.

3. Locate a photo you want to delete, and then tap the Trash Can icon. In the confirming dialog that appears, tap the Delete Photo button to finish the deletion.

 If you delete a photo on Photo Stream, it is deleted on all devices you shared it with.

Getting the Most Out of Video Features

*U*sing the Videos app, you can watch down-loaded movies or TV shows, as well as media you've synced from iCloud or your Mac or PC.

In addition, iPhone 5 sports both a front and rear video camera you can use to capture your own videos, and by downloading the iMovie app for iPhone (a more limited version of the longtime mainstay on Mac computers), you add the capability to edit those videos. The four-inch Retina display on iPhone 5 and later, which offers even more pixels than iPhone 4S, and an 8MP iSight camera that can record high-definition video make iPhone 5/5S/5C one of the best phones ever for viewing and capturing images, both still and moving.

In this chapter, I explain all about shooting and watching video content from a variety of sources. For practice, you might want to refer to Chapter 12 first to find out how to purchase or download one of many available TV shows or movies from the Videos Store and Chapter 13 for help with downloading the iMovie app.

Capture Your Own Videos with the Built-In Cameras

The camera lens that comes on iPhone 5S has perks for photographers, including a larger aperture and improved sensor, which makes for better images all around. In addition, auto image stabilization makes up for any shakiness in the hands holding the phone, and autofocus has speeded up due to the faster A7 processor chip. For videographers, you'll appreciate a faster frames per second capability as well as a new slow motion feature.

1. To capture a video, tap the Camera app on the Home screen. In iPhone, two video cameras are available for capturing video, from either the front or back of the device, making it possible for you to take videos using one of these perspectives that you can then share with others or edit with third-party apps. (See more about this topic in the next task.)

2. The Camera app opens (see **Figure 17-1**). Tap and slide the camera type options above the red Record button to the right until Video rests above the button to switch from the still camera to the video camera.

3. If you want to switch between the front and back cameras, tap the Switch Camera button in the top-right corner of the screen (refer to **Figure 17-1**).

4. To turn on the slow motion feature, select the Slo-Mo camera type.

5. Tap the red Record button to begin recording the video. (The red dot in the middle of this button turns into a red square when the camera is recording.) When you're finished, tap the Record button again. Your new video is now listed in the bottom-left corner of the screen. Tap the video to play it, share it, or delete it. In future you can find and play the video in your Camera Roll when you open the Photos app.

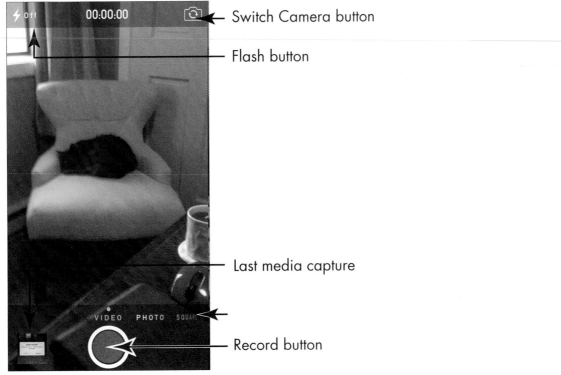

Switch Camera button

Flash button

Last media capture

Record button

Figure 17-1

 Before you start recording, remember where the camera lens is — while holding the iPhone and panning, you can easily put your fingers directly over the lens!

Play Movies or TV Shows with Videos

1. When you first open the Videos app, you may see relatively blank screens with a note that you don't own any videos and a link to the iTunes Store. After you've purchased TV shows and movies or rented movies from the iTunes Store (see Chapter 12 to learn how) or other sources, you'll see tabs of the different kinds of content you own. Tap the Videos app icon on the Home screen to open the application.

2. On a screen like the one shown in **Figure** 17-2, tap the appropriate category at the bottom of the screen (TV, Podcasts, or Movies depending on the content you've downloaded) and then tap the video you want to watch. Information about the movie or TV show episodes appears, as shown in **Figure** 17-3. TV Shows include an Episodes, Details, and Related tab; Movies contain a Details, Chapters, and Related tab.

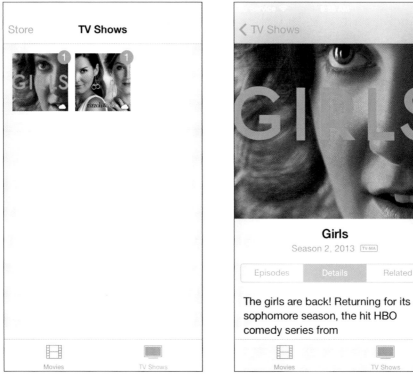

Figure 17-2   Figure 17-3

3. For TV Shows, tap the Episodes tab to display episodes which you can tap to play (see **Figure 17-4**); for Movies, the Play button appears no matter which tab is selected. Tap the Play button and the movie, TV show, or podcast begins playing (if you see a small cloud-shaped icon instead of a Play button, tap it and the content is downloaded from iCloud). Note that the progress of the playback is displayed on the Progress bar showing how many minutes you've viewed and how many remain. If you don't see the bar, tap the screen once to display it briefly, along with a set of playback tools at the bottom of the screen.

Figure 17-4

4. With the playback tools displayed, take any of these actions:

- Tap the Pause button to pause playback.

- Tap either Go to Previous Chapter or Go to Next Chapter to move to a different location in the video playback. Note that if a video has chapter support, there will be another button here for displaying all chapters so that you can move more easily from one to another.

- Tap the circular button on the Volume slider and drag the button left or right to decrease or increase the volume, respectively.

5. To stop the video and return to the information screen, tap the Done button to the left of the Progress bar.

 Note that if you've watched a video and stopped it partway, it opens by default to the last spot you were viewing. To start a video from the beginning, tap and drag the circular button (called the *playhead*) on the Progress bar all the way to the left.

 If your controls disappear during playback, just tap the screen, and they'll reappear.

 If you download the free iTunes U app, you can access educational video content that you can play back using the Videos app.

Turn On Closed-Captioning

1. iTunes and iPhone offer support for closed-captioning and subtitles. If a movie has either closed-captioning or subtitles, you can turn on the feature in iPhone. Look for the CC logo on media you download to use this feature; be aware that video you record won't have this capability. Begin by tapping the Settings icon on the Home screen.

2. Tap General↷Accessibility. On the screen that appears, scroll down and tap Subtitles & Captioning.

3. On the menu that displays (see **Figure 17-5**), tap the Closed Captioning + SDH On/Off button to turn on the feature. Now when you play a movie with closed-captioning, you can tap the Audio and Subtitles button to the left of the playback controls to manage these features.

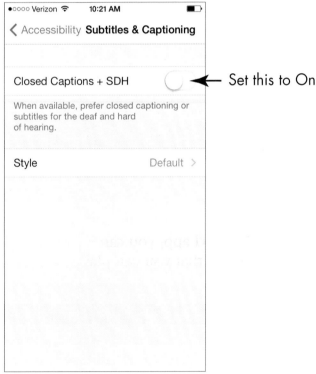

Figure 17-5

Delete a Video from the iPhone

You can buy videos directly from your iPhone, or you can sync via iCloud or iTunes to place content you've bought or created on another device on your iPhone.

When you want to get rid of video content on your iPhone because it's a memory hog, you can delete it using iTunes and then sync again, removing it from your iPhone. If you buy a video using iTunes and sync to download it to your iPhone and then delete it from your iPhone, it's still saved in your iTunes library. You can sync your computer and iPhone again to download the video once more. Remember, however, that rented movies, once deleted, are gone with the wind and that video doesn't sync to iCloud as photos and music do.

 iPhone has much smaller storage capacity than your typical computer, so downloading lots of TV shows or movies can fill its storage area quickly. If you don't want to view an item again, delete it to free up space.

Let Others Know about Your Favorite Videos

1. You can share your opinion about a video using AirDrop, Mail, Message, Twitter, or Facebook. Tap the Videos app to open it and then tap the Store button. Find a video you want to share and tap it.

2. In the information screen shown in **Figure 17-6,** tap the Share button (a box with an arrow at the top of it at the top of the screen). Tap AirDrop, Mail, Message, Twitter, or Facebook to use one of these methods of sharing your enthusiasm for the item (see **Figure 17-7**).

3. In the corresponding form, enter a recipient in the To field and add to the message, if you like. If you chose to post to your Facebook page, enter your message in the Facebook form.

Share button

Figure 17-6   **Figure 17-7**

4. Tap the appropriate Send button to send your recommendation by your preferred method.

 When you're viewing information about a video in the iTunes Store, you can tap the Related tab to find information about other movies or TV shows watched by those who watched this one.

Playing Games

Chapter 18

*T*he iPhone is super for playing games, with its bright screen, portable size, and ability to rotate the screen as you play and track your motions. You can download game apps from the App Store and play them on your device. You can also use the preinstalled Game Center app to help you find and buy games, add friends to play against, share, and track scores.

In this chapter, you get an overview of game playing on your iPhone, including opening a Game Center account, adding a friend, purchasing and downloading games, and playing basic games solo or against friends.

 Of course, you can also download games from the App Store and play them on your iPhone without having to use Game Center. What Game Center provides is a place where you can create a gaming profile, add a list of gaming friends, keep track of and share your scores and perks, and shop for games (and only games) in the App Store, which includes listings of top-rated games and game categories to choose from.

Get ready to . . .

Open an Account in Game Center

1. Using the Game Center app, you can search for and buy games, add friends with whom you can play those games, and keep records of your scores for posterity. From the Home screen, tap the Game Center icon. If you've never used Game Center, you're asked whether to allow *push notifications.* If you want to receive these notices alerting you that your friends want to play a game with you, tap OK. You should, however, be aware that push notifications can drain your iPhone's battery.

2. On the Game Center opening screen you're asked to sign in (see **Figure 18-1**). If you want to use Game Center with another Apple ID, tap Create New Apple ID and follow the onscreen instructions which ask you to enter your birthdate, agree to terms, choose a security question and so forth; or enter your current account information and tap the Go button.

3. The screen that appears once you've signed in shows games you've downloaded, requests from other players, friends, and so on (see **Figure 18-2**). You can tap any of the floating balloons to get to these categories, or tap a button along the bottom of the screen.

 When you first register for Game Center, if you use an e-mail address other than the one associated with your Apple ID, you may have to create a new Apple ID and verify it using an e-mail message that's sent to your e-mail address. See Chapter 3 for more about creating an Apple ID when opening an iTunes account.

Figure 18-1

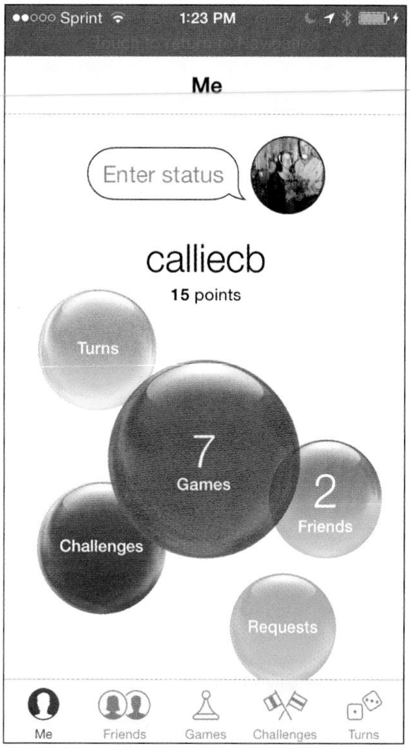

Figure 18-2

Create a Profile

1. When you have an account with which you can sign into Game Center, you're ready to specify some account settings. On the Home screen, tap Settings.

2. Tap Game Center, and in the dialog that appears (see **Figure 18-3**), if you don't want other players to be able to invite you to play games when Game Center is open, tap the Allow Invites On/Off button to turn off the feature.

3. Tap the account name under Game Center Profile.

4. If you want your friends to be able to send you requests for playing games via e-mail, check to see if the Primary e-mail address listed in this dialog is the one you want them to use (see **Figure 18-4**). If not, tap Add Another Email and enter another e-mail address.

5. In the Nickname field, enter the handle you want to be known by when playing games.

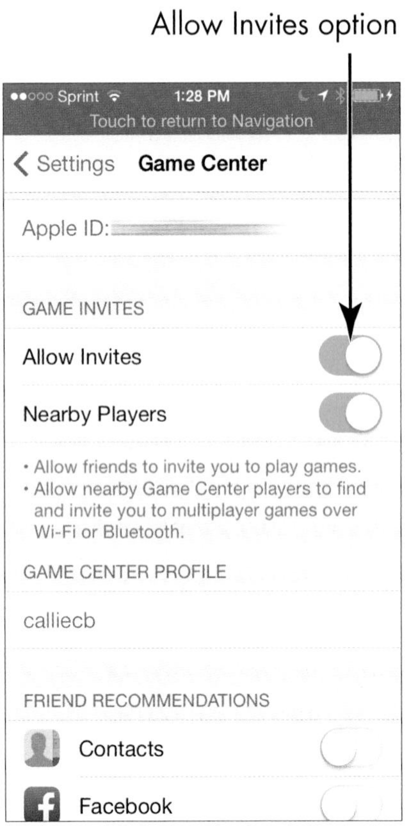

Allow Invites option   Primary e-mail address

Figure 18-3

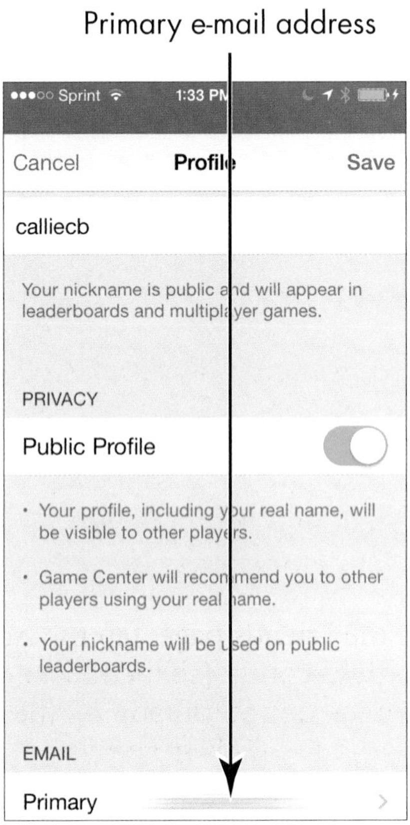

Figure 18-4

6. Tap to Allow Invites or to allow Nearby Players to find you and invite you to games.

7. If you want others to see your profile including your real name, tap the Public Profile On/Off button to turn on public profile (refer to **Figure 18-4**).

8. Tap Done when you're finished with the settings and then tap Game Center on the Home screen. You return to the Game Center home screen, already signed in to your account with information displayed about friends, games, and gaming achievements (all at zero initially).

 After you create an account and a profile, whenever you go to the Game Center, you log in by entering your e-mail address and password and then tapping Sign In.

Add Friends

1. If you want to play Game Center games with others who have an Apple ID and an iPad, iPod touch, Mac running Mountaint Lion or Mavericks, or iPhone, add them as friends so that you can invite them to play. From the Game Center home screen, tap the Friends button at the bottom of the screen.

2. On the Friends page, tap the Add Friends button in the top right corner (shaped like a plus sign). (Note that you have the option of tapping the Requests button and tapping Add Friends from there.)

3. Enter an e-mail address in the To field (see **Figure 18-5**) and edit the invitation, if you like.

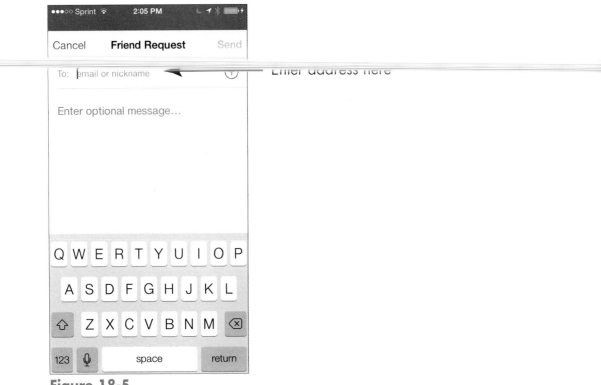

Figure 18-5

4. Tap the Send button. After your friend accepts your invitation, his or her name is listed on the Friends screen.

With iOS 5, Game Center gained a Friend Recommendations feature. Tap the Friends tab, and then tap the A-Z button in the top-left corner. A Recommendations section appears above the list of your current friends. These are people who play the same or similar games, so if you like, try adding one or two as friends. You can tap the Points tab to view the points these folks have accumulated so you can stay in your league.

You will probably also receive requests from friends who know you're on Game Center. When you get one of these e-mail invitations, be sure that you know the person sending it before you accept; otherwise, you could be enabling a stranger to communicate with you.

While a few games have versions for both Mac and iOS users, the majority are either Mac version only or iOS version only, something to be aware of when you buy games.

Purchase and Download Games

1. Time to get some games to play! Open Game Center and sign in to your account.

2. Tap the Games button at the bottom of the screen and under the Recommended category tap Show More.

3. Scroll through the list of games that appears and tap on one that appeals to you, and then tap on the Details tab to display details about it (see **Figure 18-6**). Note that you can tap the Store button from here to go to the iTunes Store to view more games.

4. To buy a game, tap the button labeled with either the word *free* or the price (such as $1.99). Then tap the button again, which is now labeled Buy if it has a price or Install if it's free.

5. A dialog appears, asking for your Apple ID and password. Enter these and tap OK.

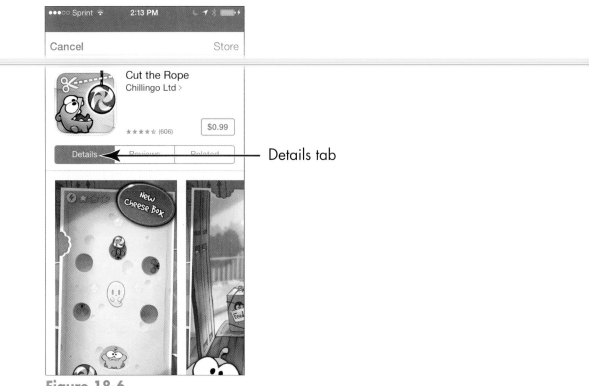

Details tab

Figure 18-6

6. Another verification dialog appears, asking you to sign in. Follow the instructions on the next couple of screens to enter your password and verify your payment information if this is the first time you've signed in to your account from this device.

7. When the verification dialog appears, tap Buy. The game downloads.

 If you've added friends to your account, you can go to the Friends page and view games that your friends have downloaded. To purchase one of these games, just tap it in your friend's list and, at the top of the screen that appears, tap the button labeled with the game's price.

Master iPhone Game-Playing Basics

It's almost time to start playing games, but first let me give you an idea of iPhone's gaming strengths. For many reasons, iPhone is a good, smaller-screen gaming device because of the following strengths:

⟶ **Fantastic-looking screen:** First, the iPhone screen offers bright colors for great gaming. In-Plane Switching (IPS) technology lets you hold your iPhone at almost any angle (it has a 178-degree viewing angle) and still see good color and contrast.

⟶ **Faster processor:** The super-fast A7 processor chip in your iPhone 5S is ideal for gaming. The A6 processor on iPhone 5 and 5C also handles games quite nicely.

⟶ **Long battery life:** A device's long battery life means that you can tap energy from it for many hours of gaming fun.

⟶ **Specialized game-playing features:** Some newer games have features that take full advantage of the iPhone's capabilities. For example, *Nova* (from Gameloft) features Multiple Target Acquisition, which lets you to target multiple bad guys in a single move to blow them out of the water with one shot. In *Real Racing Game* (Firemint), for example, you can look in your rearview mirror as you're racing to see what's coming up behind you, a feature made possible by the iPhone's large screen.

⟶ **The M7 sensor:** In iPhone 5S there's a motion-detecting sensor that can interpret data about your motion when walking or driving. Look for game and fitness app designers to begin to take advantage of that capability in the near future.

➠ **Great sound:** The built-in iPhone speaker is a powerful little item, but if you want an experience that's even more up close and personal, you can plug in a headphone, some speaker systems, or a microphone using the built-in jack.

 In addition to M7 motion sensor in iPhone 5S, most later iPhone models have a built-in motion sensor — the *three-axis accelerometer* — as well as a gyroscope. These features provide lots of fun for people developing apps for the iPhone, as they use the automatically rotating screen to become part of the gaming experience. For example, a built-in compass reorients itself automatically as you switch your iPhone from landscape to portrait orientation. In some racing games, you can grab the iPhone as though it were a steering wheel and rotate the device to simulate the driving experience.

Play Against Yourself

Many games allow you to play a game all on your own. Each has different rules and goals, so you'll have to study a game's instructions and help to learn how to play it, but here's some general information about these types of games:

➠ Often a game can be played in two modes: with others or in a *solitaire version* where you play yourself or the computer.

➠ Many games you may be familiar with in the offline world, such as Carcassonne or Scrabble, have online versions. For these, you already know the rules of play, so you simply need to figure out the execution. For example, in the online Carcassonne solitaire game, you tap to place a tile on the board, tap the placed tile to rotate it, and tap the check mark to complete your turn and reveal another tile.

➡ All the games you play on your own record your scores in Game Center so you can track your progress.

Challenge Friends in Game Center

1. After you have added a friend and both of you have downloaded the same games, you can challenge your friends to beat your scores. Tap the Game Center app icon on the Home screen and sign in, if necessary.

2. Tap Friends. The Friends page (see **Figure 18-7**) appears.

3. Tap the name of the friend you want to challenge.

4. Tap the Game bubble and then tap the name of a game you have in common.

5. Tap the Achievements tab for your friend, and then tap on one of her achievements. On the screen that appears (see **Figure 18-8**), tap Send Challenge.

6. At this point, some games offer you an invitation to fill out with a message and send to the friend — if so, wait for your friend to respond, which he can do by tapping Accept or Decline on his device.

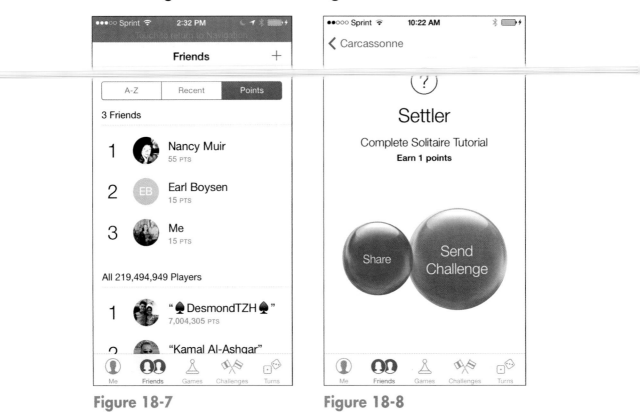

Figure 18-7

Figure 18-8

Finding Your Way with Maps

The Maps app was reimagined with iOS 6, and you'll find in its latest incarnation in iOS 7 it has lots of useful functions. You can find directions with suggested alternate routes from one location to another. You can bookmark locations to return to them again. And the Maps app makes it possible to get information about locations, such as the phone numbers and web links to businesses. You can even add a location to your Contacts list or share a location link with your buddy using Mail, Messages, Twitter, or Facebook.

You're about to have lots of fun exploring Maps in this chapter.

Go to Your Current Location

1. iPhone can figure out where you are at any time and display your current location. From the Home screen, tap the Maps icon. Tap the Current Location button (the small arrow in the bottom-left corner; see **Figure 19-1**).

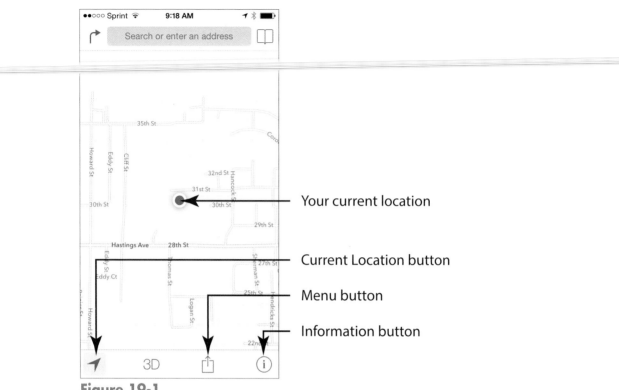

Figure 19-1

2. A map is displayed with a blue pin indicating your current location (refer to **Figure 19-1**). Depending on your connection, Wi-Fi or 3G/4G (sometimes noted as LTE in Maps), a circle may appear around the pin indicating the area surrounding your location based on cell tower triangulation — your exact location can be anywhere within the area of the circle, and it's likely to be less accurate using a Wi-Fi connection than with your phone's 3G/4G connection.

3. Double-tap the screen to zoom in on your location. (Additional methods of zooming in and out are covered in the "Zoom In and Out" task, later in this chapter.)

As mentioned above, if you access Maps via a Wi-Fi connection, your current location is a rough estimate based on a triangulation method. By using your 3G/4G data connection, you access the global positioning system (GPS), which can more accurately pinpoint where you are. Still, if you type a starting location and an ending location to get directions, you can get pretty accurate results even with a Wi-Fi–connected iPhone.

Change Views

1. The Maps app offers three views: Standard, Satellite, and Hybrid. iPhone displays the Standard view (see the top-left image in **Figure 19-2**) by default the first time you open Maps. To change views, with Maps open, tap the Information button in the bottom-right of the screen (refer to **Figure 19-1**) to reveal the Maps menu, shown in **Figure 19-3**.

2. Tap the Satellite option. The Satellite view (refer to the top-right image in **Figure 19-2**) appears.

3. Tap the Settings button to reveal the menu again, and then tap Hybrid. In Hybrid view, Satellite view is displayed with street names superimposed (refer to the bottom-left image in **Figure 19-2**).

4. Finally, you can display a 3D effect on any view (refer to the bottom-right image in **Figure 19-2**) by tapping the 3D button in the lower-left corner of the screen.

 On the Maps menu, you can also access a Traffic overlay feature. If you live in a larger metropolitan area (this feature doesn't really work in small towns or rural settings), turn on this feature by tapping the Show Traffic button. The traffic overlay shows red dashes on roads indicating accidents or road closures to help you navigate your rush hour commute or trip to the mall.

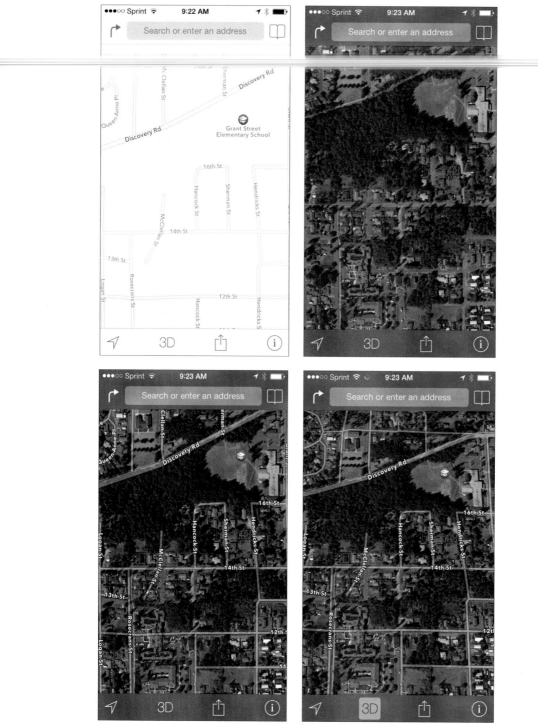

Figure 19-2

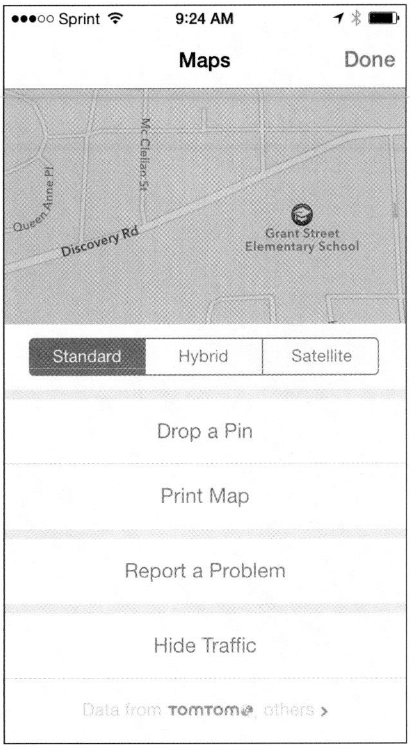

●●●○○ Sprint 🌐   9:24 AM   ✈ ✳ 🔋

Maps   Done

Mc-Clellan St

Queen Anne Pl

Discovery Rd

Grant Street
Elementary School

| Standard | Hybrid | Satellite |

Drop a Pin

Print Map

Report a Problem

Hide Traffic

Data from **TOMTOM**, others ›

Figure 19-3

 You can drop a pin to mark a location on a map that you can return to. See the task "Drop a Pin," later in this chapter, for more about this topic.

 To print any displayed map to an AirPrint-compatible wireless printer, just tap the Print Map button on the Maps menu.

Zoom In and Out

1. You'll appreciate the Zoom feature because it gives you the capability to zoom in and out to see more or less detailed maps and to move around a displayed map. With a map displayed, double-tap with a single finger to zoom in (see **Figure 19-4**; the image on the left shows the map before zooming in while the image on the right shows the map after zooming).

Figure 19-4

2. Double-tap with two fingers to zoom out, revealing less detail.

3. Place two fingers positioned together on the screen and move them apart to zoom in.

4. Place two fingers apart on the screen and then pinch them together to zoom out.

5. Press your finger to the screen and drag the map in any direction to move to an adjacent area.

It can take a few moments for the map to redraw itself when you enlarge, reduce, or move around it, so be patient. Areas that are being redrawn look like blank grids but are filled in eventually. Also, if you're in Satellite or Hybrid view, zooming in may take some time; wait it out because the blurred image resolves itself.

Go to Another Location

1. With Maps open, tap in the Search field (see **Figure 19-5**); the keyboard opens. If you have displayed directions for a route, you won't see the Search field in the top of the screen; you may have to tap the Clear button on a directions screen to get back to the Search field.

2. Type a location, using a street address with city and state, a stored contact name, or a destination such as *Empire State Building* or *Detroit airport*. Maps may make suggestions as you type if it finds any logical matches. Tap the result you prefer, and the location appears with a red pin inserted in it and an information bar with the location, a Directions button to the left and an arrow to the right (see **Figure 19-6**) which displays more information, and in some cases, the Street view icon. Note that if several locations match your search term, several pins may be displayed in a suggestions list.

Try asking for a type of business or location by zip code. For example, if you crave something with pepperoni in Spokane, WA, you might enter **99208 pizza**.

Search field · Directions button · Information bar · Bookmark icon

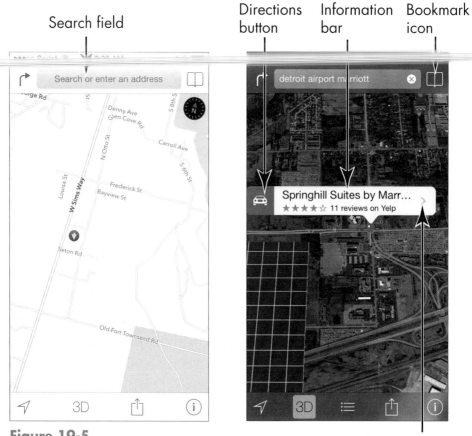

Figure 19-5

Figure 19-6

Information icon

3. You can also tap the screen and drag in any direction to move to a nearby location.

4. Tap the Bookmark icon (the little book symbol to the right of the Search field; refer to **Figure 19-6**), and then tap the Recents tab to reveal recently visited sites. Tap a bookmark to go there.

As you discover later in this chapter, in the "Add and View a Bookmark" task, you can also quickly go to any location you've previously visited and saved using the Bookmarks feature.

 If you enter a destination such as *Bronx Zoo*, you might want to also enter its city and state. Entering *Bronx Zoo* landed me in the Woodland Park Zoo in Tacoma because Maps looks for the closest match to your geographical location in a given category.

Drop a Pin

1. Pins are markers: A green pin marks a start location, a red pin marks a search result, and a blue pin (referred to as the *blue marker*) marks your iPhone's current location. If you drop a pin yourself, it appears in a lovely purple. Display a map that contains a spot where you want to drop a pin to help you find directions to or from that site.

2. If you need to, you can zoom in to a more detailed map to see a better view of the location you want to pin.

3. Press and hold your finger on the screen at the location where you want to place the pin. The pin appears, together with an information bar (refer to **Figure 19-6**).

4. Tap the arrow (refer to **Figure 19-6**) on the information bar to display details about the pin location (see **Figure 19-7**).

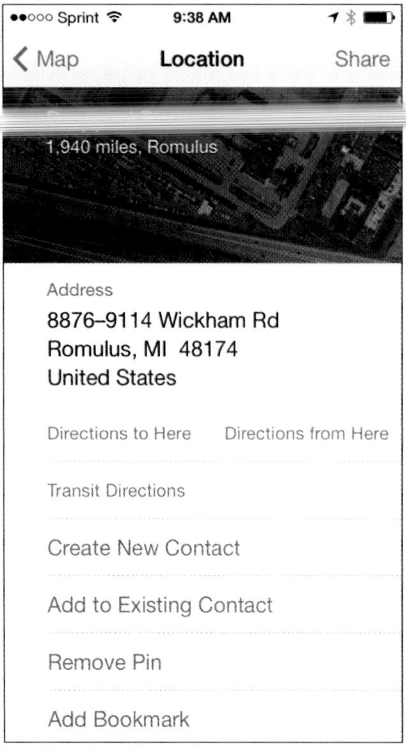

●●○○○ Sprint 📶   9:38 AM   ⬆ ⚹ ■)

❮ Map   **Location**   Share

1,940 miles, Romulus

Address

8876–9114 Wickham Rd
Romulus, MI 48174
United States

Directions to Here   Directions from Here

Transit Directions

Create New Contact

Add to Existing Contact

Remove Pin

Add Bookmark

Figure 19-7

If a location has associated reviews on sites such as
the restaurant review site Yelp (www.yelp.com),
you can tap the Reviews tab and then tap the Check
In on Yelp button in its information dialog to install
the Yelp app and read the reviews.

Add and View a Bookmark

1. A *bookmark* provides a way to save a destination so you
can display a map or directions to it quickly. To add a
bookmark to a location, first place a pin on it, as
described in the preceding task.

2. Tap the arrow on the information display to open the
Information dialog.

3. Tap Add Bookmark.

4. The Add Bookmark dialog (see **Figure 19-8**) and the keyboard appear. If you like, you can modify the name of the bookmark.

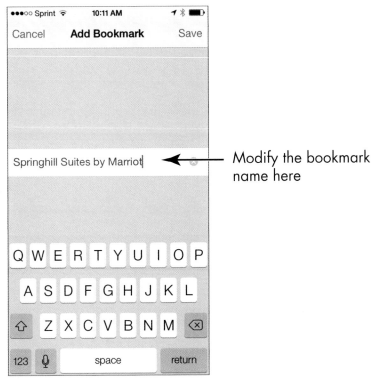

Modify the bookmark name here

Figure 19-8

5. Tap Save.

6. To view your bookmarks, tap the Bookmark icon (it looks like a little open book; refer to **Figure 19-6**) at the top of the Maps screen. Be sure that the Bookmarks tab is selected; a list of bookmarks is displayed.

7. Tap on a bookmark to go to that location in Maps.

You can also view recently viewed locations, even if you haven't bookmarked them. Tap the Bookmark icon; then at the bottom of the Bookmarks dialog that appears, tap Recents. Locations you've visited recently are listed there. Tap one to return to it.

Delete a Bookmark

1. Tap the Bookmark icon, and then tap the Bookmarks tab at the bottom of the dialog that appears to be sure you're viewing Bookmarks.

2. Tap the Edit button. A red minus icon appears to the left of each of your bookmarks, as shown in **Figure 19-9**. Note that a dropped pin item, which isn't a bookmark, doesn't display a minus icon.

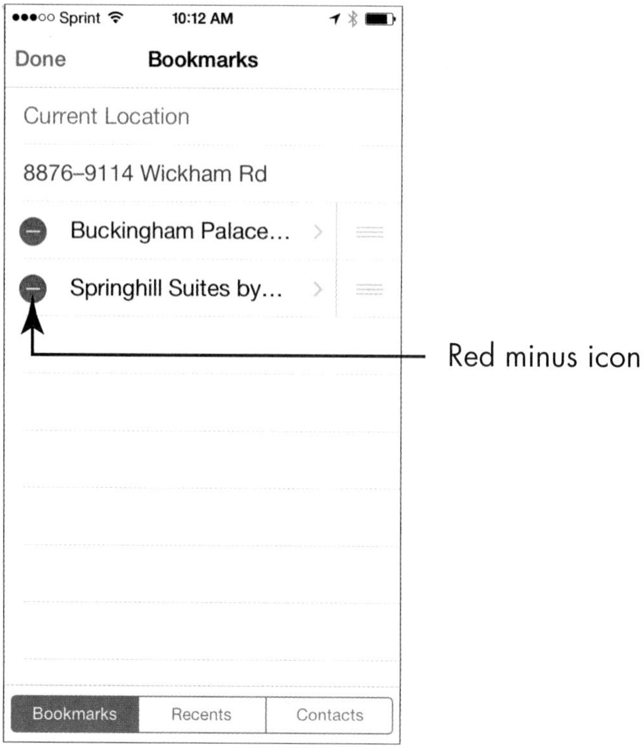

●●●○○ Sprint 📶	10:12 AM ✈ ✳ 🔋
Done	**Bookmarks**

Current Location

8876–9114 Wickham Rd

⊖ Buckingham Palace... > ≡

⊖ Springhill Suites by... > ≡ ———— Red minus icon

| Bookmarks | Recents | Contacts |

Figure 19-9

3. Tap a red minus icon.

4. Tap Delete. The bookmark is removed.

 You can also use a touchscreen gesture after you've displayed the Bookmarks in Step 1 in the preceding list to delete a bookmark. Simply swipe across a bookmark item and then tap the Delete button.

 You can clear out all recent locations stored by Maps to give yourself a clean slate. Tap the Bookmark icon and then tap the Recents tab. Tap Clear and then confirm by tapping Clear All Recents.

Find Directions

1. You can get directions in a couple of different ways. With at least one pin on your map in addition to your current location or a dropped pin, tap the Directions button in the top-left corner and then tap Route. A line appears, showing the route between your current location and the closest pin (see **Figure 19-10**).

2. To show directions from your current location to another pin, tap the other pin, and in the dialog that appears, tap Route; the route is redrawn.

3. You can also enter two locations to get directions from one to the other. Tap the Directions button in Maps and then tap in the Start field (see **Figure 19-11**). The keyboard appears.

4. Enter a different starting location.

5. Tap in the End field and enter a destination location. If you like, you can tap the Pedestrian or Public Transit buttons to get walking or bus/train routes rather than driving directions. Tap the Route button on the keyboard. The route between the two locations is displayed.

Line indicating your route

Start field

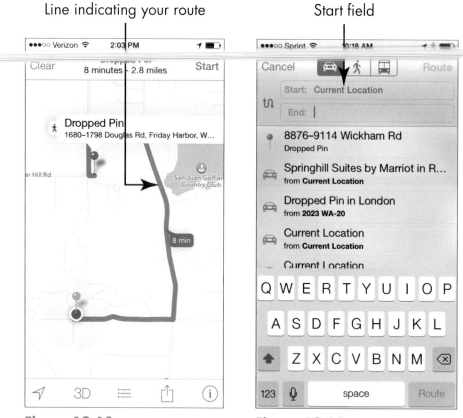

Figure 19-10

Figure 19-11

6. When a route is displayed, a bar appears along the top of the Maps screen (refer to **Figure 19-10**) with information about the distance and time it takes to travel between the two locations. Here's what you can do at this point:

- Tap the Directions button (it's the middle icon at the bottom of the screen that looks like a numbered list) to display written directions.

- Tap Start to begin turn-by-turn direction narration (see **Figure 19-12**).

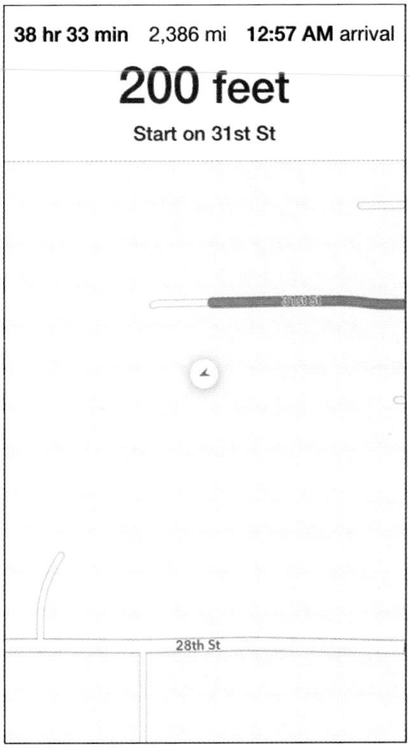

38 hr 33 min 2,386 mi **12:57 AM** arrival

200 feet

Start on 31st St

31st St

28th St

Figure 19-12

7. If there are alternate routes, Maps notes the number of alternate routes in the Directions informational display and shows the routes on the map. Tap a route number to make it the active route.

View Information About a Location

1. You displayed the Information dialog for locations to add a bookmark or get directions in previous tasks. Now you focus on the useful information displayed there. Go to a location and tap the pin.

2. On the information bar that appears above the pinned location, tap the arrow (refer to **Figure 19-6**).

3. In the Information dialog (refer to **Figure** 19-7), tap the web address listed in the Home Page field, which you can use to go the location's web page, if one is associated with it.

4. You can also press and hold either the Phone or Address field and use the Copy button (see **Figure** 19-13) to copy the phone number, for example, so that you can place it in a Notes document for future reference.

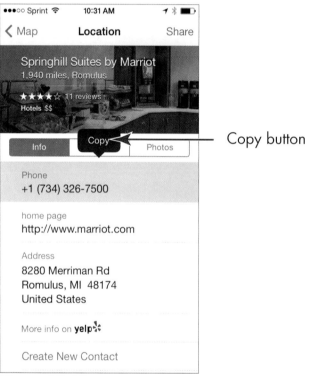

Copy button

Figure 19-13

5. Tap outside the Information dialog to close it.

 Rather than copy and paste information, you can easily save all information about a location in your Contacts address book. See the next task, "Add a Location to a New Contact," to find out how it's done.

Add a Location to a New Contact

1. Tap a pin to display the information bar.

2. Tap the arrow.

3. In the Information dialog that appears, tap Create New Contact or Add to Existing Contacts.

4. In the resulting dialog, tap Create New Contact. The New Contact dialog appears (see **Figure 19-14**). (Note if you choose Add to an Existing Contact here, you can choose a contact from your Contacts list to add the location information to).

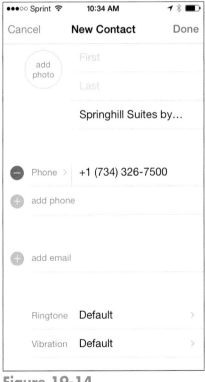

Figure 19-14

5. Whatever information was available about the location has already been entered. Enter any additional information you need, such as a name, phone number, or e-mail address.

6. Tap Done. The information is stored in your Contacts address book.

Share Location Information

1. Tap a pin to display the information bar.

2. Tap the arrow to display more information.

3. In the Information dialog that appears, tap Share in the upper right corner. In the dialog that appears (see **Figure 19-15**), you can choose to share via AirDrop, text message, Mail, Twitter, or Facebook. Tap Mail to see how this option works.

4. On the form that appears, use the onscreen keyboard to enter a recipient's information (if you're using Facebook or Twitter, you enter recipient information as appropriate to the service you choose to use).

5. Tap Send. A link to the location information in Google Maps is sent to your designated recipients.

 If you choose Twitter or Facebook in Step 3, you must have already installed and set up the Twitter or Facebook app and have a Twitter or Facebook account set up using iPhone Settings before sharing Maps content using those services. You also must have an account with these services to use them to share content.

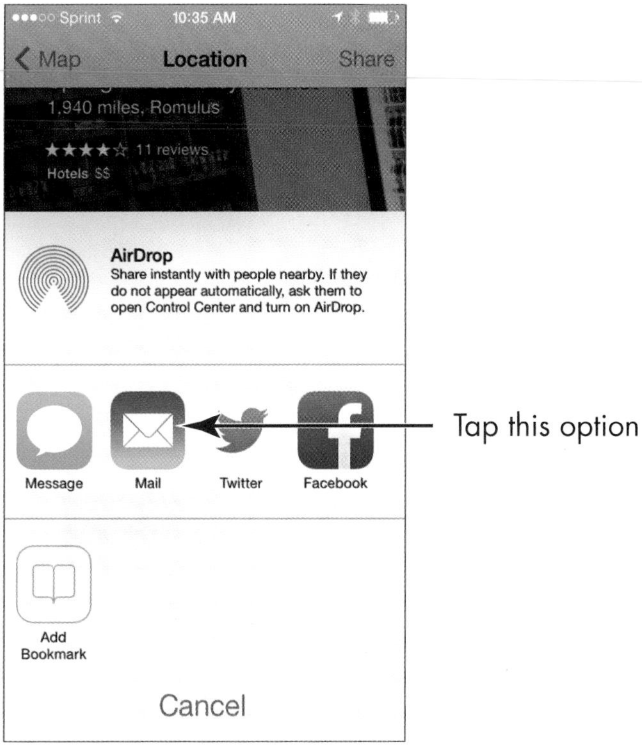

Tap this option

Figure 19-15

Get Turn-By-Turn Navigation Help

1. When you enter directions for a route and display that route, you can then begin listening to turn-by-turn navigation instructions that can be helpful as you're driving. Tap the Start button in the upper-right corner.

2. The narration begins and large text instructions are displayed. Continue driving according to the route until the next instruction is spoken.

3. For an overview of your route (as shown in **Figure 19-16**), at any time you can tap the screen and then tap the Overview button that appears in the upper-right corner.

Figure 19-16

 To adjust the volume of the spoken navigation aid, tap Settings on the Home screen, tap Maps, and then adjust the Navigation Voice Volume settings to No Voice, Low, Normal, or Loud.

 To change route information from miles to kilometers, go to Settings⇨Maps and tap In Kilometers to change the setting.

Part V

Managing Your Life and Your iPhone

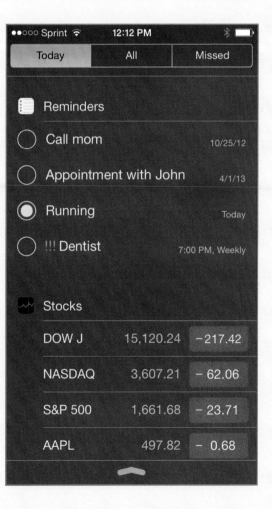

Visit http://www.dummies.com/extras/iphoneforseniors for instructions on how to set up the Stocks app to reflect your personal investment portfolio in Notifications Center.

Keeping On Schedule with Calendar and Clock

Whether you're retired or still working, you have a busy life full of activities (even busier if you're retired, for some unfathomable reason). You may need a way to keep on top of all those activities and appointments. The Calendar app on your iPhone is a simple, elegant, electronic daybook that helps you do just that.

In addition to being able to enter events and view them in a list or by the day, week, or month, you can set up Calendar to send alerts to remind you of your obligations and search for events by keywords. You can even set up repeating events, such as birthdays, monthly get-togethers with the girls or guys, or weekly babysitting appointments with your grandchild. To help you coordinate calendars on multiple devices, you can also sync events with other calendar accounts.

Another preinstalled app that can help you stay on schedule is Clock. Though simple to use, Clock helps you view the time in multiple locations, set alarms, check yourself with a stopwatch feature, and use a timer.

In this chapter, you master the simple procedures for getting around your calendar, entering and editing events, setting up alerts, syncing, and searching. You also learn the simple ins and outs of using Clock.

View Your Calendar

1. Calendar offers several ways to view your schedule. Start by tapping the Calendar app icon on the Home screen to open it. Depending on what you last had open, you may see today's calendar, an open event, or the Search screen with all appointments displayed.

2. Tap the Today button at the bottom of the screen to display Today's view (if it's not already displayed) and then tap the Search button to see all scheduled events. This view, shown in **Figure 20-1,** displays all events for the current day with times listed on the left. Tap an event in the list to get more event details, or tap the + symbol to add an event.

 If you'd like to display events only from a particular calendar, such as the Birthday or US Holidays calendars, tap the Calendars button at the bottom of the List view and select a calendar to base the list on.

3. Tap Back, and then tap the Today button to view your daily appointments for every day in a list, as shown in **Figure 20-2.** In this view, appointments appear like a page in a daily appointment book. (Note that in landscape orientation, you see the day as a column in a set of columns for the days of the week.)

Events listed by hour   Calendars button

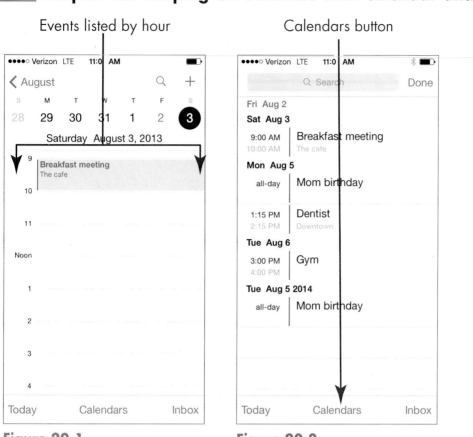

Figure 20-1   **Figure 20-2**

4. Tap the Month button; for example, if the month displayed at the top of the screen is August, tap the word August to get an overview of your busy month (see **Figure** 20-3). In this view, you see the calendar for the month with any events shown as gray dots.

5. To move from one month to the next in Month view, scroll up or down the screen with your finger.

6. To jump back to today, tap the Today button in the bottom-left corner of Calendar.

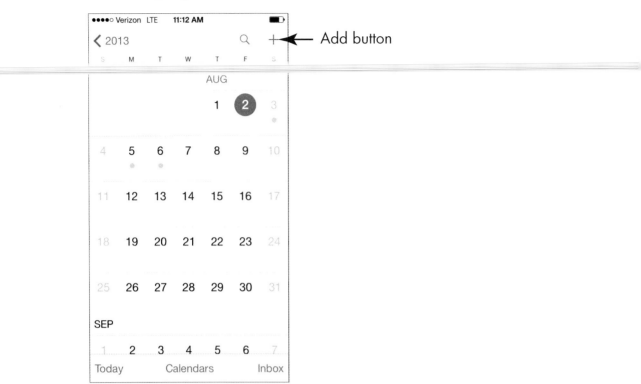

Add button

Figure 20-3

 To view any invitation that you accepted, which placed an event on your calendar, tap Inbox, and a list of invitations is displayed. Tap Done to return to the calendar.

Add Calendar Events

1. With any view displayed, tap the plus symbol-shaped Add button (refer to **Figure 20-3**) to add an event. The Add Event dialog, shown in **Figure 20-4,** appears.

2. Enter a title for the event and, if you want, a location.

3. Tap the All-day button, or tap the Starts or Ends field; the scrolling setting for day, hour, and minute appears.

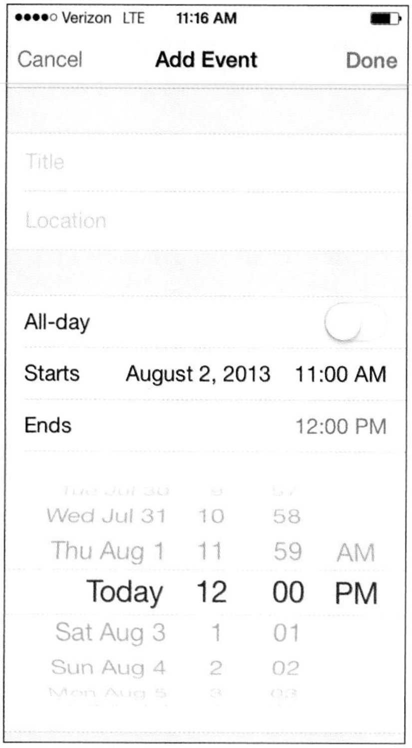

●●●●○ Verizon LTE   11:16 AM

Cancel   **Add Event**   Done

Title

Location

All-day

Starts   August 2, 2013   11:00 AM

Ends   12:00 PM

Wed Jul 31   10   58
Thu Aug 1   11   59   AM
Today   12   00   PM
Sat Aug 3   1   01
Sun Aug 4   2   02
Mon Aug 5   3   03

Figure 20-4

4. Place your finger on the date, hour, minute, or AM/PM column and move your finger to scroll up or down. (Note that, if the event will last all day, you can simply tap the All-Day On/Off button and forget about setting start and end times.)

5. If you want to add notes, use your finger to scroll down in the Add Event dialog and tap in the Notes field. Type your note, and then tap the Done button to save the event.

 You can edit any event at any time by simply tapping it in any view of your calendar and, when the details are displayed, tap Edit. The Edit dialog appears, offering the same settings as the Add Event dialog. Tap the Done button to save your changes or Cancel to return to your calendar without saving any changes.

Create Repeating Events

1. If you want an event to repeat, such as a weekly or monthly appointment, you can set a repeating event. With any view displayed, tap the Add button to add an event. The Add Event dialog (refer to **Figure 20-4**) appears.

2. Enter a title and location for the event and set the start and end dates and times, as shown in the earlier task "Add Calendar Events."

3. Scroll down the page if necessary and then tap the Repeat field; the Repeat dialog, shown in **Figure 20-5**, is displayed.

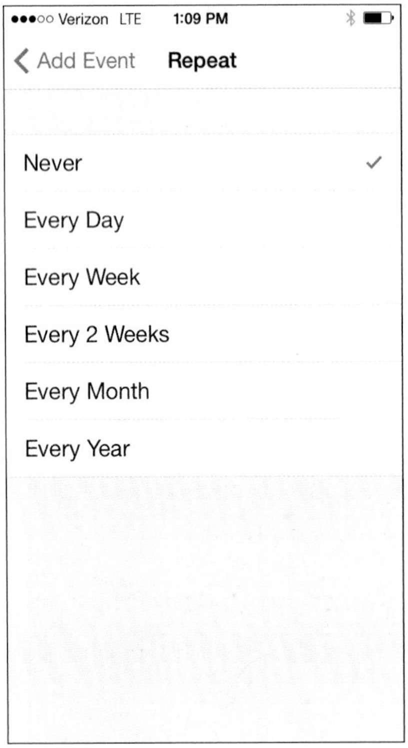

Figure 20-5

4. Tap a preset time interval: Every Day, Week, 2 Weeks, Month, or Year, and you return to the Add Event dialog.

5. Tap Done. You return to the Calendar.

 Other calendar programs may give you more control over repeating events; for example, you might be able to make a setting to repeat an event the fourth Tuesday of every month. If you want a more robust calendar feature, you might consider setting up your appointments in an application such as Outlook or the Mac version of Calendar and syncing them to iPhone. But, if you want to create a simple repeating event in iPhone's Calendar app, simply add the first event on a Tuesday and make it repeat every week. Easy, huh?

Add Alerts

1. If you want your iPhone to alert you when an event is coming up, you can use the Alert feature. First tap the Settings icon on the Home screen and choose Sounds.

2. Scroll down to Calendar Alerts and tap it; then tap any Alert Tone, which causes iPhone to play the tone for you. When you've chosen the alert tone you want, tap Sounds to return to Sounds settings.

3. Press the Home button and then tap Calendar and create an event in your calendar or open an existing one for editing, as covered in earlier tasks in this chapter.

4. In the Add Event (refer to **Figure 20-4**) or Edit dialog, tap the Alert field. The Event Alert dialog appears, as shown in **Figure 20-6**.

5. Tap any preset interval, from 5 Minutes to 2 Days Before or At Time of Event. (Remember that you can scroll down in the dialog to see more options.)

6. Note that the Alert setting is shown in the Edit dialog (see **Figure 20-7**).

7. Tap Done in the Edit dialog to save all settings.

8. Tap the Day button to display Day view of the date of your event.

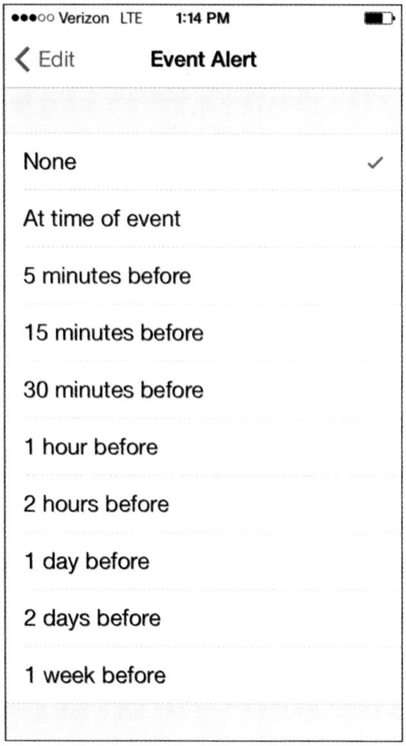

Alert setting for an event

Figure 20-6

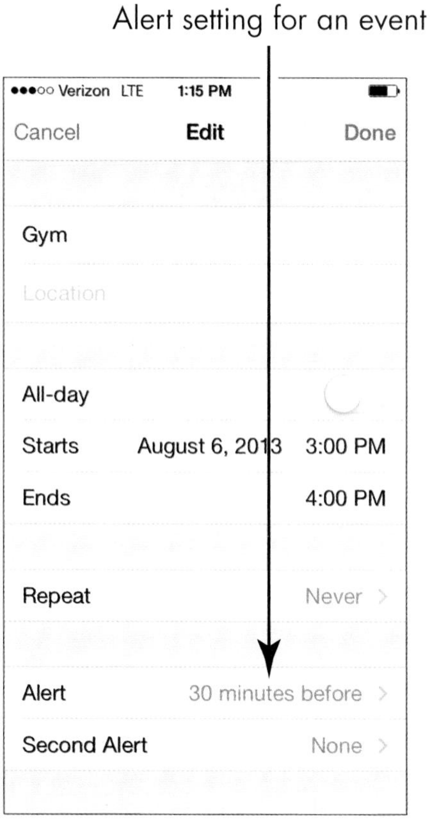

Figure 20-7

If you work for an organization that uses a Microsoft Exchange account, you can set up your iPhone to receive and respond to invitations from colleagues in your company. When somebody sends an invitation that you accept, it appears on your calendar. Check with your company network administrator (who will jump at the chance to get her hands on your iPhone) or the *iPhone User Guide* to set up this feature if it sounds useful to you. Note that iCloud offers similar functionality to individuals.

Subscribe To and Share Calendars

1. If you use a calendar available from an online service such as Yahoo! or Google, you can subscribe to that calendar to read events saved there on your iPhone. Note that you can only read, not edit, these events. Tap the Settings icon on the Home screen to get started.

2. Tap the Mail, Contacts, Calendars option. The Mail, Contacts, Calendars settings pane appears.

3. Tap Add Account. The Add Account options, shown in **Figure 20-8,** appear.

4. Tap an e-mail choice, such as Gmail or Yahoo!.

5. In the dialog that appears (see **Figure 20-9**), enter your name, e-mail address, and e-mail account password.

6. Tap Next. iPhone verifies your address.

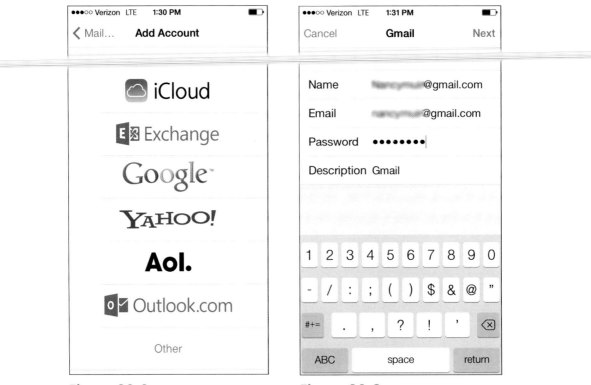

Figure 20-8

Figure 20-9

7. On the following screen (see **Figure 20-10**) tap the On/ Off button for the Calendars field; your iPhone retrieves data from your calendar at the interval you have set to fetch data. To review these settings, tap the Fetch New Data option in the Mail, Contacts, Calendars dialog.

8. In the Fetch New Data dialog that appears, be sure that the Push option's On/Off button reads *On* and then choose the option you prefer for how frequently data is pushed to your iPhone.

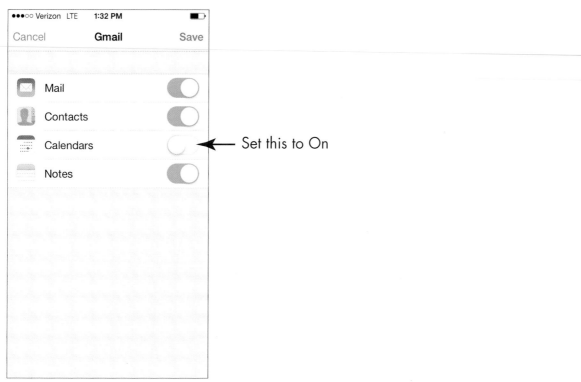

Figure 20-10

 If you use Microsoft Outlook's calendar or Calendar on your main computer, you can sync it to your iPhone calendar to avoid having to reenter event information. To do this, use iCloud settings to sync automatically (see Chapter 3) or connect your iPhone to your computer with the lightening connector or wirelessly and use settings in your iTunes account to sync with calendars — or use Wi-Fi syncing if you eschew cables. Click the Sync button, and your calendar settings will be shared between your

computer and iPhone (in both directions). Read
more in Chapter 3 about working with iTunes to
manage your iPhone content.

 If you store birthdays for people in the Contacts app,
the Calendar app then displays these when the day
comes around so you won't forget to pass on your
congratulations!

 Though you can have calendar events pushed to you
or synced from multiple e-mail accounts, remember
that having data pushed to your iPhone may drain
your battery more quickly.

Delete an Event

1. When an upcoming luncheon or meeting is canceled,
you should delete the appointment. With Calendar open,
tap an event, and then tap the Edit button in the dialog
that appears (see **Figure 20-11**). The Edit dialog opens.

2. In the Edit dialog, tap the Delete Event button at the bottom (see **Figure 20-12**).

3. If this is a repeating event, you have the option to delete
this instance of the event or this and all future instances
of the event (see **Figure 20-13**). Tap the button for the
option you prefer. The event is deleted, and you return to
Calendar view.

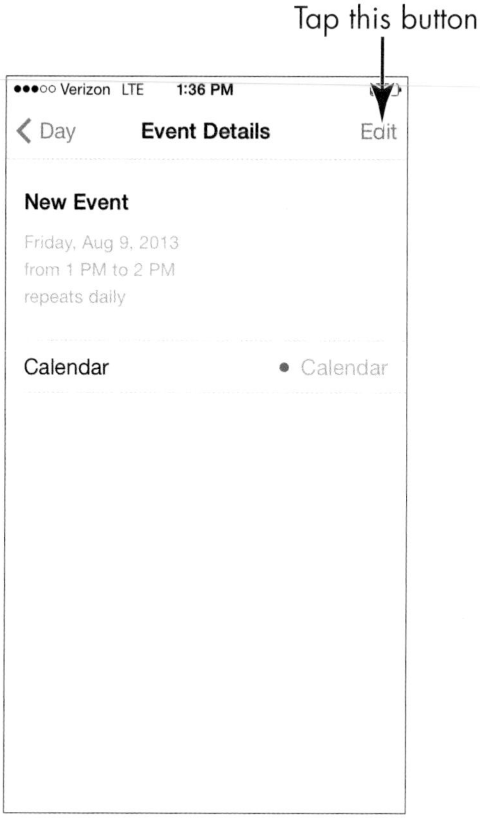

Tap this button   Tap this button

●●●○○ Verizon LTE   1:36 PM

‹ Day   **Event Details**   Edit

New Event

Friday, Aug 9, 2013
from 1 PM to 2 PM
repeats daily

Calendar   • Calendar

Figure 20-11

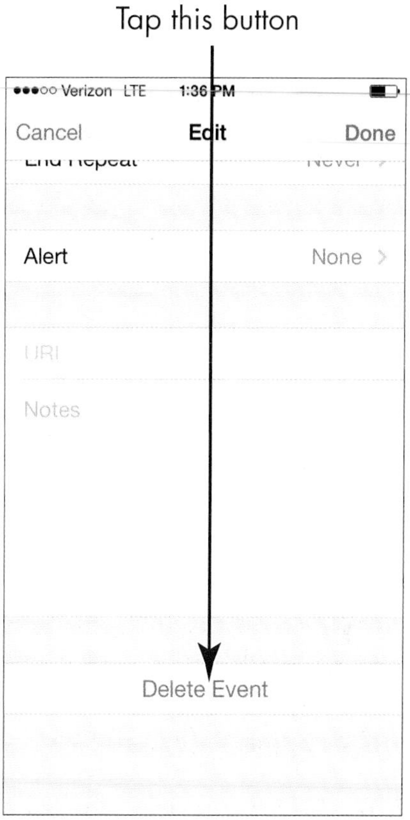

●●●○○ Verizon LTE   1:36 PM

Cancel   **Edit**   Done

End Repeat   Never ›

Alert   None ›

URL

Notes

Delete Event

Figure 20-12

 If an event is moved but not canceled, you don't have to delete the old one and create a new one. Simply edit the existing event to change the day and time in the Event dialog.

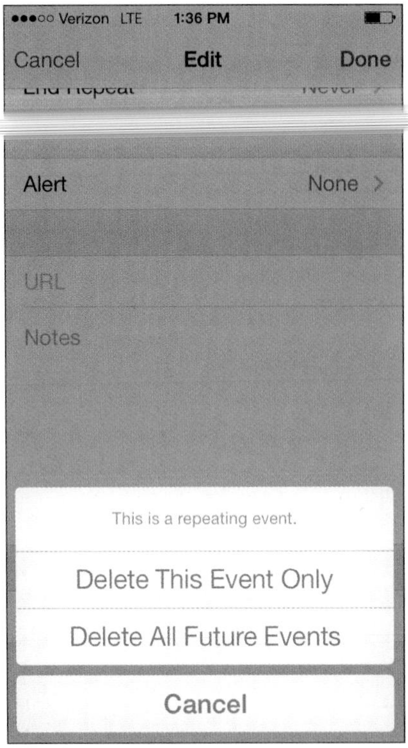

Figure 20-13

Display Clock

1. Clock is a preinstalled app that resides on the Home screen along with other preinstalled apps such as Videos and Camera. Tap the Clock app to open it. Preset locations are displayed (see **Figure 20-14**).

2. You can add a clock for many (but not all) locations around the world. With Clock displayed, tap the Add button.

3. Tap a city on the list or tap a letter on the right side to display locations that begin with that letter (see **Figure 20-15**) and then tap a city. You can also tap in the search field and begin to type a city name to find and tap on a city. The clock appears in the last slot at the bottom.

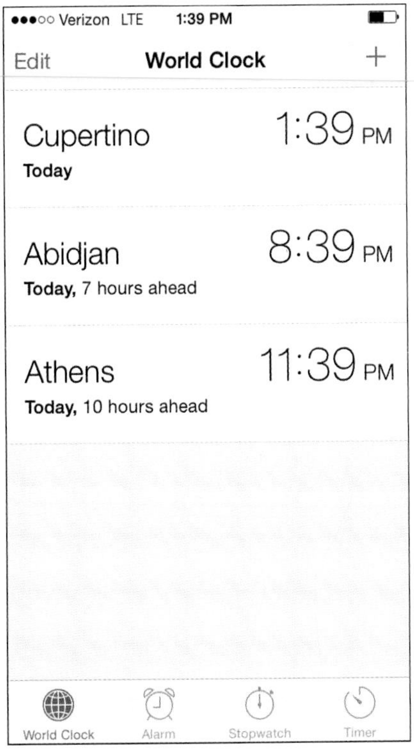

Figure 20-14

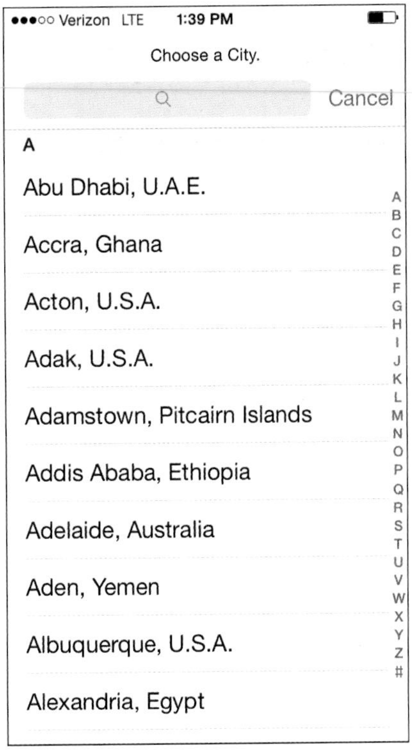

Figure 20-15

Delete a Clock

1. To remove a location, tap the Edit button in the top-left corner of the World Clock screen.

2. Tap the minus symbol next to a location and then tap Delete (see **Figure 20-16**).

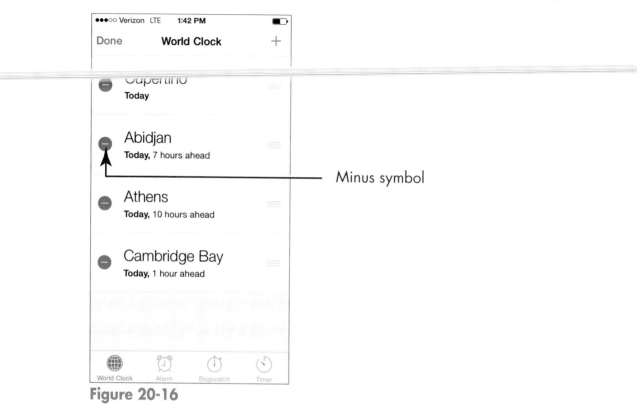

Figure 20-16

Set an Alarm

1. With the Clock app displayed, tap the Alarm tab.

2. Tap the Add button. In the Add Alarm dialog shown in **Figure 20-17,** take any of the following actions, tapping Back after you make each setting to return to the Add Alarm dialog:

- Tap Repeat if you want the alarm to repeat at a regular interval, such as every Monday or every Sunday.

- Tap Sound to choose the tune the alarm will play.

- Tap the On/Off button for Snooze if you want to use the Snooze feature.

- Tap Label if you want to name the alarm with a name such as "Take Pill" or "Call Helen."

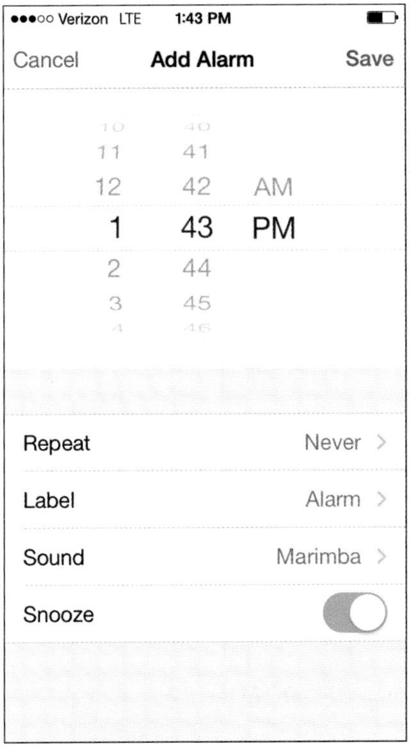

●●●○○ Verizon LTE	1:43 PM	■▷
Cancel	**Add Alarm**	Save

10	40	
11	41	
12	42	AM
1	43	PM
2	44	
3	45	
4	46	

Repeat	Never ⟩
Label	Alarm ⟩
Sound	Marimba ⟩
Snooze	⬤

Figure 20-17

3. Place your finger on any of the three columns of sliding numbers at the top of the dialog and scroll to set the time you want the alarm to occur and tap Save. The alarm appears on the calendar on the Alarm tab.

 To delete an alarm, tap the Alarm tab and tap Edit. All alarms appear. Tap the red circle with a minus in it and then tap the Delete button.

Use Stopwatch and Timer

Sometimes life seems like a countdown or a ticking clock, counting the minutes you've spent on a certain activity. You can use the Timer and Stopwatch tabs of the Clock app to do a countdown to a specific time such as the moment when your chocolate chip cookies are done cooking or to time an activity such as a walk.

These two work very similarly: Tap the Stopwatch or Timer tab from Clocks World Clock screen and then tap the Start button. When you set the Timer, iPhone uses a sound to notify you when time's up. When you start the Stopwatch, you have to tap the Stop button when the activity is done (see **Figure 20-18**).

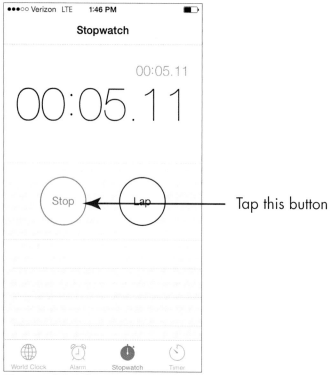

Figure 20-18

Stopwatch allows you to log intermediate timings, such as a lap in the pool or the periods of a timed game. With Stopwatch running, just tap the Lap button and the first interval of time is recorded. Tap Lap again to record a second interval, and so forth.

Working with Reminders and Notifications

Chapter
21

*W*ith the arrival of iOS 5, the Reminders app and the Notification Center feature appeared, warming the hearts of those who need help remembering all the details of their lives.

Reminders is a kind of to-do list that lets you create tasks and set reminders so you don't forget important commitments.

You can even be reminded to do things when you arrive at or leave a location. For example, you can set a reminder so that, when your iPhone detects that you've left the location of your golf game, an alert reminds you to pick up your grandchildren, or when you arrive at your cabin, iPhone reminds you to turn on the water . . . you get the idea. Notifications allows you to review all the things you should be aware of in one place, such as mail messages, text messages, calendar appointments, and alerts.

If you occasionally need to escape all your obligations, try the Do Not Disturb feature, new as of iOS 6. Turn this feature on, and you won't be bothered with alerts until you turn it off again.

Get ready to . . .

In this chapter, you discover how to set up and view tasks in Reminders and how the Notification Center can centralize all your alerts in one easy-to-find place, including the new Today, All ~~help you view all your notifications in an organized way.~~

Create a Task in Reminders

1. Creating a task in Reminders is pretty darn simple. Tap Reminders on the Home screen.

2. On the screen that appears, tap Scheduled or tap a category of reminders you've created such as Exercise or Club, and then tap a blank slot in the displayed list to add a task (see **Figure 21-1**). The onscreen keyboard appears.

3. Enter a task name or description using the onscreen keyboard.

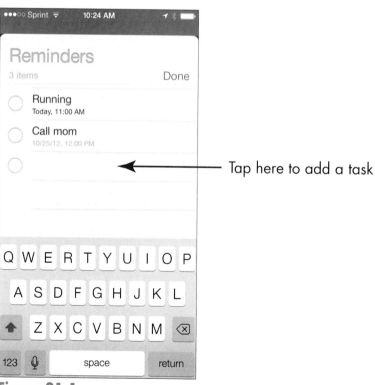

Tap here to add a task

Figure 21-1

See the next task to discover how to add more specifics about an event for which you've created a reminder.

Edit Task Details

1. Tap a task and then tap the Details button that appears to the right of it to open the Details dialog shown in **Figure 21-2**. (Note that I deal with reminder settings in the following task.)

2. Tap a Priority: None, Low (!), Medium (!!), or High (!!!) from the choices that appear.

3. Tap Notes and enter any notes about the event (see **Figure 21-3**).

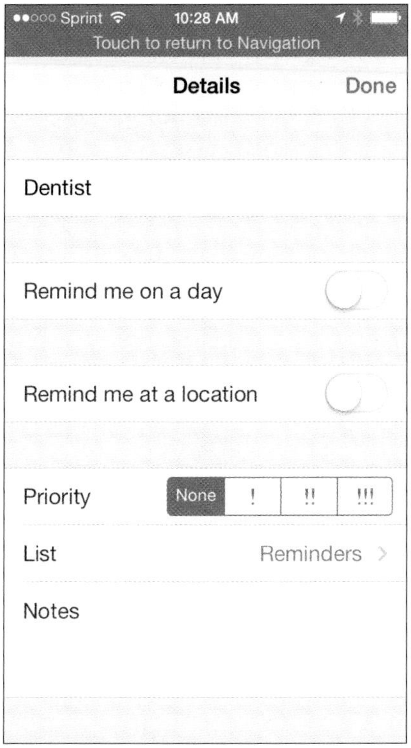

Enter notes here

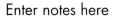

Figure 21-2

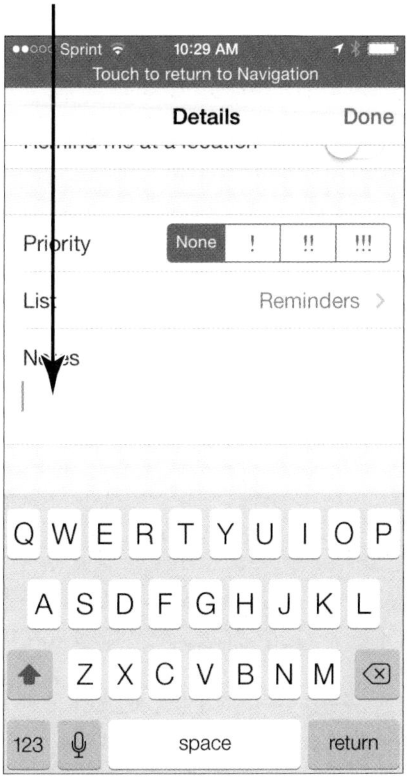

Figure 21-3

4. Tap List and then tap which list you want the Reminder saved to. Tap Details to return to the Details dialog.

5. Tap Done to save the task.

 With this version of the app, priority settings now display the associated number of exclamation points on a task in a list to remind you of its importance.

Schedule a Reminder by Time or Location

1. One of the major features of Reminders is to remind you of upcoming tasks. To set a reminder, tap a task and then tap the Details button that appears to the right of the task.

2. In the dialog that appears (refer to **Figure 21-2**), tap Remind Me On a Day to turn the feature on.

3. Tap the Alarm field that appears below this setting (see **Figure 21-4**) to display date settings.

4. Tap and flick the day, hour, and minutes fields to scroll to the date and time for the reminder.

5. Tap Remind Me Location and then tap the Location field. If prompted, tap OK to let Reminders use your current location.

6. Use the field labeled Search or Enter Address to find or enter a location. Tap Details to return to the task detail screen.

7. Tap Done to save the settings for the reminder.

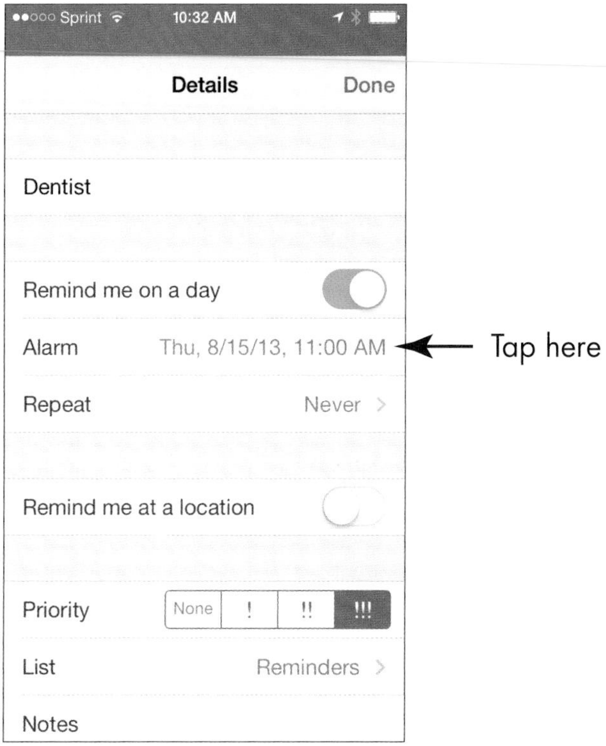

Details   Done

Dentist

Remind me on a day

Alarm   Thu, 8/15/13, 11:00 AM   ◀— Tap here

Repeat   Never >

Remind me at a location

Priority | None | ! | !! | **!!!** |

List   Reminders >

Notes

Figure 21-4

 If you want a task to repeat with associated reminders, tap the Repeat field in the Details dialog, and from the dialog that appears tap Every Day, Week, 2 Weeks, Month, or Year (for those annual meetings or great holiday get-togethers with the gang). Tap Done to save the setting. To stop the task from repeating, tap the End Repeat field, tap End Repeat Date, and select a date from the scrolling calendar.

 You have to be in range of a connection for GPS for the location reminder to work properly.

Create a List

1. You can create your own lists of tasks to help you keep different parts of your life organized and even edit the tasks on the list in List View. Tap Reminders on the Home screen to open it. If a particular list other than Reminders is open, tap its name to return to the List View.

2. Tap New List to display the New List form shown in **Figure 21-5.**

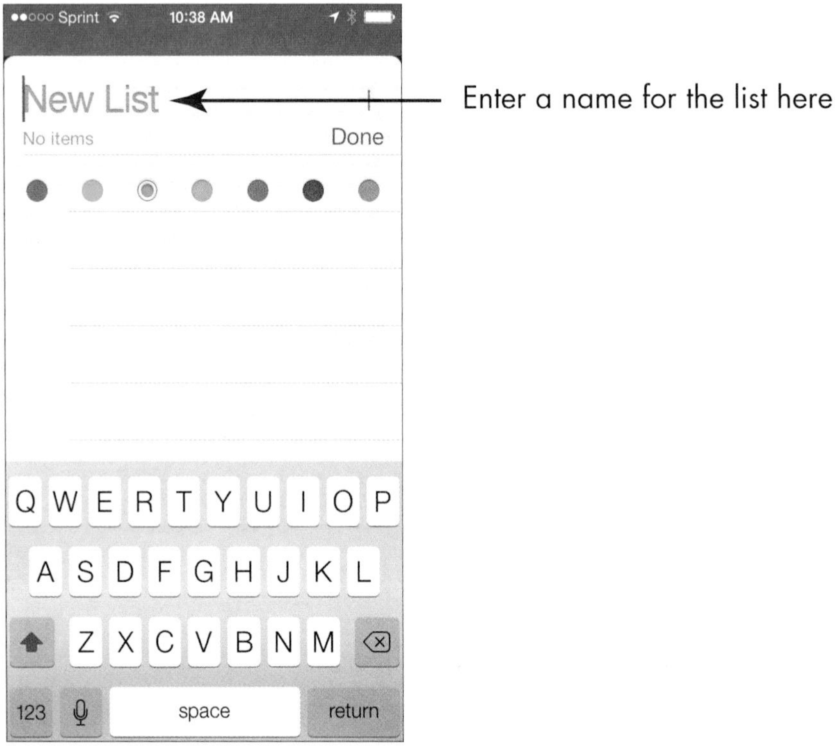

Enter a name for the list here

Figure 21-5

3. Enter a name for the list and tap a color; the list name will appear in that color in List View.

4. Tap Done to save the list. Tap on a blank line to enter a task, or tap the list name to return to the List View.

Sync with Other Devices and Calendars

 Note that to make all these settings work, you should set up your default Calendar in the Mail, Contacts, Calendar settings, and set up your iCloud account under Accounts in those same settings.

1. To determine which tasks are brought over from other devices or calendars such as Outlook, tap the Settings button on the Home screen.

2. Tap iCloud. In the dialog that appears, be sure that Reminders is set to On.

3. Tap Settings to return to the main settings list, and then tap Reminders.

4. Tap the Sync field and then choose how far back to sync Reminders.

Mark as Complete or Delete a Reminder

1. You may want to mark a task as completed or just delete it entirely. With Reminders open and a list of tasks displayed, tap the check box to the left of a task to mark it as complete. When you tap Show Completed, the task now appears as completed and is removed from the Reminders category.

2. To delete more than one reminder, with the list of tasks displayed, tap Select and in the screen shown in **Figure 21-6,** tap the red minus icon to the left of any task.

3. Tap Done. In the confirming dialog, tap Delete again.

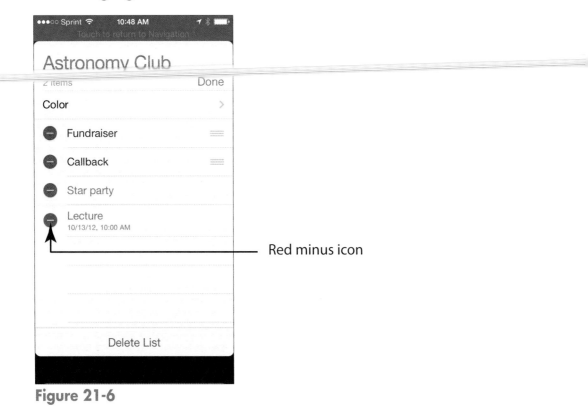

Red minus icon

Figure 21-6

Set Notification Types

1. Notification Center is a list of various alerts and scheduled events you can display by swiping down from the top of your iPhone screen. Notification Center is on by default, but you don't have to include every type of notification there if you don't want to; for example, you may never want to be notified of incoming messages but always want to have reminders listed here — it's up to you. There are some settings you can make to control what types of notifications are included. Tap Settings, and then tap Notification Center.

2. In the settings that appear (see **Figure 21-7**), note that there is a list of items to be included in Notification Center and a list of items to not be included. For example, Messages and Reminders may be included, but alerts in game apps may not.

3. Tap any item and, in the settings that appear, tap the On/Off button (see **Figure 21-8**) for Show In Notification Center to include or exclude an item from Notification Center.

Items in Notification Center

Include/Exclude from Notification Center

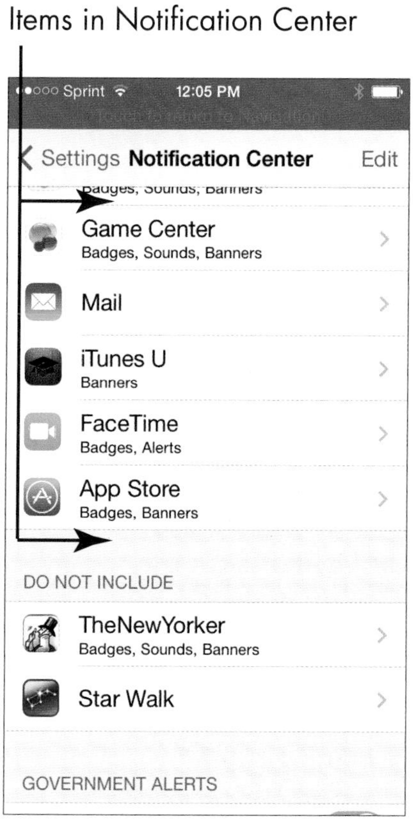

Figure 21-7

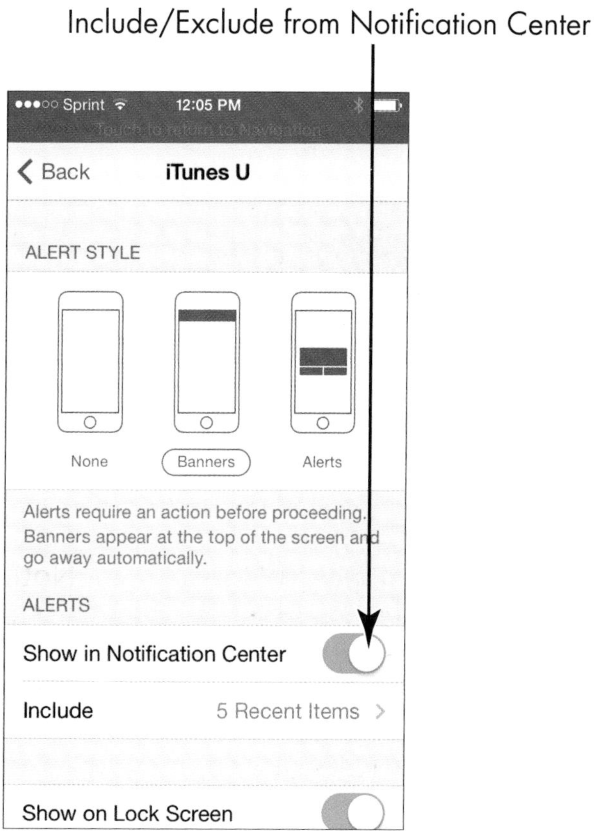

Figure 21-8

4. Tap an Alert Style to have no alert, a banner across the top of the screen, or a boxed alert appear. If you choose Banner, it will appear and then disappear automatically. If you choose Alert, you have to take an action to dismiss the alert when it appears.

5. Tap the Back button to return to the Notification Center home screen.

6. If you want to be able to view alerts when the Lock Screen is displayed, turn on the Access on Lock Screen setting for Notifications View or Today View (if you only want to see today's notifications there). When you've finished making settings press the Home button.

 You can drag across an alert to go to its source to see more details about it.

View Notification Center

1. After you've made settings for what should appear in Notification Center, you'll regularly want to take a look at those alerts and reminders. From any screen, tap and hold the black Status bar on top and drag down to display Notification Center (see **Figure 21-9**).

2. Note that items are divided into lists by type — for example, you'll see items categorized as Reminders, Mail, Calendar, and so on.

3. To close Notification Center, swipe upward from the bottom center of the screen.

 To determine what is displayed in Notification Center, see the previous task.

 You can display Stocks in Notification Center by tapping Settings, Notification Center, and making sure Stocks is set to on.

Figure 21-9

View Notifications from the Lock Screen

1. You will receive notifications on your Lock screen when a message has been received or you've missed a phone call, for example. There are two possibilities here:

- Slide to unlock your phone, and then tap and drag down from the Status bar to view Notification Center.

- Slide across a notification on the Lock screen to unlock the phone and go to the originating app for that notification in one action. Note that this only works if you have two or more notifications on the Lock screen. When you're taken to the originating app, take the appropriate action: Create and send a return message, initiate a phone call, or whatever.

Check Out All and Missed Views

1. With the latest Notifications feature in iOS 7, you get three views to play with: Today, All, and Missed. Tap and swipe down from the top of the screen to display Notifications.

2. Tap Today to show all Reminders and other items you've selected to display in Notification Center (see the previous task) that occur today.

3. Tap the All tab to see items for today plus missed and future items (see **Figure 21-10**). Tap Missed to see only those items that are in the past that you never deleted or marked as complete in their originating app.

Figure 21-10

Go to an App from Notification Center

1. You can easily jump from Notification Center to any app that caused an alert or reminder to appear. Tap the Status bar and drag down to display Notification Center.

2. Tap any item category such as Reminders or Stocks; it opens in its originating app. If you tap a message such as an e-mail, you can then reply to the message using the procedure described in Chapter 11.

Clear Notifications

1. To get rid of old notifications for an app, tap the Status bar and drag down to display Notification Center.

2. Tap the pale gray X to the right of a notification category, such as Mail. The button changes to read Clear.

3. Tap the Clear button, and the notifications from that category are removed from Notification Center.

Get Some Rest with Do Not Disturb

1. Do Not Disturb is a simple but useful setting you can use to stop any alerts and FaceTime calls from appearing or making a sound. You can make settings to allow calls from certain people or several repeat calls from the same person in a short time period to come through. (The assumption here is that such repeat calls may signal an emergency situation or urgent need to get through to you.) Tap Settings and then tap Do Not Disturb.

2. Tap the Manual On/Off switch to turn the feature on.

3. In the other settings shown in **Figure 21-11,** do any of the following:

- Tap Scheduled to allow alerts during a specified time period to appear.

- Tap Allow Calls From and then from the next screen select Everyone, No One, Favorites, or Groups such as All Contacts.

- Tap Repeated Calls to allow a second call from the same person in a three-minute time period to come through.

4. Press the Home button to return to the Home screen.

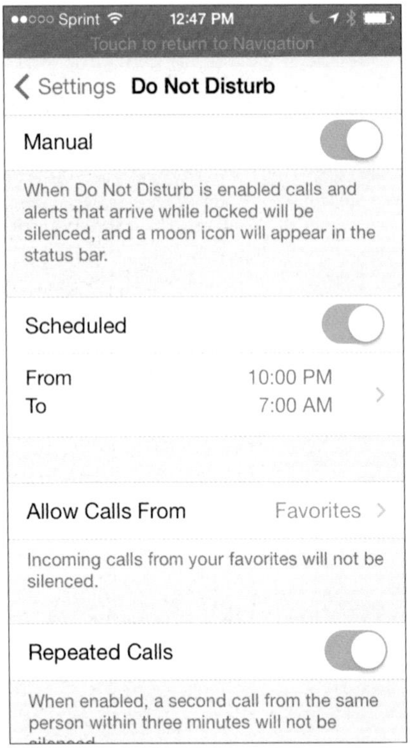

Figure 21-11

Making Notes

*N*otes is the included app that you can use to do everything from jotting down notes at meetings to keeping to-do lists. It isn't a robust word processor (such as Apple Pages or Microsoft Word) by any means, but for taking notes on the fly, jotting down shopping lists, or writing a few pages of your novel-in-progress while you sit and sip a cup of tea on your deck, it's a useful option.

In this chapter, you see how to enter and edit text in Notes and how to manage those notes by navigating among them, searching for content, or sharing or deleting them.

Open a Blank Note

1. To get started with Notes, tap the Notes app icon on the Home screen. If you've never used Notes, it opens with a blank notes list displayed. (If you have used Notes, it opens to the last note you were working on. If that's the case, you might want to jump to the next task to display a new, blank note.) You see the view shown in **Figure 22-1**.

2. Tap New. The onscreen keyboard, shown in **Figure 22-2**, appears.

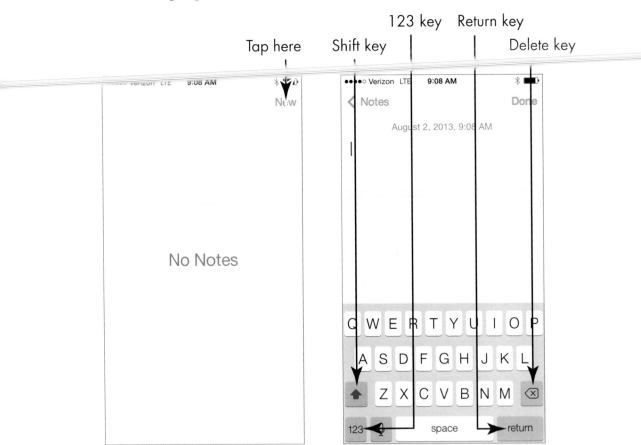

Tap here   Shift key   123 key   Return key   Delete key

Figure 22-1   **Figure 22-2**

3. Tap keys on the keyboard to enter text or, if you're using iPhone 4S or later with Siri enabled, tap the Dictation key (the one with the microphone on it) to speak your text. If you want to enter numbers or symbols, tap the key labeled *123* on the keyboard (refer to **Figure 22-2**). The numeric keyboard, shown in **Figure 22-3**, appears. Whenever you want to return to the alphabetic keyboard, tap the key labeled *ABC*.

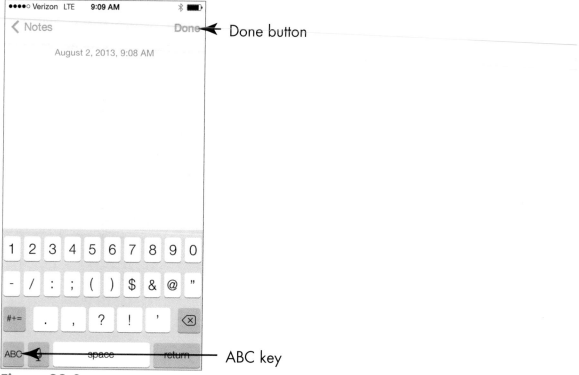

Figure 22-3

4. To capitalize a letter, tap the Shift key (refer to **Figure 22-2**) and then tap the letter. You can activate the Enable Caps Lock feature in the General Keyboard Settings so that you can then turn Caps Lock on by double-tapping the Shift key (an upward pointing arrow only available in the letter keyboard); tap the Shift key once to turn the feature off.

5. When you want to start a new paragraph or a new item in a list, tap the Return key (refer to **Figure 22-2**).

6. To edit text, tap to the right of the text you want to edit and either use the Delete key (refer to **Figure 22-2**) to delete text to the left of the cursor or enter new text.

When you have the numerical keyboard displayed (refer to **Figure 22-3**), you can tap the key labeled # to access more symbols, such as the percentage sign or the euro symbol, or additional bracket styles.

No need to save a note — it's kept automatically until you delete it.

Create a New Note

1. With one note open, to create a new note, tap the Done button (refer to **Figure 22-3**) and then tap New.

2. A new, blank note appears (refer to **Figure 22-1**). Enter and edit text as described in the previous task.

You can tap the Notes button to see a list of all notes you've created. Tap an individual note to display it.

Use Copy and Paste

1. The Notes app includes two essential editing tools you're probably familiar with from other word processors: Copy and Paste. With a note displayed, press and hold your finger on a word. The toolbar shown in **Figure 22-4** appears.

2. Tap the Select button. The toolbar shown in **Figure 22-5** appears.

3. Tap the Copy button.

4. Tap in the document where you want the text to go and then press and hold your finger on the screen.

Tap this button   Tap this button

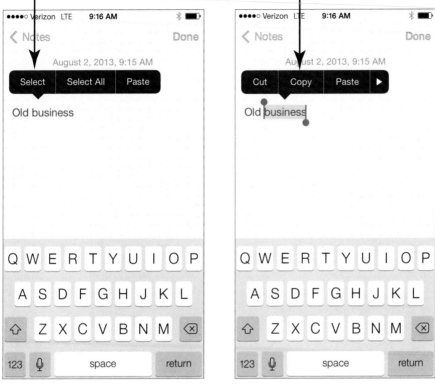

Figure 22-4   **Figure 22-5**

5. On the toolbar that appears (see **Figure 22-6**), tap the Paste button. The copied text appears.

 If you want to select all text in a note to either delete or copy it, tap the Select All button on the toolbar shown in **Figure 22-4**. All text is selected, and the toolbar shown in **Figure 22-5** appears again. Tap a button to Cut or Copy the selected text.

 To extend a selection to adjacent words, press one of the little handles that extends from the selection and drag to the left, right, up, or down.

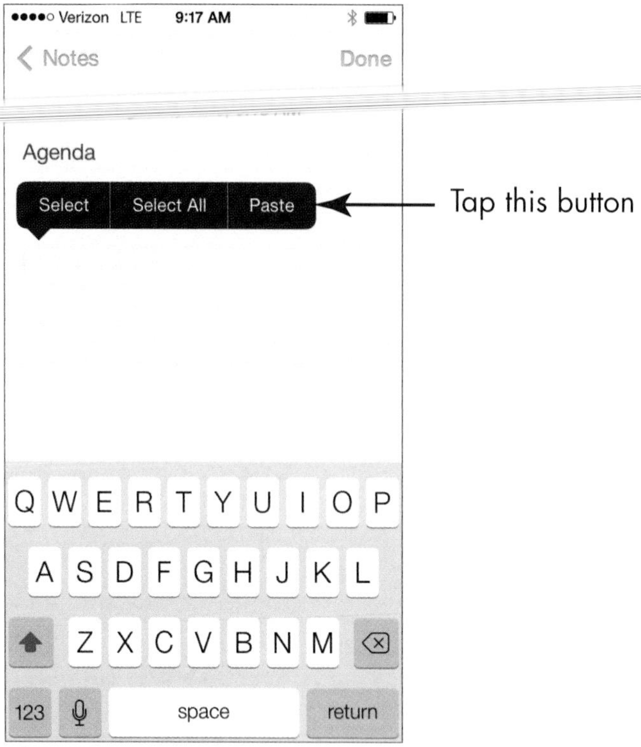

•••••○ Verizon LTE   9:17 AM   ⚹ ■▪

‹ Notes   Done

Agenda

| Select | Select All | Paste |

⟵——— Tap this button

Q W E R T Y U I O P

A S D F G H J K L

⬆ Z X C V B N M ⌫

123 🎤   space   return

Figure 22-6

To delete text, you can also choose text using the
Select or Select All command and then tap the Delete
key on the onscreen keyboard.

Display the Notes List

1. Tap the Notes app icon on the Home screen to open
Notes.

2. Tap the Notes button in the top-left corner of the screen;
the notes list appears, as shown in **Figure 22-7**. This list
is organized chronologically (the date isn't indicated if
you created the note today).

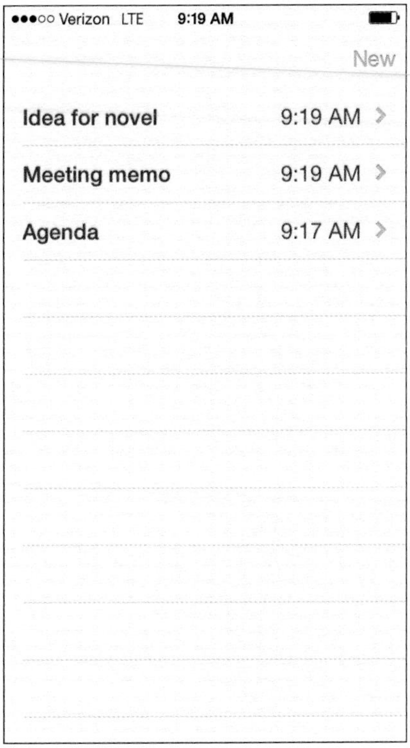

●●●○○ Verizon LTE   9:19 AM

New

Idea for novel	9:19 AM >
Meeting memo	9:19 AM >
Agenda	9:17 AM >

Figure 22-7

3. Tap any note on the list to display it.

 Notes names your note, using the first line of text. If you want to rename a note, first display the note, tap at the start of the first line of text, and then enter a new title and tap Return on the keyboard; the new first line is now reflected as the name of your note in the notes list.

Move Among Notes

1. Tap the Notes app icon on the Home screen to open Notes.

2. With the notes list displayed (see the previous task), tap a note to open it.

~~**3.**~~ To move among notes, tap the Notes button and tap another note in the list to open it.

 Because Notes lets you enter multiple notes with the same title — which can cause confusion — name your notes uniquely!

Search for a Note

1. You can search to locate a note that contains certain text. The Search feature lists only notes that contain your search criteria and only highlights the first instance of the word or words you enter when you open a note. Tap the Notes app icon on the Home screen to open Notes.

2. Tap the Notes button in the top-left corner to display the notes list if it isn't already displayed.

3. Press your finger on the middle of the screen and swipe down. The Search field appears above the notes list, as shown in **Figure 22-8**.

4. Tap in the Search field. The onscreen keyboard appears (see **Figure 22-9**).

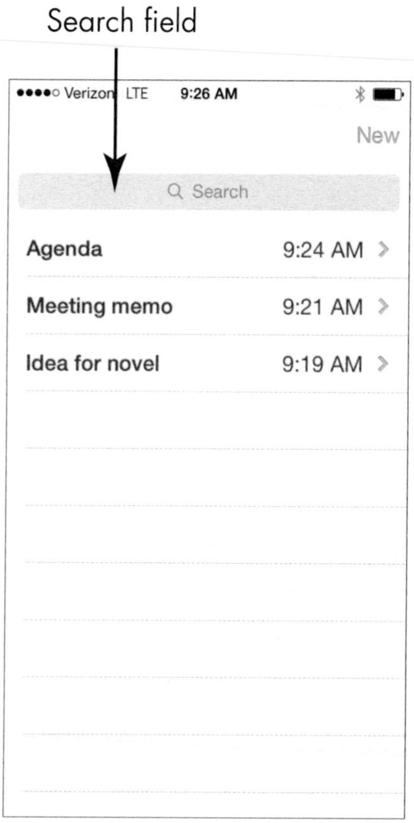

Search field

Figure 22-8

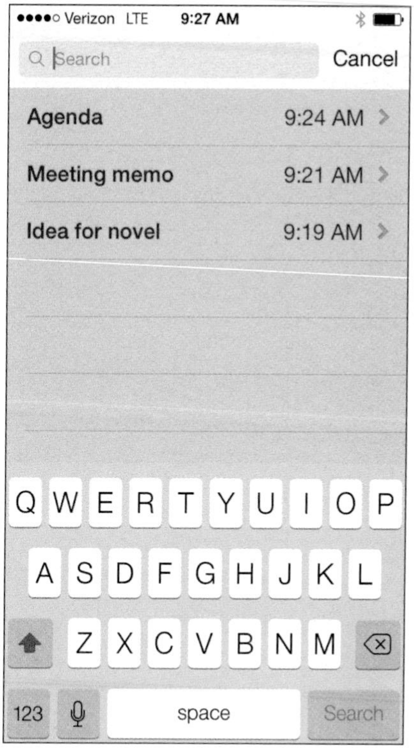

Figure 22-9

5. Begin to enter the search term. All notes that contain matching words appear on the list, as shown in **Figure 22-10.**

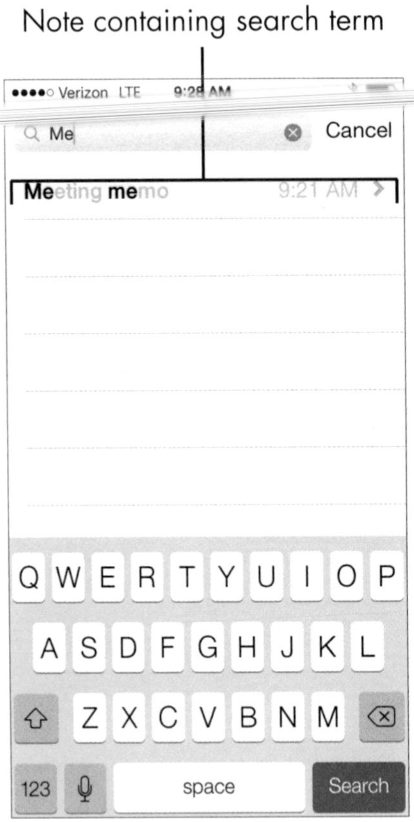

Note containing search term

Figure 22-10

6. Tap a note to display it with the first instance of the search term highlighted; locate other instances of the matching word the old-fashioned way — by skimming to find it.

Share a Note

1. If you want to share what you wrote with a friend or colleague, you can easily use AirDrop (iPhone 5 or later), Mail, or Message the contents of a note. With a note displayed, tap the Menu button at the bottom of the screen, and a menu appears as shown in **Figure 22-11**.

2. Tap Mail or Message. In the e-mail or message form that appears (see **Figure 22-12**), type one or more addresses in the appropriate fields. At least one address must appear in the To field.

3. If you need to make changes to the subject or message, tap in either area and make the changes.

4. Tap the Send button, and your e-mail is on its way.

5. To send via AirDrop to an AirDrop-enabled device nearby, tap AirDrop in Step 2 above and then tap the detected device you want to send the note to.

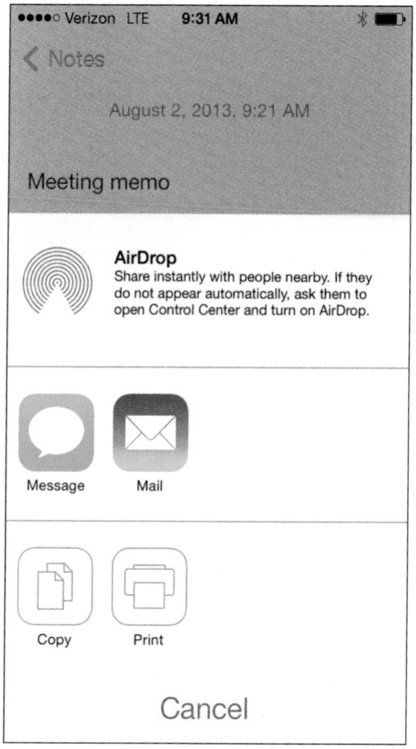

Figure 22-11

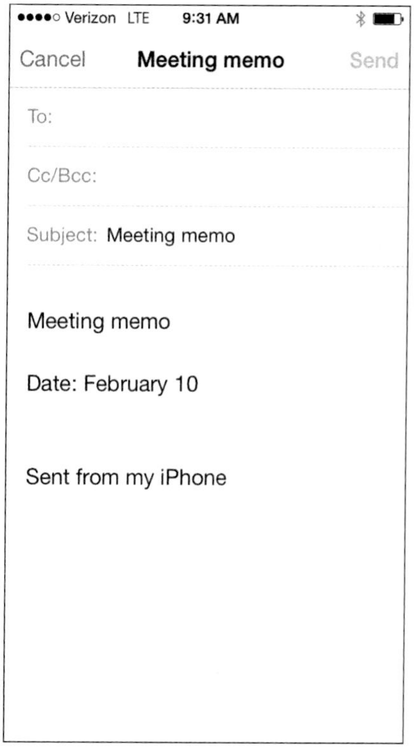

Figure 22-12

If you want to print a note, in Step 2, choose Print rather than Mail. Complete the Printer Options dialog by designating an AirPrint-enabled wireless printer (or shared printer on a network that you can access using AirPrint) and how many copies to print, and then tap Print.

To cancel an e-mail message and return to Notes without sending it, tap the Cancel button in the e-mail form and then tap Delete Draft on the menu that appears. To leave a message but save a draft so that you can finish and send it later, tap Cancel and then tap Save Draft. The next time you tap the e-mail button with the same note displayed in Notes, your draft appears.

Delete a Note

1. There's no sense in letting your notes list get cluttered, making it harder to find the ones you need. When you're done with a note, it's time to delete it. Tap the Notes app icon on the Home screen to open Notes.

2. Tap a note in the notes list to open it.

3. Tap the Trash Can button, shown in **Figure 22-13**.

4. Tap the Delete Note button that appears (see **Figure 22-14**). The note is deleted.

Notes is a nice little application, but it's limited. It offers no formatting tools, for example. You can't paste pictures into Notes. (You can try, but it won't work. Only the filename appears, not the image.) So, if you've made some notes and want to graduate to building a more robust document in a word processor, you have a couple of options. One way is to buy the Pages word-processor application for iPad, which costs about $9.99, and copy your note (using the copy-and-paste feature discussed earlier in this chapter). Alternatively, you can send the note to yourself in an e-mail message or sync it to your computer. Open the e-mail or note and copy and paste its text into a full-fledged word processor, and you're good to go.

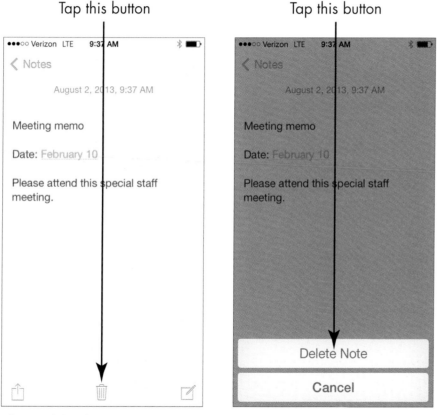

Tap this button   Tap this button

Figure 22-13   **Figure 22-14**

Troubleshooting and Maintaining Your iPhone

*i*Phones don't grow on trees — they cost a pretty penny. That's why you should learn how to take care of your iPhone and troubleshoot any problems it might have so that you get the most out of it.

In this chapter, I provide some advice about the care and maintenance of your iPhone, as well as tips about how to solve common problems, update iPhone system software, and even reset the iPhone if something goes seriously wrong. In case you lose your iPhone, I even tell you about a feature that helps you find it, activate it remotely — or even disable it if it has fallen into the wrong hands. Finally, you get information about backing up your iPhone settings and content using iCloud and the new fingerprint reader feature, Touch ID.

Keep the iPhone Screen Clean

If you've been playing with your iPhone, you know (despite Apple's claim that the iPhone has a fingerprint-resistant screen) that it's a fingerprint magnet. Here are some tips for cleaning your iPhone screen:

➠ **Use a dry, soft cloth.** You can get most fingerprints off with a dry, soft cloth such as the one you use to clean your eyeglasses or a cleaning cloth that's lint- and chemical-free. Or try products used to clean lenses in labs such as Kimwipes or Kaydry, which you can get from several major retailers such as Amazon.

➠ **Use a slightly dampened soft cloth.** To get the surface even cleaner, very slightly dampen the soft cloth. Again, make sure that whatever cloth material you use is free of lint.

➠ **Remove the cables.** Turn off your iPhone and unplug any cables from it before cleaning the screen with a moistened cloth.

➠ **Avoid too much moisture.** Avoid getting too much moisture around the edges of the screen, where it can seep into the unit.

➠ **Don't use your fingers!** That's right, by using a stylus rather than your finger, you avoid smearing oil from your skin or cheese from your pizza on the screen entirely.

➠ **Never use household cleaners.** They can degrade the coating that keeps the iPhone screen from absorbing oil from your fingers.

 Do *not* use premoistened lens-cleaning tissues to clean your iPhone screen. Most brands of wipe contain alcohol, which can damage the screen's coating.

Protect Your Gadget with a Case

Your screen isn't the only element on the iPhone that can be damaged, so consider getting a case for it so you can carry it around the house or around town safely. Besides providing a bit of padding if you drop the device, a case makes the iPhone less slippery in your hands, offering a better grip when working with it.

Several types of cases are available, but be sure you get one that will fit your model iPhone, as iPhone 5, 5S, and 5C have a larger 4-inch screen, and some models have slightly different thicknesses. You can choose covers from manufacturers such as Griffin (`www.griffin technology.com`) that come in materials ranging from leather to silicone.

Cases range from a few dollars to $70 or more for leather (with some outrageously expensive designer cases upward of $500). Some provide a cover for the screen and back, and others protect only the back and sides. If you carry your iPhone around much, consider a case with a screen cover to provide better protection for the screen or use a screen overlay, such as InvisibleShield from Zagg (`www.zagg.com`). If you're the literary type, try the BookBook case that looks like a well-worn leather book.

Extend Your iPhone's Battery Life

The much-touted battery life of the iPhone is a wonderful feature, but you can do some things to extend it even further. Here are a few tips to consider:

➡ Keep tabs on remaining battery life. You can estimate the amount of remaining battery life by looking at the Battery icon on the far-right end of the Status bar, at the top of your screen.

➡ Use standard accessories to charge your iPhone most effectively. When connected to a modern Mac or Windows computer for charging, the iPhone can slowly charge; however, the most effective way to charge your iPhone is to plug it into a wall outlet using the Lightening to USB Cable and the 10W USB Power Adapter that come with your iPhone.

➡ **Use a case with an external battery pack.** These cases are very handy when you're traveling or unable to reach an electric outlet easily.

➡ **The fastest way to charge the iPhone is to turn it off while charging it.**

➡ **The Battery icon on the Status bar indicates when the charging is complete.**

 Your iPhone battery is sealed in the unit, so you can't replace it, as you can with many laptops or cellphone batteries. If the battery is out of warranty, you have to fork over about $79 to get a new one. See the "Get Support" task, later in this chapter, to find out where to get a replacement battery.

 Apple has introduced AppleCare+. For $99 you get two years of coverage, which even covers you if you drop or spill liquids on your iPhone (Apple covers up to two incidents of accidental damage). If your iPhone has to be replaced, it will only cost you $49, rather than the $250 it used to cost with garden variety AppleCare. You can purchase AppleCare+ when you buy your iPhone or within a month of the date of purchase. See `www.apple.com/support/ products/iphone.html` for more details.

Find Out What to Do with a Nonresponsive iPhone

If your iPhone goes dead on you, it's most likely a power issue, so the first thing to do is to plug the Lightning to USB Cable into the 10W USB Power Adapter, plug the 10W USB Power Adapter into a wall outlet, plug the other end of the Mini-USB Cable into your iPhone, and charge the battery.

Another thing to try — if you believe that an app is hanging up the iPhone — is to press the Sleep/Wake button for a couple of seconds. Then press and hold the Home button. The app you were using should close.

You can always try the tried-and-true reboot procedure: On the iPhone, you press the Sleep/Wake button on top until the red slider appears. Drag the slider to the right to turn off your iPhone. After a few moments, press the Sleep/Wake button to boot up the little guy again.

If the situation seems drastic and none of these ideas works, try to reset your iPhone. To do this, press the Sleep/Wake button and the Home button at the same time until the Apple logo appears onscreen.

 If your phone has this problem often, try closing out some active apps that may be running in the background and using up too much memory. Also check to see that you haven't loaded up your phone with too much content, such as videos, which could be hogging your memory.

Update Software

1. Apple occasionally updates the iPhone system software to fix problems or offer enhanced features. You should occasionally check for an updated version (say, every month). You can do so by hooking up your iPhone to a computer with iTunes installed, but it's even easier to just update from your iPhone Settings, though it's a tad slower. Tap Settings.

2. Tap General and then tap Software Update (see **Figure 23-1**).

3. A message tells you if your software is up to date; if it's not, the phone is updated to the latest software version.

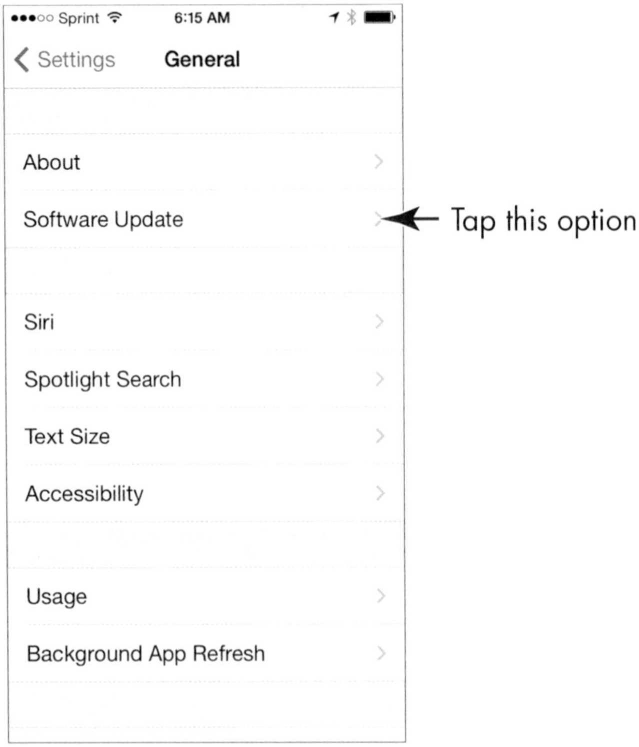

●●●○○ Sprint 🛜	6:15 AM	✈ ✲ 🔋

❮ Settings General

About	＞
Software Update	＞	← Tap this option

Siri	＞
Spotlight Search	＞
Text Size	＞
Accessibility	＞

Usage	＞
Background App Refresh	＞

Figure 23-1

 If you're having problems with your iPhone, you can use the Update feature to try to restore the current version of the software. Follow the preceding set of steps, and then tap the Restore button instead of the Update button in Step 3.

 If you've chosen to back up and restore iPhone via iCloud when you first set up the device, restoring and updating your device happens automatically.

Restore the Sound

On the morning I wrote this chapter, as my husband puttered with our iPhone, its sound suddenly (and ironically) stopped working. We gave ourselves a quick course in sound recovery, so now I can share some tips with you. Make sure that

➠ **You haven't touched the volume control buttons on the side of your iPhone.** They're on the left side of the phone. Be sure not to touch the volume decrease button and inadvertently lower the sound to a point where you can't hear it.

➠ **You haven't flipped the Silent switch.** Moving the switch located on the left side above the volume buttons mutes sound on the iPhone.

➠ **The speaker isn't covered up.** It may be covered in a way that muffles the sound.

➠ **A headset isn't plugged in.** Sound doesn't play over the speaker and the headset at the same time.

➠ **The volume limit is set to Off.** You can set up the volume limit in the Music settings to control how loudly your music can play (which is useful if you have teenagers around). Tap the Settings icon on the Home screen and then, on the screen that displays, tap Music and then tap Volume Limit control and use the slider that appears (see **Figure 23-2**) to set the volume limit.

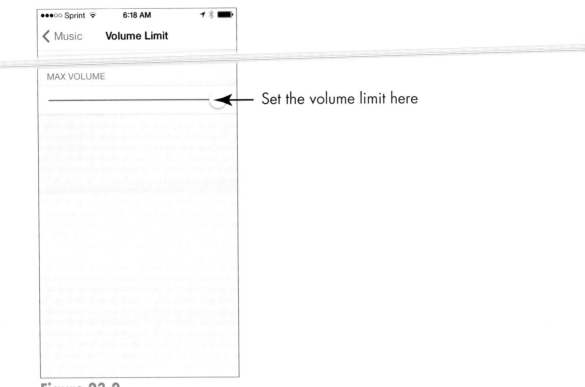

Set the volume limit here

Figure 23-2

When all else fails, reboot. This strategy worked for us — just press the Sleep/Wake button until the red slider appears. Press and drag the slider to the right. After the iPhone turns off, press the Sleep/Wake button again until the Apple logo appears, and you may find yourself back in business, sound-wise.

Get Support

Every single new iPhone comes with a year's coverage for repair of the hardware and 90 days of free technical support. Apple is known for its helpful customer support, so if you're stuck, I definitely recommend that you try it out. Here are a few options you can explore for getting help:

➡ **The Apple Store:** Go to your local Apple Store (if one is handy) to see what the folks there might know about your problem. Call first and make an appointment at the Genius Bar to be sure you get prompt service.

➡ **The Apple support website:** It's at `www.apple.com/support/iphone`. You can find online manuals, discussion forums, and downloads, and you can use the Apple Expert feature to contact a live support person by phone.

➡ **The *iPhone User Guide*:** You can use the bookmarked manual on the Safari browser to view the user guide that comes with your iPhone.

➡ **The Apple battery replacement service:** If you need repair or service for your battery, visit `www.apple.com/batteries/replacements.html`. Note that your warranty provides free battery replacement if the battery level dips below 50 percent and won't go any higher during the first year you own it. If you purchase the AppleCare service agreement, this is extended to two years.

Apple recommends that you have your iPhone battery replaced only by an Apple Authorized Service Provider.

Find a Missing iPhone

You can take advantage of the Find My iPhone feature to pinpoint the location of your iPhone. This feature is extremely handy if you forget where you left your iPhone or someone steals it. Find My iPhone not only lets you track down the critter but also lets you wipe out the data contained in it if you have no way to get the iPhone back.

Follow these steps to set up the Find My iPhone feature:

1. Tap the Settings icon on the Home screen.

2. In the Settings pane, tap iCloud.

3. In the iCloud settings, tap the On/Off button for Find My iPhone to turn the feature on (see **Figure 23-3**).

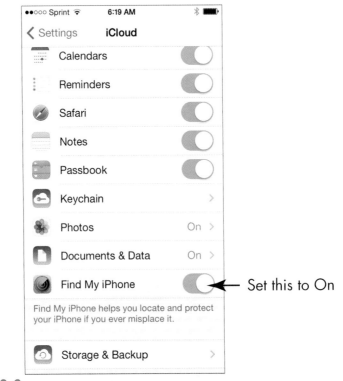

Figure 23-3

4. From now on, if your iPhone is lost or stolen, you can go to https://www.iCloud.com from your computer and enter your ID and password.

5. The iCloud screen appears. Click the Devices button and then click the device you want to locate to display a map of its location and some helpful tools (see **Figure 23-4**).

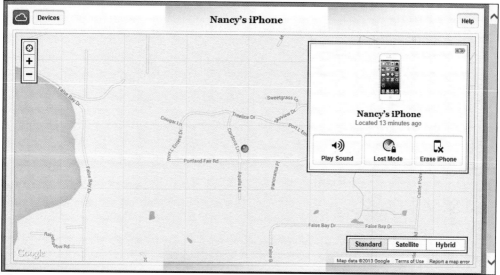

Figure 23-4

6. To wipe information from the iPhone, click the Erase iPhone button. To lock the iPhone from access by others, click the Lost Mode button. Tap Play Sound to have your phone play a sound that might help you locate it if you're in its vicinity.

 Erase iPhone will delete all data from your iPhone, including contact information and content such as music. However, even after you've erased your iPhone it will display your phone number on the Lock screen along with a message so any good Samaritan who finds it can contact you.

The Lost mode feature allows you to send whoever has your iPhone a note saying how to return it to

~~you. If you choose to play a sound, it plays for two~~

minutes, helping you track down your phone if you left it on top of the refrigerator or if anybody holding your iPhone is within earshot.

Tap the Notify Me When Found check box if you want to receive a notification when your device is found. This is handy if you have, say, an iPad and iPhone and one is lost; you can still get a notification on the other device.

Back Up to iCloud

You used to be able to back up your iPhone content using only iTunes, but with Apple's introduction of iCloud with iOS 5, you can back up via a Wi-Fi network to your iCloud storage. You get 5GB of storage (not including iTunes-bought music, iTunes Match and Photo Stream content, video, apps, and e-books) for free or you can pay for increased storage (an additional 10GB for $20 per year, 20GB for $40 per year, or 50GB for $100 per year).

1. To perform a backup to iCloud, first set up an iCloud account (see Chapter 3 for details on creating an iCloud account) and then tap Settings on the Home screen.

2. In Settings tap iCloud and then tap Storage & Backup (see **Figure 23-5**).

3. In the pane that appears (see **Figure 23-6**), tap the iCloud Backup On/Off switch to enable automatic back-ups. To perform a manual backup, tap Back Up Now. A progress bar shows how your backup is moving along.

If you get your iPhone back after it wanders and you've erased it, just enter your Apple ID and password and you can reactivate it.

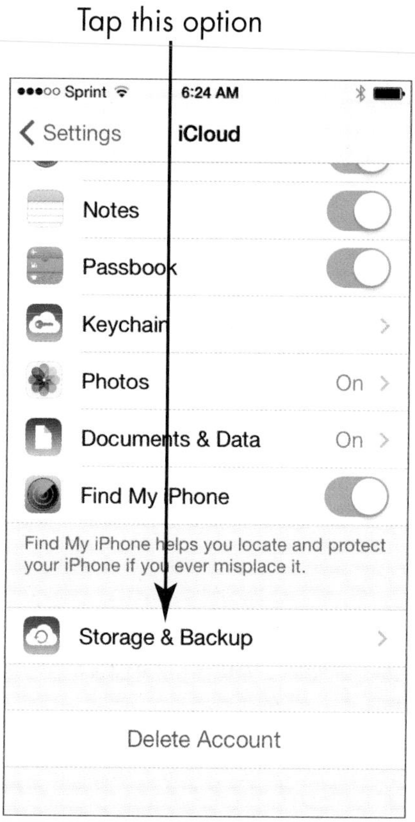

Tap this option

Set this to On

Figure 23-5

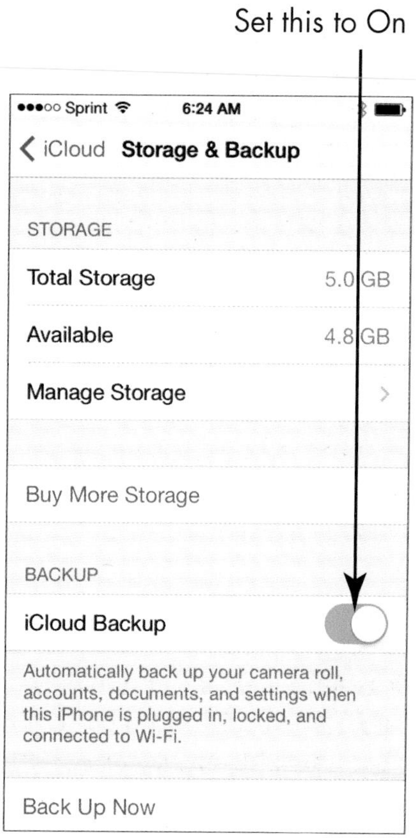

Figure 23-6

Understand Touch ID

Up to now you had to set a password to protect the contents of your phone from others, and input that password every time your phone went to sleep. iPhone 5S sports a new feature called Touch ID which allows you to unlock your phone by placing your finger on the redesigned Home button. That button now contains a sophisticated fingerprint sensor. As your fingerprint is unique, this is one of the most foolproof ways to protect your data.

You have to educate iPhone about your fingerprint on your finger of choice by placing it on the Home button several times from different angles. Then, with the featured turned ~~~~~~~~~~~~~~~~~~~~~~~~~~~~ place your finger on the Home button to unlock the phone.

Touch ID also works with the iTunes Store; instead of entering your Apple ID and password every time you want to buy something, when prompted, just place your finger to the Home button. Easy!

Index

About the Author

Nancy Muir is the author of over 100 books on technology and business topics. In addition to her writing work, Nancy runs a companion website for her iPad books in the *For Dummies* series, iPadMadeClear.com. She writes a regular column on computers and the Internet on Retirenet.com and is Senior Editor for the website UnderstandingNano.com. Prior to her writing career Nancy was a manager at several publishing companies and a training manager at Symantec.

Dedication

To Blair and Dennis, my partners in crime, for all their help.

Author's Acknowledgments

I was lucky enough to have Blair Pottenger, the absolute best editor in the world, assigned to lead the team on this book. Blair, I hope you don't get tired of me saying that I couldn't have gotten through this rush schedule without you, not to mention the other four rush schedules that coincided with this book. Thanks also to Dennis Cohen for his able work as technical editor, and to Laura Miller, the book's copy editor. Last but never least, thanks to Kyle Looper, Acquisitions Editor, for giving me the opportunity to write this book.

Publisher's Acknowledgments

Acquisitions Editor: Kyle Looper

Project Editor: Blair J. Pottenger

Copy Editor: Laura Miller

Technical Editor: Dennis Cohen

Editorial Assistant: Annie Sullivan

Sr. Editorial Assistant: Cherie Case

Project Coordinator: Patrick Redmond

Cover Images: Front Cover Image: ©Image Source/jupiterimages. Back Cover Images: Wiley

Apple & Mac

iPad For Dummies,
5th Edition
978-1-118-49823-1

iPhone 5 For Dummies,
6th Edition
978-1-118-35201-4

MacBook For Dummies,
4th Edition
978-1-118-20920-2

OS X Mountain Lion
For Dummies
978-1-118-39418-2

Blogging & Social Media

Facebook For Dummies,
4th Edition
978-1-118-09562-1

Mom Blogging
For Dummies
978-1-118-03843-7

Pinterest For Dummies
978-1-118-32800-2

WordPress For Dummies,
5th Edition
978-1-118-38318-6

Business

Commodities For Dummies,
2nd Edition
978-1-118-01687-9

Investing For Dummies,
6th Edition
978-0-470-90545-6

Personal Finance
For Dummies
7th Edition
978-1-118-11785-9

QuickBooks 2013
For Dummies
978-1-118-35641-8

Small Business Marketing Kit
For Dummies,
3rd Edition
978-1-118-31183-7

Careers

Job Interviews
For Dummies,
4th Edition
978-1-118-11290-8

Job Searching with
Social Media
For Dummies
978-0-470-93072-4

Personal Branding
For Dummies
978-1-118-11792-7

Resumes For Dummies,
6th Edition
978-0-470-87361-8

Success as a Mediator
For Dummies
978-1-118-07862-4

Diet & Nutrition

Belly Fat Diet For Dummies
978-1-118-34585-6

Eating Clean For Dummies
978-1-118-00013-7

Nutrition For Dummies,
5th Edition
978-0-470-93231-5

Digital Photography

Digital Photography
For Dummies,
7th Edition
978-1-118-09203-3

Digital SLR Cameras &
Photography For Dummies,
4th Edition
978-1-118-14489-3

Photoshop Elements 11
For Dummies
978-1-118-40821-6

Gardening

Herb Gardening
For Dummies,
2nd Edition
978-0-470-61778-6

Vegetable Gardening
For Dummies,
2nd Edition
978-0-470-49870-5

Health

Anti-Inflammation Diet
For Dummies
978-1-118-02381-5

Diabetes For Dummies,
3rd Edition
978-0-470-27086-8

Living Paleo For Dummies
978-1-118-29405-5

Hobbies

Beekeeping
For Dummies
978-0-470-43065-1

eBay For Dummies,
7th Edition
978-1-118-09806-6

Raising Chickens
For Dummies
978-0-470-46544-8

Wine For Dummies,
5th Edition
978-1-118-28872-6

Writing Young Adult Fiction
For Dummies
978-0-470-94954-2

Language &
Foreign Language

500 Spanish Verbs
For Dummies
978-1-118-02382-2

English Grammar
For Dummies,
2nd Edition
978-0-470-54664-2

French All-in One
For Dummies
978-1-118-22815-9

German Essentials
For Dummies
978-1-118-18422-6

Italian For Dummies,
2nd Edition
978-1-118-00465-4

Available in print and e-book formats.

Math & Science

Algebra I For Dummies,
2nd Edition
978-0-470-55964-2

Anatomy and Physiology
For Dummies,
2nd Edition
978-0-470-92326-9

Astronomy For Dummies,
3rd Edition
978-1-118-37697-3

Biology For Dummies,
2nd Edition
978-0-470-59875-7

Chemistry For Dummies,
2nd Edition
978-1-1180-0730-3

Pre-Algebra Essentials
For Dummies
978-0-470-61838-7

Microsoft Office

Excel 2013 For Dummies
978-1-118-51012-4

Office 2013 All-in-One
For Dummies
978-1-118-51636-2

PowerPoint 2013
For Dummies
978-1-118-50253-2

Word 2013 For Dummies
978-1-118-49123-2

Music

Blues Harmonica
For Dummies
978-1-118-25269-7

Guitar For Dummies,
3rd Edition
978-1-118-11554-1

iPod & iTunes
For Dummies,
10th Edition
978-1-118-50864-0

Programming

Android Application
Development For
Dummies, 2nd Edition
978-1-118-38710-8

iOS 6 Application
Development For Dummies
978-1-118-50880-0

Java For Dummies,
5th Edition
978-0-470-37173-2

Religion & Inspiration

The Bible For Dummies
978-0-7645-5296-0

Buddhism For Dummies,
2nd Edition
978-1-118-02379-2

Catholicism For Dummies,
2nd Edition
978-1-118-07778-8

Self-Help & Relationships

Bipolar Disorder
For Dummies,
2nd Edition
978-1-118-33882-7

Meditation For Dummies,
3rd Edition
978-1-118-29144-3

Seniors

Computers For Seniors
For Dummies,
3rd Edition
978-1-118-11553-4

iPad For Seniors
For Dummies,
5th Edition
978-1-118-49708-1

Social Security
For Dummies
978-1-118-20573-0

Smartphones & Tablets

Android Phones
For Dummies
978-1-118-16952-0

Kindle Fire HD
For Dummies
978-1-118-42223-6

NOOK HD For Dummies,
Portable Edition
978-1-118-39498-4

Surface For Dummies
978-1-118-49634-3

Test Prep

ACT For Dummies,
5th Edition
978-1-118-01259-8

ASVAB For Dummies,
3rd Edition
978-0-470-63760-9

GRE For Dummies,
7th Edition
978-0-470-88921-3

Officer Candidate Tests,
For Dummies
978-0-470-59876-4

Physician's Assistant Exam
For Dummies
978-1-118-11556-5

Series 7 Exam
For Dummies
978-0-470-09932-2

Windows 8

Windows 8 For Dummies
978-1-118-13461-0

Windows 8 For Dummies,
Book + DVD Bundle
978-1-118-27167-4

Windows 8 All-in-One
For Dummies
978-1-118-11920-4

Available in print and e-book formats.

Take Dummies with you everywhere you go!

Whether you're excited about e-books, want more from the web, must have your mobile apps, or swept up in social media, Dummies makes everything easier .

Visit Us

Like Us

Follow Us

Watch Us

Join Us

Pin Us

Circle Us

Shop Us

Dummies products make life easie

- DIY
- Consumer Electronics
- Crafts
- Software
- Cookware
- Hobbies
- Videos
- Music
- Games
- and More!

For more information, go to **Dummies.com**® and search the store by category.

FOR
DUMMIE

A Wiley Bra